ON BEING HUMAN

FRITZ MEDICUS

[Menschlichkeit. English]

ON BEING HUMAN

The Life of Truth and Its Realization

Translated by
FRITZ MARTI
Southern Illinois University, Edwardsville

FREDERICK UNGAR PUBLISHING CO.
NEW YORK

Translated from the original German
Menschlichkeit
by arrangement with the author's heirs

Copyright © 1973
by Frederick Ungar Publishing Co., Inc.

Printed in the United States of America
Library of Congress Catalog Card No. 72-178170
ISBN 0-8044-5673-9

TRANSLATOR'S PREFACE

Fritz Medicus was born April 23, 1876, at Stadtlauringen in Franconia, the northern part of Bavaria. The oldest child of a pharmacist, he attended the classical Gymnasium at Hildburghausen. He then began to study Protestant theology but soon turned to philosophy, though remaining all his life a deeply religious thinker. He studied at the Universities of Jena, Kiel, and Strassburg, returning to Jena for his doctorate, granted in 1898. He began his teaching career as a Privatdozent or lecturer at the University of Halle, where he soon stressed the philosophical importance of Fichte. His first book, thirteen lectures collected as *J.G. Fichte*, was published in 1905 and translated into Japanese in 1931. Medicus edited the main works of Fichte in six volumes, published 1908-1912. The introduction, a biography of Fichte, was also brought out as a separate volume, *Fichtes Leben*, and enlarged in a second edition in 1922. The renewed interest in Fichte was largely due to the writings of Medicus who, for his part, came to see Schelling as the most profound of the thinkers who had taken their cue from Kant. One of Medicus' early students at Halle was Paul Tillich, with whom he kept up a friendship all his life. Together they drew new attention to Schelling.

Medicus' work on Fichte, and many articles on a wide range of subjects, earned him a professorship at Halle and, in 1911, the chair of philosophy and pedagogy at the Swiss Federal Institute of Technology in Zürich. He had not been happy in the intellectual and political climate of the era of Wilhelm II, but soon felt at home in Zürich, where he spent the rest of his life. He married a Swiss, Clara Frey, and between 1915 and 1921 they had a daughter and two sons.

The Swiss Federal Institute of Technology has an illustrious history; Jacob Burkhardt and Carl Gustav Jung have been among the teachers in its Division of Electives in the humanities. Medicus' lectures drew large crowds, both from the Institute and from the University of Zürich, located across the street. The Institute offered no degrees in philosophy, and Medicus had no seminar jurisdiction. Nevertheless he influenced a new generation of thinkers, among them Hans Urs von Balthasar. Out of his lectures came books such as *Grundfragen der Aesthetik* (Fundamental Problems of Esthetics), published in 1917, and *Die Freiheit des Willens und ihre Grenzen* (Freedom of Will and Its Limits) published in 1926. The latter was written because quantum physics raised new questions regarding determinism. Medicus, whose dissertation topic had been "Kant's Transcendental Esthetics and Non-Euclidean Geometry," and who now had among his colleagues and friends the eminent mathematical physicist Hermann Weyl, was immediately attracted by the philosophical implications of the theory of relativity and of the quantum theory. Teaching at a technical university, he endeavored to bridge, or at least narrow, the gap between the humanities and science and technology. This interest led him to an intensive study of the Renaissance physician and humanist Paracelsus, and his pedagogic interests led him to a second great Swiss, Pestalozzi, whose philosophical importance Medicus expounded in a biography, *Pestalozzis Leben* (The Life of Pestalozzi), published in 1927.

Living what he preached, Medicus attempted, after 1933, to relocate refugees from Nazi Germany. In June, 1937, he wrote to me: "*You* live in a more fortunate country where it is not a dire necessity for philosophy to give strength in the fight against degrading circumstances. But the strength which issues from philosophy is just as great, even so. If philosophy is not constrained to struggle against painful obstacles, it can make life all the more substantial." His own name stood high on the list of those whom the Nazis wished to eliminate.

Despite his other activities during the war and afterward, Medicus found time for four more books: *Vom Wahren, Guten und Schönen* (About the True, the Good and the Beautiful),

Translator's Preface

published in 1943; *Das Mythologische in der Religion* (The Mythological Element in Religion), published in 1944; *Menschlichkeit,* published in 1951, and *Vom Überzeitlichen in der Zeit* (About the Supertemporal in Time), published in 1954. He died January 13, 1956. Not long before he had been elected to the Italian Accademia Nazionale dei Lincei.

In an obituary, his friend Hans Barth, professor of philosophy at the University of Zürich, observed that Medicus came from that Neo-Kantian movement which sought a comprehensive study of all three *Critiques*, seeking their unity: "And he who proceeds that way finds the way open toward a wide philosophy of art and a conception of nature not limited to an understanding which knows nothing but the law of mechanical causation. He who comes that way cannot be satisfied with the truth of the mere intellect but he will see instead that our certainty of truth concerns all aspects of the life of the spirit." For Medicus, "the kind of reckless flight of a philosophy which ignores the work of generations of thinkers in order to think as if nobody had ever thought before, was foreign and suspect. Medicus philosophized from the context of tradition, which he had mastered and would affirm in order to go forward. His tie with tradition, his deliberate stand as productive heir is manifest in the form of his books. They always deal with their respective problems on the basis of a magnificent and expert survey of the accomplishments of earlier thinkers. Yet an alive thinker cannot be a mere traditionalist. Life confronts us with new historical problems. One cannot simply apply what, at an earlier time, was validly beautiful and good, just, and true. The life of thought must prove itself in ever new adventures, and its norms must find new formulations under changed conditions. It is precisely the task of philosophy to be watchful that nothing hardens and poses as final, philosophy included. Medicus says philosophy sees everything, even itself, as problematic."

In 1951, when Medicus sent me his new book, I was impressed by its importance for our time and ultimately undertook its translation. A research grant from Southern Illinois University provided secretarial help. Grants by the Swiss cultural foundation Pro Helvetia and by the Southern Illinois University Foundation made this edition possible, as did continuing help from the publisher, Frederick Ungar, and from the author's son, Professor Heinrich Medicus of Rensselaer Polytechnic Institute.

F. M.

TRANSLATOR'S NOTE

In his preface, Medicus advises the reader to start at the beginning. He had in mind continental European readers. American readers might prefer to postpone their reading of the historical introduction. Readers with systematic interests in philosophy but who are not familiar with Kant and Fichte might find it helpful to start with Chapters 9 and 10 of the First Part. Readers whose main interest is the state and society might wish to read first Chapters 3 and 4 of the Second Part, readers coming from ethical interests Chapter 5 of the Second Part; readers most keenly interested in religion might even begin with the last chapters of the book, starting with Chapter 6 of the Second Part. Although Medicus rightly says these sections are not treatises independent of the context of the whole book, they could indeed be so read.

CONTENTS

Preface   xi
Historical-Philosophical Introduction   1

First Part: Foundation

1. Science and Our View of the World   15
2. The Supertemporally True and Its Forms   24
3. The Faith in Truth under the Changes of History   39
4. Trials in the Awareness of Truth: Trials of Humanity   47
5. Dionysos and Apollo   62
6. True Knowledge of God   73
7. About the Mystery of the Non-Finite   80
8. The Problematic Nature of the Certainty of Self   86
9. The Role of the Intelligence in the Life of the Spirit   97
10. Personal Wholeness   105
11. About the Super-Objective   115
12. Concerning the Truth of Faith   125

Second Part: The Realm of Truth

1. On Being at One with Oneself   135
2. The Foundation in the Realm of Truth   154
3. Concerning Injustice and the Resistance to It   171
4. Concerning Humanity and Inhuman "Duties"   186
5. Inhuman Truths and Human Untruths   203
6. The Claim That the Depths of Truth Make on Man   217
7. About the Goal of Mankind   228

8	About Humanity: Its Ontological Ground, the Dangers to It, and Its Height	232
9	Confirmations	246
10	Religion and Culture	257

Notes	285
Index of Names	313
Index of Topics	316

PREFACE

Humanitatis studia, id est philosophia—"philosophy is the study of what is meant by being human." With this statement Ludovicus Vives, a thinker of the Renaissance and Reformation period who was able to stand above the turmoil of his century, supplied a formula for the modern meaning of philosophy. It is true, of course, that the centuries which followed would continue to witness the movements of that metaphysical curiosity which fancied it could penetrate by the power of the intelligence the veil of "appearances" said to conceal "true being." Fichte was the first to see the absurdity of that kind of metaphysical endeavor with full clarity, but it was precisely this insight which met with a rigid barrier in minds incapable of understanding him. The misunderstandings are now being eliminated, yet much remains to be accomplished. The aim of the present book is to contribute to that end. As a beginning, we must clarify Vives' dictum that *humanity*, what is meant by being human, is the proper theme for philosophy.

For the "intellectualists"—those who hold that knowledge is derived purely from the operations of the intellect—philosophy is one discipline alongside others; to their minds, the word *truth* has a precise meaning only in the form of statements. But statements are man-made and contingent. The comprehensive depths of truth cannot be compressed in any statement. Art searches and in a way reveals these depths; and human action, when it is fully human, accepts the actual situation seen for what it is in its profoundest reality. The statements of the intellect, however, grasp neither the truth of artistic revelation nor the truth of purely human experience discovered in a situation which is a call for action. The philosophy which has humanity as its theme acknowledges that truth lays claim to the whole man, and not just to his intelligence.

One pointer: the chapters of the book should be read in the sequence in which they appear (and in which they were written). What they have to say they say in their respective place; they are not self-contained essays.

The book appears at a time which is difficult for Swiss publishers. I owe profound thanks to the Foundation for Art and Research of the Swiss National Exhibition of 1939 in Zürich, for its liberal help in overcoming the obstacles of publication.

Zürich, April 1951   FRITZ MEDICUS

HISTORICAL-PHILOSOPHICAL INTRODUCTION

Towards the end of the year 1793, Fichte, writing to Niethammer, later his colleague in Jena, expressed his fear that an understanding of Kant would never be achieved by those "who were in a hurry to finish their own systems, having studied nothing but the *Critique of Pure Reason* alone."[1] In this respect, of course, Fichte himself was in a more favorable position. When the *Critique of Pure Reason* was published, Fichte, a mere student of nineteen, had no reason even to notice the book. Nor did he advert to the appearance of the *Critique of Practical Reason*, for at that time he was fully occupied in earning his frugal livelihood as a private tutor. When the *Critique of Judgment* appeared Fichte's circumstances had improved hardly at all; he was actually "worried about his daily bread."[2] However, at that moment destiny knocked at his door in the shape of a student who wanted tutoring in Kantian philosophy. Fichte now read the three Critiques in quick succession, and so, almost unwittingly, he saw the *Critique of Pure Reason* within the context of a total structure which included the other two works. It is clear to Fichte that Kant's procedure, starting from the conditions of objective existence and leading to a clear awareness of the opposition between those conditions of objectivity and the direct certainty of freedom, had to have its term in the recognition of reality as *living and experienceable*.

Kant's *Critiques* opened up a new life for Fichte, yet it would not be correct to say that Fichte had understood the three books in the exact meaning of their author. It may well be said, however, that the comprehensive context within which Fichte saw the details gave them each a greater and more profound significance than had appeared to the minds of those who had read the

Critique of Practical Reason fully seven years after the *Critique of Pure Reason* and the *Critique of Judgment* two years after that. For of course these readers had drawn their own conclusions about the meaning of the first Critique, and long afterwards about the second; now they found it difficult or outright impossible to let go of their earlier interpretations. Thus it was the third Critique in particular which could not be seen for what it was— the magnificent conclusion of the whole undertaking;[a] instead, it was regarded as an appendix. Fichte, however, knew that it was the third Critique which must contain the matter of greatest importance. In September of 1790 (the year of the third Critique) he was already at work on a "Tentative Explanatory Epitome of Kant's *Critique of Judgment*." The plan to publish this essay was still on his mind in the summer of the following year.[3] The book was never finished. Many years later Fichte referred to the time when he related his own doctrine to the *Critique of Judgment* as the "historical point" at which he had become independent of Kant.[4] To be sure, Fichte's efforts to banish the vaguely glimpsed obscurities into which that first reading of the third Critique led him had proved, at that time, to be in vain;[5] nevertheless he never ceased to hold the work in the highest esteem. In a letter of 1806 he calls it "the summit of Kantian speculation."[6]

Anyone who opens the *Critique of Judgment* for the first time and tries to learn from the table of contents what it is all about finds himself faced by something rather puzzling. If he should happen to have in hand a first edition, he would find the outline of the "Subdivisions of the Whole Work" preceded by the rather lengthy introduction (which Fichte called "what is most important in this very important book"). Kant does not mention the introduction among the subdivisions of the book. Moreover, the reader can find in the outline only distinctions between an aesthetic and teleological power of judgment (the former referring to the beautiful and the sublime), both dealt with first in an analytic and then in a dialectic, in analogy with the two earlier Critiques. He will also find that the theory of the teleological power of judgment has been supplied with a doctrine of method in the form of an appendix. The reader will be intrigued by the question, how do aesthetics and teleology come under the same roof?

The hint of an explanation may be found in the subtitles of the introduction. There one reads that the *Critique of Judgment* is "a means of connecting the two parts of philosophy into a whole" and that the concept of "purposiveness" (*Zweckmässigkeit*) is important in aesthetics as well as in teleology. The first of these two pieces of information makes one think of the contrast between the first two Critiques; the affirmation of freedom in the *Critique of Practical Reason* seems to contradict the strict emphasis on the necessity of nature in the *Critique of Pure Reason*. However, the contradiction does not hold true at the level of an ultimate depth, for the necessity of nature involves the order of objective phenomena exclusively. The central concern of the *Critique of Pure Reason* was the concept of the object. As an emphatically stressed passage in the preface to the second edition says, the book expounds the paradoxical assumption that "objects must conform to our way of understanding them."[7] On the other hand, "the structure of phenomena according to necessary rules, that is, according to laws," constitutes the objectivity of things for our knowledge.[8]

But now for this concept of purposiveness! It has no relation to the necessary rules which determine the structure of the objective world, the world where the "universal laws of the mechanism of matter" apply.[9] Hence in order to speak in terms of "purposiveness," and by means of this concept to establish a link between the "two parts of philosophy," another way of looking at existence is required than that which consists in looking at "objects." But to clarify this fresh approach Kant had to draw upon the resources of a language still lacking in flexibility, and in this ordeal the unity he envisioned between aesthetics and teleology becomes obscure. Afterwards the nineteenth century (at the beginning of the 1870s at the latest) minted the concept of experience (*Erlebnis*), thus providing the key to the riddle.

If a painting interests us, it stands over against our consciousness as an "object" as long as we are ascertaining the technique with which it has been painted, or its height, or its width, or what it represents, or whether it is for sale and at what price. The relation of consciousness to the object which faces it ceases, however, as soon as the painting becomes our aesthetic "experience."

Now object and subject, object and consciousness, become an undivided unity; our experience is in us, it is our own immediacy.

Our relation to nature is in some respects comparable to this twofold relationship with the work of art. In the *Critique of Pure Reason* nature is called "the aggregate of the objects of experience."[10] But nature as a living reality cannot be seized by this concept; what "life" means cannot be expressed objectively; we grasp the sense of the word only from the immediate experience of our own life.

The readers who came upon the *Critique of Pure Reason* before the appearance of the *Critique of Judgment* assumed as a matter of course that the first Critique was a complete, self-contained work. When, later on, they read the *Critique of Practical Reason*, they tended to take the doctrine of free will as an antithesis to the doctrine of natural necessity found in the earlier book. The antithesis was not necessarily disturbing, for both books made it sufficiently clear how the apparent contradiction was to be resolved: the world of objective phenomena is not the ultimate reality. What is, in the last analysis, necessary is our faith in reason, which gives us a certitude in the moral sphere that is beyond the reach of intelligence bent upon objects.[11] The possibility of freedom existing alongside the causality of nature would be excluded only by the "deceptive, though all too common, assumption that phenomena have an *absolute reality*."[12] "The laws furnished by human reason . . . contain the law of nature as well as the law of morality, considered first in two separate systems but finally in one single philosophical system."[13] With these words the *Critique of Pure Reason* has already pointed beyond its limited sphere of interest. And by the time Fichte had begun his study of Kant the *Critique of Judgment* had just appeared, and with it the outline of that "one philosophical system." For Fichte it was a matter of course that the first two Critiques reached their conclusion in the third. "Herewith, therefore, I terminate my entire critical undertaking," Kant wrote in the preface to the *Critique of Judgment*. And Fichte realized that even the two earlier books depended for their proper meaning on this conclusion. Here it is quite unimportant that Fichte's interpretation did not tally with Kant's precise meaning. What is important is that

Historical-Philosophical Introduction

for Fichte philosophy was always the interpretation of life, and this, above all, is what is involved when the I, the positing I, became forthwith the starting point of his systematic endeavors.[14]

The impact of Fichte's new doctrine was extraordinary. It could be seen both in his crowded lecture halls and in the fierce rejections, devoid of comprehension, which he met in Jena;[15] but it was most evident of all in the fact that Fichte's point of departure in immediate experience soon acquired important adherents who advanced further in the same direction. In 1795 Schelling's ingenious *Letters on Dogmatism and Criticism* had already shown Kant's contribution in a new light by distinguishing it sharply from what those who had "hitherto gone on dogmatizing on Kant's credit"[16] had found in him. A few years later (1799) Schleiermacher published his discussions *About Religion*; thus he initiated the assault on the old dogmatism which, basing itself on quotations from the Bible, undertook to provide an objective knowledge of God and of divine things by means of philosophical speculation. In Schleiermacher's discussions, religious life speaks out of its own immediacy. Dogmas are secondary, and "all sacred scripture is only a mausoleum of religion.... It is not the believer in sacred scripture who is the religious man, but the one who has no need of such scripture and might be able to write one himself."[17] How far removed Schleiermacher is from the traditional Protestant veneration of the "Word" and the "pure doctrine"! Schleiermacher's later doctrine concerning faith is presented with a distinct awareness of its own historical conditionality. The sovereign theme of dogmatics is not concerned with timeless formulas with a claim to objective validity; rather, it is the task of dogmatics to serve its own time by interpreting pious feeling as it is found living in the congregation of the church. Soon thereafter, Hegel came before the public. In 1801 he praised Fichte for having distinguished between the spirit and the letter of Kantian philosophy, and for boldly affirming "the identity of subject and object in the form I=I." "As for the needs of the time, the Fichtean philosophy has been so sensational and epoch-making that even those who took a stand against it and endeavored to start their own speculative systems succumbed to the principle of the Fichtean philosophy, and could not reject it although their systems were murkier and less pure." Hegel was not satisfied with the exposition which Fichte gave to the principle; he said it was outstripped by Schelling. And in Schleiermacher's discussions about religion Hegel recognizes a kindred spirit.[18]

Could one raise the objection that any philosophizing which takes experience (*Erleben*) as its starting point is condemned from the very outset as individualistic objectivism and, on that account, is motivated by no serious desire for truth? One can reply that philosophers have at all times taken their own experience as their point of departure. If they have not explicitly said so, then in that respect they were destined to be kinsmen of that Monsieur Jourdain who had to learn from his Master of Philosophy that for more than forty years he has been speaking prose. If water had not become an *experience* for Thales, nor the proportions of lengths of sounding strings experiences for the Pythagoreans, they would not have established their doctrines. How could any consciousness be concerned with something which had not entered its experience! To be sure, pre-Kantian philosophy took this very little into account. Since all experience implies an experiencing subject, all philosophizing, too, is subjectively conditioned. This becomes manifest in the divergences between the different philosophies. But the endeavors to resolve such divergences sought to go beyond the mere oppositions as such. And the fact that the centuries-old classics of philosophy have survived the changes brought by many intellectual reorientations and are read even today in the awareness that they have important things to say to us indicates that the effort to bring the factor of subjective conditioning under control can attain a high degree of success. Every philosopher will try to transcend those elements belonging to what is contingent in his personality. He does not philosophize like a "windowless monad," but in distinguishing his own position from the stand taken by others, and in discussion with them, he endeavors to interpret and express, as seen from the highest attainable summit, the truth of his time. Where he meets with unacceptable theses he seeks to penetrate to their fundamental principles in order to attain greater clarity about his own views, and perhaps to improve his own theses. Thus the history of philosophy is fertilized and fostered by the very experience of

Historical-Philosophical Introduction 7

differences. If we were submerged in the contingency of subjectivity, we should lose truth; but the danger of this diminished, rather than increased, when critical philosophy made us aware of the inevitability of starting from our own experience. Thales did not say to himself that it was an intensive *experience* of water which gave the direction to his philosophizing; but Fichte, Schelling, Schleiermacher, and Hegel were very clearly and expressly aware of the point of departure of their systems. Even today we are not free of the danger of individualistic subjectivism, nor shall we be tomorrow. But if we acknowledge the necessity of starting from experience the danger is less than if we do not acknowledge it.

Ordinarily the word experience (*Erlebnis*) is used in that emphatic sense which would distinguish it from the passive sensation which constitutes experience in animals, for from the latter no occasions for philosophizing would issue. Rather, the word denotes a living personal experience enhanced by the activity of intellect (*geistige Tätigkeit*). The intellect's activity is, in Fichte's phrase, "activity directed upon itself and determining itself."[19] Inherent in it is something like a law ordered towards a goal. This goal is often unattained—and not only in philosophizing. Strong animal urges may present a hindrance to the spirit, and a man may act contrary to what he knows is right. Or, his intellectual powers may be insufficiently developed with respect to the goal towards which they are directed: the reader of a scientific work may struggle in vain to understand it; a tourist, say, who is a stranger to Italy and unversed in cultural history may with conscientious docility (but without cultural profit) go to each site which his Baedeker, with its asterisks, assures him he must not miss. But whether, in such instances, the spirit gains the mastery or the situation is beyond the capacities of the spirit's imperfect human vehicles, what man is experiencing is that necessity within which he is to discover his own freedom. He experiences this as logical necessity if, for instance, he clarifies a mathematical proof to his own satisfaction or strives to make it clear. When listening to a symphony he experiences this necessity as aesthetic in the measure in which the music actually speaks to him. And when, faced with a situation which is of genuine concern to him, he tries to conform his response to the truth it contains, his action is the effect of his concrete experience of moral necessity. In short, the experience of reality manifests norms which, if they are obeyed, lead to our experiencing a given situation seized at its highest. But even when the movement of the spirit is without real success, those norms are immanent in the experience.

Down to the time of Kant and often thereafter it was assumed that these norms could be expressed without ambiguity, in immutable formulas. Men searched for a canon of artistic creation; and many, moreover, adhered to the view that classical art might be used as a criterion for all epochs. If one were not a skeptic or a libertine, one believed in both a morality valid for all times (disguised, so to speak, in changing conventions) and a perennial "natural right." Moreover, with regard to logic, Kant himself said that (inessentials aside) "it was not at liberty to take a step backward after Aristotle" and "could not take a step forward."[20] But at the very summit at which Kant brought his "whole critical business" to its conclusion, the orientation which he gave philosophy towards a concern with life itself experienced in its immediacy was soon productive of entirely new formulations of the old problems. Twenty-five years after Kant had praised Aristotelian logic for being, so it seemed to him, "closed and finished," Hegel took issue with these words, declaring that we must instead infer from the long stagnation of logic that "a total revision" was now required, "for the continuous activity of the intellect over two thousand years should have provided it with a higher degree of awareness of its own thinking."[21] The so-called laws of thought were dethroned.[22] For they took their bearings not from the immediate experience of thinking but from objectified concepts—thoughts set up as lifeless forms. Hegel points out that no consciousness operates in accordance with the law of identity as the schoolmen teach it: "Everything is identical with itself. A equals A; or, negatively, A cannot simultaneously be A and not A."[23]

Every living thing substantiates its identity with itself only by becoming other; it remains the same only by changing. We who are reading these words are the same persons we were ten years ago, and yet we are no longer the same. Had we wanted to remain changelessly the same—identical with ourselves without any alteration—we should have had to achieve this through a kind of numbness and rigidity (though assuredly this would not have prevented the ravages of time from effecting their own changes in us). In fact, we have been able to maintain our own identity only by constantly emerging from identity considered as unchanging sameness. According to Hegel the law of identity contains "only an incomplete truth." But this very judgment "implies at once that the truth is complete only in the unity of identity with difference, and therefore consists only in this unity."[24] Already Fichte, working within the schematism of thesis-antithesis-synthesis, was trying to understand what was meant by living thought, and even to probe the meaning of life itself. Seeing the *Critique of Judgment* as the climax of Kant's work, he realized that one must take life itself as one's starting point in order to enter worthily into the great legacy of Kant. It became fully evident to him that the point of departure for philosophy (a problem which Kant left untouched) must be at a level inaccessible to the grasp of mere intelligence. As far as life is concerned, there cannot be an "objective" concept of it, that is, a concept which is objectively valid; here the objective forms of thought prove inadequate. The word "life" receives its meaning only from the immediate experience of our own life.[25] In the *Addresses to the German Nation* Fichte castigates a kind of philosophizing which would discover "in the perceivable phenomenon itself a perceivable basis for perception" (*eine in der Erscheinung erscheinende Grundlage dieser Erscheinung*), a kind of philosophizing which would assume as such a basis "a fixed being, which simply is what it is and nothing else, fettered in itself and tied to its own being." Such turgid philosophizing would declare death to be the "original and ultimate"![26] "The true philosophy, however, which has attained its end in itself and which has penetrated through the phenomenon to its true core, must start from the one, pure, divine life."[27]

According to a doctrine which goes back to Aristotle,[28] truth in the strict sense is a matter of statements. This thesis has been reiterated down to the most recent times. True, the Christian philosophy of the Middle Ages, particularly at its height, identified truth with God and thus opened the widest vistas for the doctrine of truth. But in the subsequent centuries the labors dedicated to Thomistic tradition (but lagging behind Thomas) had confined the problem of truth within narrow intellectualistic limits. The reconquest of an unhampered view, which brings into experience the limitlessness of the problem, is the merit of thinkers like A.-D. Sertillanges, O.P.,[29] and after him, Hans Urs von Balthasar. Balthasar has especially in mind the Christian philosophy of the modern age when he writes: "The reduction of the problem of truth to a purely theoretical evidence which carefully excludes all living personal and ethical decisions limits the scope of truth so severely that, through this limitation alone, truth is robbed of its universality and thus of its proper essence."[30] The all-embracing, ontological significance of the problem of truth has been acknowledged in the philosophy of idealism by the movement starting with Fichte (although in the domain of German culture this movement has almost died because the doctrines of Hegel and Schelling were ignored). Fichte stirred traditional philosophy out of its stagnation when he made "true being" prior to the activity of judgment. (True being, of course, in the meaning which he established in his *Lectures about the Essence of the Scholar*: "There is no other being than life . . . the life of God or of the absolute."[31])

Truths exclusively concerned with the "phenomenon" as such require only an intelligence which moves within its own set forms for their understanding. But as soon as truths reach beyond the domain of the objective—for instance, truths concerned with artistic or moral experience—the possibility of their becoming evident is bound to the condition that the one who encounters them has overcome the death in himself. "The living acts only upon the living," one reads in the *Addresses to the German Nation* in a passage wherein Fichte is attacking the "newer German philosophy" in an effort to explain its still prevailing sterility.[32] This same conviction had evoked from him, quite early in his career (1797), the much-quoted dictum: "The philosophy a man chooses depends on the kind of man he is."[33] And even earlier Schelling had spoken in the same vein.[34]

Fichte charges the philosophers he attacks in his *Addresses to*

Historical-Philosophical Introduction

the German Nation with deviation from the line of development of the German national genius which leads from Leibniz through Kant to Fichte. He reproaches them for harboring a faith not in life but in death.[35] What a philosopher "believes in" reveals his point of departure (whether or not it is acknowledged by him). The starting point of a philosophy is its basis derived from nothing else. Fichte demands that man shall "acknowledge his life to be an eternal link in the chain of revelation of the divine life, and hence consider it holy, and likewise acknowledge every other life of the spirit as just such a link."[36] Fichte believes in the divine life, of which he has an immediate certainty. He regards the reality of nature as secondary and conditional; if nature did not have its relation to the moral task of mankind, it would be a mere phenomenon without essence. Here Schelling follows other paths; he believes in the reality of nature; he finds nature in God. Nature is not, for him, a mere object; it belongs to the immediate experience of his own being. Nature is the *ground* of human existence—nay, God himself has nature in himself as the ground of his existence. Nature is not divine, but it is in God and it could not exist if God did not *exist*.[37]

FIRST PART
FOUNDATION

1
SCIENCE AND OUR VIEW OF THE WORLD

The propositions of science, in the broader sense of science which embraces all the branches of learning, must be evaluated as cognitions (*Erkenntnisse*); that is, they must be referred to the critical consciousness for confirmation of their claim to universal validity. Professions of belief (*Bekenntnisse*), on the other hand, present themselves as marking a position which transcends the sphere of the various scholarly disciplines; a position, therefore, from which the limits and the bearing of scientific knowledge can be seen, and hence its true meaning clarified. This principle becomes important when we come to the distinction between "philosophy as a strict discipline" and "philosophy as a world view." Cognitions, it is said, are rational, professions of belief are not. Rational propositions can be scrutinized and proved. Propositions based on belief cannot; any assent which we can give to them comes from our personal experience. Rational truth is timeless. Whatever is irrational and a matter of belief is subject to time and conditioned by it. Beliefs may be shortlived, but they are not necessarily so, since they depend for their duration on historically conditioned life situations. Indeed it is the needs that arise from our historically conditioned human existence which determine the extent to which specific beliefs can continue to hold sway over the thought of an age; and it is on such needs, too, that beliefs always depend for their efficacy.

Everyone knows that professed beliefs arise out of faith and appeal to faith for their confirmation. But what about scientific knowledge? First let us consider the objective knowledge aimed at by mathematics and the natural sciences; but secondly, the point we are making here applies likewise to those disciplines known as the "humanities" (*Geisteswissenschaften*), for their wordings, though they are necessarily "perspectives" and often have a pronounced character of statements of belief, nevertheless do have scientific value to the precise degree in which they clarify facts.

Through Kant's *Critique of Pure Reason* science became a problem for philosophy (in fact it had already become a problem for the predecessors of Kant, about whom Alois Riehl makes decisive statements in the first volume of his *Philosophical Criticism*[1]). Kant showed that the fundamental concepts which determine the structure of scientific thinking prove their validity only within finite conditional contexts. They become obscure if they are "extended to the unconditional."[a] These concepts are not fully clear, and the "truths" of science are therefore fraught with problems, and hence cannot furnish an unclouded realization of the *idea* of what is true; they have only a conditional truth value. Moreover that which conditions them is beyond the reach of science. (We shall have to talk about that later on.) This problematicity which weighs on science as such is always ignored wherever philosophy itself poses as science. In other words, "scientific philosophy" rests on the faith in science, faith in scientific intelligence. But is it permissible in philosophy to respect faith where only conditional truths are within its reach—and to direct faith to no higher goal than that? Conditional truths always have only a preliminary validity; as they enter our consciousness, they always point beyond themselves; for in consciousness dwells, in full clarity, the idea of that truth which is true unconditionally. We may obtain the elucidation of that idea of truth from the form of absolute identity. Since it is a form, we are at liberty to pour into it any contents we wish, and by so doing find satisfaction in the manifestation of unconditional truth: "A is A"; "an atom is an atom." But in order to be able to pour a content into a logical form, we must have turned the form into an object, that is, we must have robbed it of the immediate life without which it cannot bring about a cognition. That form which is really effective in intellectual experience is not separated from its content. And thus it does not merely assert an identity but always a relation to something else. For instance, if in a geometric proof there is occasion to say that a triangle ABC is equal to itself, then that occasion occurs precisely because the triangle must be conceived in two different relationships, and because thus its identity with itself is not absolute. The sheer assertion of identity ("an atom is an atom") is an empty abstraction which has only the form (with optional content) of truth but which does not furnish any cognition—no full, no living truth.

Husserl has spoken about "the low methodological rank" of the results which the "philosophers of world-view" (*Weltanschauungsphilosophen*) can produce.[2] But we are entitled to ask whether what Husserl calls a philosophy of world-view makes any claim to "scientific rank." For the greatest task which faces such a philosophy, with regard to science, is to show what science signifies for the context within which man can shape his life and, presumably, seeks to shape it in a human way, in a way worthy of man. If philosophy were to take this task for a scientific task, then this would amount to a judgment of science about itself. To be sure, one who puts his belief in science cannot take offense at this; he will be of the opinion that he is entitled to claim for himself the truth of the doctrine of Spinoza that when truth sheds its light it brings with it its own certainty: *Qui veram habet ideam, simul scit se veram habere ideam . . . sicut lux se ipsam et tenebras manifestat, sic veritas norma sui et falsi est.*[3] ("One who has a true idea knows in the same act that he has a true idea. . . . As light manifests both itself and darkness, truth is the norm both of itself and of the false.") But the light which shines in science does not suffice to clear up the obscurity which is spread over those fundamental concepts which are presupposed by scientific thinking. And therefore one would have to dispute the title of the scientist who would appeal to the words of Spinoza.

In science the decision as to the validity of a statement belongs to the intelligence alone, but the decision concerning a world-view is a matter for the whole man. Husserl ignores this basic distinction. He tries to understand the difference by relating it to history. He says, "The 'idea' of every world-view is different for every age. The 'idea' of science, however, is not limited by any relation to the spirit of an age."[4] Certainly, world-views are subject to the movements of history (in the last resort, subject to the personal history of those who hold them). However, in history the doctrines of science themselves are also subject to change. But Husserl speaks of the *ideas* of both. "The life of the spirit of mankind always goes on with its profusion of ever-new forms, new intellectual contests, new experiences, new evaluations and renewed goals. Thus, within the widening horizon of life, where all the new psychic formations have their place, man's culture, his wisdom, and his world-view, change."[5] Certainly. But in this historical process science changes, too. It does not merely increase in content and extend the reach of its doctrines; it changes its proper character (one may think of astronomy before and after Copernicus, of zoology before and after Darwin, of physics of the nineteenth and then of the twentieth century). And what also changes is the measure of the significance of science for the formation of human life. What remains unchanged is merely the formal relationship of science to the idea of the truth—yet this relation is no less important for a world-view than it is for science; nay, it is important in a more comprehensive sense which is not restricted to the insights of the intelligence. Theodor Litt declares, "Truth is not a view of the foreground; it does not leave in the background what is really decisive and ultimate with regard to man and the world."[6] And therefore, looking back upon the ghastly years of devastation of culture in Germany, Litt says: "Along with the evasion of truth, humanity, too was set aside."[7]

Husserl's concept of science abstracts from the movements of history—movements which, in life, cannot be separated from science. By proposing problems these movements affect science; and, in return, they receive impulses from the very doctrines derived from the intrinsic law of science. According to Husserl, the concept takes its bearing from the abstract idea of changeless truth. "Science is a name for absolute, timeless values."[8] But scientific doctrines undergo revisions upon the discovery of facts which invalidate the claim to validity made by theories hitherto appearing plausible. Scientific doctrines can hold their own not because they take their orientation from the idea of timeless truths (which they can do only in a historically conditioned manner) but because they square with the facts available at their particular time. Even such cogently evident propositions as those of Euclidean geometry have acquired a new relation to space, and therewith to the idea of truth, owing to the appearance of non-Euclidean geometries. Even for geometry it is true that history conditions the intellectual experience in which alone the geometric "truth" can be verified and maintained. All human reality is historically conditioned, and science is a piece of human reality. When new evidence contains, or seems to contain, significant implications for our world-view—that is, for the meaning which goes beyond what is merely of academic interest—then science itself changes. The time-conditioned intellectual life to which science belongs will put a stress different from the hitherto prevailing emphasis on that which determines what is important in a given science and which therefore determines the way in which the science must formulate its questions. Science continues to seek truth, but the direction in which it seeks is no longer the same in every respect as it was before. A physics for which the strictest determinism of events is no longer an axiomatic presupposition, a physics which, therefore, takes its place in the life of the mind with assertions whose orientation is different from before, is a physics which is no longer what it was. It is obvious that our exposition has its ground in a "philosophy of world-view," while Husserl starts from a rationalistic "idea" of science. A philosophy of world-views can and must make room, within its structure, for the rights of rationalistic understanding. In contrast a "scientific philosophy" cannot but reject a philosophy of world-views as an unscientific affair; at best it can tolerate such views alongside its own; it cannot understand them.

A scientific doctrine presents itself to the contemporary world in a conceptual formulation which is always historically conditioned. But usually the presentation makes no explicit mention of this conditionality; it abstracts from the historical situation. Owing to this simplification, the thought appears more transparent, clearer—clearer than its object as it appeared to the researcher bent on it. Moreover, this abstract formulation (though it may be the only one of interest) always throws light on the real from one side only. The very abstract concept of science supported by Husserl (and by many others) ignores the fact that science is woven into the structure of human endeavor, and that this endeavor changes the concrete goals of science as it pursues them.

If we acknowledge the fact of world-views, are we not implicitly admitting the validity of sheer subjectivity, mere contingency? Although it is true that science is fraught with obscure problems with respect to its most fundamental concepts and in the course of its history undergoes profound and far-reaching changes, the fact remains that it constantly seeks confirmation for its doctrines in experience. It may be that for a time science will move along erroneous paths; yet in the long run the correction of the error will not fail to come. For what seems to be an objective confirmation, but is only a deceptive appearance of confirmation, cannot forever support the subjective concepts it involves. (A good example is Georg Ernst Stahl's doctrine of phlogiston.) On the other hand, a world-view does not easily meet with such a correction—strictly speaking it never does. The prophecy that Hitler's Third Reich would last for a thousand years has been confuted; but the confutation could touch only the intellectual, the impersonal, element of the world-view of National Socialism; and it is precisely this element which can be detached from the essence of the view. "Logic can neither create nor destroy world-views," Nietzsche wrote to Deussen, in the year 1867, and again similarly in 1868.[9] An adherent of Irving[b] was asked what her Adventist faith could be if, contrary to her conviction, Jesus should not appear again at the announced time; this woman replied: "Then, the fact would have been a trial."

But how about the non-intellectual elements of the world-views? Are they merely subjective? Is what seems to give firmness, or at least the appearance of firmness, to those views merely subjective? Gabriel Marcel speaks about a "knowledge which, far from being confined within the sphere of immediate subjectivity, even transcends objectivity."[10] Scientific knowledge seeks objectivity; but objectivity rests on fundamental concepts which are fraught with problems. Objectivity offers no ultimately valid truth. It is the *necessity* of its form which gives objectivity its priority over the merely subjective. But is this undeniable superiority over the merely subjective also a superiority over the nature of a world-view? The fact that a world-view depends on the entire personality (not on mere theoretical reason) does not mean that its nature is a product of arbitrariness and of contingency and is merely subjective in *that* sense. To be sure, one must acknowledge that a world-view belongs to the most intimate depths of unexchangeable personality. Gabriel Marcel tells how an early experience of antagonism among his closest relatives—"divergences of views and of temperaments"—made clear to him how mutual understandings can be difficult, nay impossible. "I believe nothing better prepared me for understanding that on one same plane, there can exist incompatible perspectives, each of which a mind committed to justice and truth is obliged to adopt, without hoping to discover a unifying and conciliating formula. This led me directly and without technical reflection to the acknowledgment of a certain weakness in the nature of judgment. I had to acknowledge the necessity not only of conceiving but of affirming a certain beyond, an area beyond discursive reason, where a harmony can be foreseen and even restored in some manner without ratiocinating reason being able to impose those forms which satisfy it and which it claims, unduly perhaps."[11] A world-view is not something objective, nor can it become objective. Therefore, such a view can not be transmitted to other men (like an object or like an objectively proved proposition). We are challenged to transcend what is merely subjective, arbitrary, contingent in our outlook on reality. But this must be achieved by personal struggle, and the product of the struggle retains the mark of our personal characteristics. This does not mean that the individual stands alone in the fight; for all that is personal finds its true development within the structures of the community, in mutual relationships with others. The responsibility always belongs to all, and all are responsible for all. However, each individual bears the responsibility as his own, in his own situation. And one who is aware that he is responsible for his world-view seeks to secure and clarify the particular rightness of his own position while he is struggling to attain the world-view.

Here the words of Theodor Litt are apposite: "In every conceivable concrete situation, reality demands that the mind shall see the aspect of the world which comes with the situation as a strictly unique view and interpretation."[12] We can help each other in our struggle for the achievement of a world-view; yet what is ultimately decisive each one has to do for himself. The whole man is the one who has attained his world-view; but in what different measures are men whole.

In general—that is, without taking into consideration the difference between men's values—one may say that world-views are determined by the individual's life course in such a way that they appear as summaries of whatever seems capable of furnishing the feeling of intellectual satisfaction—satisfaction furnished for each one in *his* life and on the basis (cultivated with more or less seriousness) of *his* possibilities, and therefore "satisfying" in very different individual degrees. Inward alienation excludes true satisfaction. There are evil world-views. One who has evil inclinations has the natural tendency to harmonize his world-view with those inclinations: he needs definite articles of faith peculiar to himself in order to be satisfied in some measure with his life as he lives it. In this case, the articles of faith accommodate the arbitrariness of the conduct of life. One cannot seriously raise the question of their truth. One who affirms in practice the world-view of a libertine may try to justify his intellectual inclination with arguments of some kind. However, such arguments never go beyond the domain determined by the correlation of the subjective and the objective; therefore they can tell us nothing about that truth which "transcends objectivity" and which must furnish the norm for a world-view. Paul Tillich points in the direction of this norm when he speaks of the "understanding of the structure of reality," of the "immediately creative power of cognition," and of man's "relation to the unconditional, a relation which is freedom as well as fate, and from which flow both, action and cognition." In order to prevent any relativistic misinterpretation, Tillich adds the following statement: "The responsibility for truth is as great as the responsibility for the good, or rather, it is one responsibility."[13]

In his first main work, Fichte explicitly expressed the intentional trend toward a world-view: "The doctrine of knowledge[c] is to claim the whole man; therefore, it can be apprehended only with the totality of man's powers."[14] Fichte is convinced that Kant's philosophy, too, was seeking "the whole man"; but the reader of Kant can discover that only if he is able to recognize the indissoluble interdependence of the three Critiques. Fichte says clearly that he is concerned with this unity. But he also knows the personal prerequisites which his readers must bring to his books. In the richest measure Fichte found those prerequisites in Goethe. When on June 21, 1794, Fichte sent him the first fascicle of the *Foundation of the Entire Theory of Knowledge* (*Grundlage der gesamten Wissenschaftslehre*) he wrote in the accompanying letter: "Philosophy has not reached its goal as long as the results of reflective abstraction do not conform with the purest spirituality (*Geistigkeit*) of feeling. I regard *you,* and have always regarded you, as the pre-eminent representative of that spirituality on the level which humanity has attained at present. With justice philosophy addresses itself to you. Your feeling is the touchstone of philosophy."[15] Of course, philosophy is not possible without an appeal to the strictest account of logic; but the assent of logic is no more than a *conditio sine qua non*. The validity of a philosophy which in its desire for the truth claims to be more than intellectual discipline (*Wissenschaft*) depends decisively on whether it can appeal to the whole man. And the question whether it has the right to make such an appeal must be answered by one who in his person represents "the purest spirituality of feeling on the level attained by humanity at present."

The attainment of humanness is the task which pervades the whole history of mankind, the task in which every epoch has its own particular part. The possibilities of shaping one's life change, and with them changes the concrete meaning of the word *humanity*. The great struggle demands ever new ways of fighting, and as its goals are unceasingly renewed, the problems of philosophy become new, too. Whenever philosophy attains its height, and wherever it does so, it confronts *new* questions, and man's struggle towards the height of the time can demand *new* vigor from philosophy.

2
THE SUPERTEMPORALLY TRUE AND ITS FORMS

In the structures of cultural life the *supertemporal* rules, and thus establishes historical continuity. One should not use this word supertemporal in the sense in which, like so many others, Husserl uses it, as synonymous with the *timeless*. That which is timeless has no relation to time. Thus, though surely the multiplication table was first thought out somewhere and at some time, the insights formulated by the multiplication table have nothing to do with the history of its discovery. For it was merely impersonal intelligence, independent of any specific characteristic of the historical situation, which found the multiplication table to be what it is and nothing else—in fact, had to find it as what it is and nothing else, because it is valid in timeless abstraction. The supertemporal, however, can be apprehended in the concrete works and accomplishments of art, of morality, of the law and also, in smaller measure, of science. In these accomplishments every cultural community finds its historical coinage. It is not a mere abstraction, "right," which in a historically limited sphere of culture gives unity to the different acts of the administration of justice. For example, it is a definite code on the basis of which lawsuits are carried on in a given country. Instead of an abstract concept there is manifest a concrete reality which, though historically conditioned, is yet in duty bound to a superhistorical idea —to the idea of the just—a reality which has to fulfill its necessary function for the sake of humanity.

The abstraction "right" also takes form, but as a mere matter of thought, while the right which is actually in force manifests its reality very perceptibly. This right lays claim to man as a personality; it demands *faith* from those subject to the right, even

The Supertemporally True and Its Forms 25

from those who live outside the sphere of the right's legal validity. In the first place it demands faith in the idea of justice to which it is in duty bound, but secondly (and perhaps without good reason) it also demands faith in the embodiment which the right, in its historical limitation, gives to the idea of justice. Concepts can exhaust the meaning of the abstraction "right": the abstraction directly concerns only the intelligence. (If I read the title of a book, *Swiss Constitutional Law*, then I know what this book is about; but I do not yet meet the reality of that law.) The historically conditioned reality "law" is a wide body of individual legal *actions* with their heights and with their shortcomings; the abstraction "law" is nothing but a much narrower number of *concepts* relating to law.

Only in the domain of intellectual abstraction is there anything timeless. The abstraction "art" is timeless, but there are no timeless *works of art*. We are familiar with the timeless abstract concepts "art," "morality," "science." But these are derivative formulas which refer back to superhistorical ideas in authority over the life of the mind. These life forces enter into the change of the times; they are not the product of that change but its ideal rulers. They affirm themselves in that change; during every epoch they are present with high demands, but no epoch can exhaust them; every subsequent epoch receives its own call. The works which are the exemplary products of any epoch—works which show the newly accessible height which the epoch has reached—thereby obtain superhistorical dignity. The impressiveness of the work furnishes the power, and the idea it serves confirms the right, of the work to outlast its own time. It has the power to add substance to the life even of a much later epoch. Thus the Homeric poems and the legislation of the Emperor Justinian survive and exercise their influence even today. Of no superhistorical significance are those many works which merely conform to the conditions of the time, or which answer badly, or which even defy, the challenging call of the supertemporal idea, though they are contained within the temporal manifestation of what is supertemporally real. Though they would not have been possible without that reality's manifestation in time—and although after centuries they may still interest the historian of culture who wants to find out what the life of the past was like—yet they lack superhistorical significance, since it belongs only to works which manifest the *creative* power of the ideas.

Manifest in the movements of civilization, art, morality, law, are superhistorical life forces; with them there is another: science. Insofar as science is the work of impersonal intelligence whose laws would demand for the product they have formed a validity which endures unaltered in history, science (like the multiplication table) demands recognition of its statements beyond the boundaries of the different cultures which are in some way separated from each other. (This may be why Husserl has accorded timelessness to the values of science. However, the process of theoretical reasoning itself has a history. The thinking of Aristotle with regard to causation was different from that of Robert Mayer. To be sure, an immediate conviction of timeless validity is present in all the operations of ratiocinating reason; but the history of science confirms that belief only in a limited way. To find the definite form in which new scientific tasks can be mastered is a matter left to tomorrow's struggles of the mind.) For, the scientific work is not the product of intelligence alone; imagination always plays its part, and imagination is power which has its roots in the particular conditions of historical existence; it determines the direction of the scientific quest, and it speaks more impressively, more convincingly, to a kindred than to an alien mentality. Since scientific works find their first circle of readers where the language in which they are written is spoken, they are likely to have their strongest influence within the sphere of that language. Thus the character and the interest of scientific research attain a differentiating influence on the formations of culture. But science is superhistorical because, like art, morality and law, it meets the historical conditions within which it develops —conditions whose particular character does influence science— with the force of its own superior necessity.

Every cultural epoch needs science; but the desire for it springs from different presuppositions and tendencies, and therefore the demands themselves which science seeks to satisfy are different. Even the fact that a universally human practical goal of research has but one meaning does not efface the particular character of its origin. Historian of medicine Albert Esser writes in the introduction to his edition of a sixteenth-century ophthalmological Sanskrit text whose "genuinely scientific bent" he acknowledges, that its content "may not be evaluated as an isolated fact but only in the context of the history and geography of a nation and country in general and in particular in the context of the historical development of medical thought."[1] In the West the science of antiquity was something other than the science of the Middle Ages, and the science of modern times again shows a different face. The needs of the existing social structure are of great significance for the goals of scientific research and for the time given to it. The general conditions of life can favor or hamper science in many ways. In the history of the civilized nations there have been epochs in which science meant a great deal and epochs in which it meant very little for the formation of the life of the community. And the same can also be said about art, morality, and law. These elements of life, too, have an intellectual ingredient; yet their specific character is determined by the ideas of the good, the beautiful, the just, although they use the intelligence as their indispensable servant (who at times behaves overbearingly). These ideas do not pretend to keep their manifestations in rigid subjection (as if the ideas called for precisely the same expression at all times). They find their realization in free creations which will ennoble the social order of the particular age by allowing the supertemporal to shine forth in it as a witness of the eternal, which is present in the particular circumstances of the given time in a particular manner.

Science can be mentioned along with morality, art and law, which are the representations of the good, the beautiful and the just; however, in speaking of science we should not fail to take into account what was said in the foregoing chapter when we discussed the contrast between science and philosophy; the activity of the intelligence can have only a problematic relationship to the idea of the true. If the word *truth* is being used as a predicate attributed to the accomplishments of science, then it is being deprived of its full meaning. Scientific endeavors are concerned only with ascertaining objective relationships. (Even in historiography and the humanities the objective order functions as a critical court of appeal and helps to determine the character of truth.) However, that truth which is unconditionally true is not in the least a truth about objects.[2] The individual subject, in seeking truth, finds in the object something which is opposite, foreign, to himself; finds something about which he can fashion thoughts from the outside but which he can never apprehend as-it-is-in-itself with unconditional certainty. In morality, art and law, however, the unconditional ideas which are not made relative by an inherent reference to that which is "not-I" point the direction in which immediate experience must go, though not in the sense that man could ever attain a total realization of the good, the beautiful and the just, and thus of the unconditionally true. The constitutional frailty of that intelligence which seeks its truth in objective existence, and hence can never be certain of the ultimate validity of those truths, brings its train of consequences even where reasoning is needed for merely auxiliary services. Yet, in the domains of morality, art and the administration of justice, the impersonal evidence furnished by intelligence is subjected to the personal, the human, in such a way that in immediate experience that which the subject should attain stands out in clear distinction from that which has been objectively accomplished. It is understandable that Faust can think only with melancholy regret of his activity in the time of the plague when, as his father's helper, he tried to heal the afflicted with medicaments he now knows to have been harmful; but Faust is wrong when he speaks about "brazen murderers."[a] Whatever is attained objectively is always dependent on circumstances which are not fully transparent and therefore cannot be fully controlled. The objective attainment is not a pure expression of the humanity which is operative in it. The immediacy of experience has its norms in the unrefracted ideas of the supertemporal. Nevertheless not only every realized attainment, but also every attempt to recognize the legitimacy of the endeavor, depends on the services of intelligence, which is limited structurally and also historically, whether by the history of culture or by the history of the individual. In its historical manifestations of these services even the most genuine humanity appears inadequate and often ambiguous.

The supertemporal ideas of the good, the beautiful, the just are forms and ways of realization of the unconditionally true. What become accessible in these forms are not truths *about* something (such truths are always conditional); *the* true enters radiantly into consciousness—shedding light, yet in such a way that we can at the same time become aware of how every human accomplishment falls short of the unconditionally valid.

A person performs a morally good action when he recognizes and accepts the situation which claims him for what it is in truth; and that means what the situation is for him, for his experience, which is part of the situation. (For sheer intelligence, the individual is one entity confronted with something other which is the situation. One is placed "over against" the other. But for moral experience the individual exists only as part of the situation.) To be sure, in this moral situation the intelligence is indispensable; yet it can err even in the service of good will. Thus it can happen that a man desires good but brings about evil. Perhaps in such a case a moral reprimand is justified on the ground that the agent acted rashly; but in that case the "good will" was not good enough. Perhaps the subjective limitation of one's own perspective has been accepted only too readily. But it may be that even the greatest care could not have sufficed to avoid the erroneous evaluation of the situation. And then it was precisely the *good* will which had to bring about evil. This is painful for the agent, but his conscience will absolve him—with justice, for the moral evaluation of the action is not referred to its objective success but to its subjective basis, to the will. With all his might, the agent wanted to do justice to the situation which challenged him to act; he wanted to treat it as what it was in truth; he had misunderstood it; he was not able to understand it rightly, and it was not a partisan interest which confused the understanding of the situation for him. He mistook for an unconditional truth the conditional situation which existed in his experience (an experience also conditioned by his ratiocination). In its relation to the truth, no human power reaches beyond the limit set for subjectivity by the strangeness of the objective realm which can never be made fully familiar. But the strangeness does not prevent the will from experiencing the unconditionally true, from becoming aware of its unconditional claims. That truth which science seeks must be found in the objective realm: thus it is conditioned by that realm's problematicity. But this truth which is addressed to the will in the idea of the good is unconditional.

Even in art it is not the objective as such that matters. The objective (whose representation in the work of art is a mere appearance) can be taken into consideration merely as a start. What is artistic in a work of art can be apprehended only if the work becomes the content of our aesthetic experience, and therefore does not stand "over against" us (the way a substance stands "over against" the chemist who is observing its reactions). In artistic experience the separation of subject and object is eliminated. To experience works of art means to increase our inner wealth, to be so closely touched by the very essence of reality that it loses some of its strangeness and our ability to understand it becomes greater. Cultures long lost in the depths of the past become accessible to us through their works of art, and the art of our contemporaries gives us a certain intimation of that life, ever steeped in mystery, by which we are all embraced. It has often been said that art is revelation. From the word revelation the relation to truth is inseparable. To be specific, so far as the scope of the present book is concerned (and it rests on no oath of allegiance to any ready-made revelation), revelation is inseparable from that relation to truth which is hidden from mere intelligence and cannot be expressed at all in prose. What the work of art reveals need not be a sublime truth, one of immense depths: waltz music will never have depth, yet it can be artistically valuable and it cannot be translated into prose. What art reveals is life—life itself, not its mere appearance. Truth becomes accessible, its nature—whether deep and momentous or slight and superficial—depending on the meaning of the given work of art. (One who comes to feel at home in the revealing works of art gives a greater content to his own existence and can therefore put more at stake in the struggle of life.) To be sure, each will read in the work of art only that which conforms to his character and to his level of education. And this is particularly true with regard to a comprehensive masterpiece with many meanings. Yet the work of art can lift one beyond one's level of education. And again, many may misinterpret the work. Here individual contingency sets limits.

The Supertemporally True and Its Forms

In the development of a people's genius, art is not lacking even in the most primitive cultural communities. Seen from richly developed planes of culture, it may often seem that the purpose of art is merely to let us forget the seriousness of life for a short while. But works of high art seriously lay claim to the whole man. In such works the depth of truth is revealed. Logical forms do not reach into this depth; it can become accessible to man only in symbols—in formulations of the aesthetic consciousness. All prophets are artists: they have something to say which could never be said in sober, prosaic sentences, something which, though it cannot be apprehended without reasoning, will not claim the attention merely of the intelligence. (The reverse is also true; all artists are prophets;—to be sure, not all are prophets of the true.)

Though we may at times put a somewhat hazardous trust in our openness of mind, we meet every work of art with the claim that it should speak to us—that the harmony of its elements should be aesthetically meaningful for us. The claim rests on the value distinction we make between the beautiful and the ugly, a distinction which cannot be reduced to human invention and which, on its part, helps to constitute our humanity and therewith the meaning of life. (Nobody can ignore the distinction, but how each one makes it depends on the degree of his personal culture.)

Of course, we do not demand that all works of art shall be beautiful; but the relation to that value distinction is essential for our getting into touch with the works of art so that they can speak to us. If the work of art is beautiful, then it speaks for us of perfection. To be sure, beautiful art can also be seductive; Plato already knew it; it can delude our aesthetic sensibilities by the appearance of perfection even as it repudiates aesthetic reality, "true being." Moreover, many inferior products of art present themselves to a sensitive mind as mendacious trash because they strive for an inappropriate beauty. Man is not perfect. And truth ranks above beauty—not the truth of mere intelligence, as everyone knows (or could know, and should take into account when he criticizes works of art), but the unconditional truth (which also ranks above the concepts of our intelligence). From the comprehensive significance of art arises also its role of representing the extent to which man falls short of perfection as such. Works which fulfill this task withhold from us the experience of beauty. A work of art which moves us deeply does not set out to be "beautiful." Works like Hans Baldung Grien's *Death Kissing a Woman* (in the Basel Museum), or Pieter Brueghel's *Blind Leading the Blind* (in the museum at Naples), or Goya's *The Disasters of War*, or Giraudoux's drama *Sodom and Gomorrah* have no place within the sphere of what is, properly speaking, beautiful. Nevertheless such works refer to the idea of the beautiful as a constituent of our self-awareness. But because they not only lack beauty but make us aware of its absence, our encounter with them evokes feelings and thoughts which carry us away from aesthetic enjoyment and recall us to the consciousness of human misery and human duty. The beautiful work of art, on the other hand, as belonging to the sphere of appearances, is closed within itself by its very form; it makes no demands on us which point beyond itself and which disturb our enjoyment of it. The work of art which moves us lacks this purely aesthetic self-containedness: one for whom it becomes an experience finds himself forced out of aesthetic enjoyment into that reality in which man's suffering lays claim to our humanity. Such a work calls for the response of the whole man—it confronts us with the truth. Every work of art is determined by the idea of the beautiful, which is always present in it as the moving force of the aesthetic experience. Where the idea of the beautiful is unexpressed, it nevertheless governs the experience of the ugly and awakens the longing for what really ought to be—the longing for unconditional perfection in the human sphere.

Like the ideas of the good and the beautiful, the idea of the *just* has unbounded significance in human affairs. (Among these affairs one could name, along with the tasks of the administration of justice, those in particular of the economist and the educator.) The distinction between the just and the unjust is ordered towards our immediate experience (unlike the distinction between the scientifically true and false, which is directed towards an objectified order). Everyone ought to have what is *his*, what *in truth* belongs to him. This principle applies where a title to goods must be protected or rejected, and likewise where a penalty is to be imposed or acquittal is in order. To be effective, the service rendered to the idea of the just requires power. But the indispensable connection between right and might places the actions aimed at the realization of justice in an ambiguous light; and since human weakness and human wickedness only too frequently abuse power, the connection easily weakens our faith in the possibility of a just use of power. Moreover, it is inevitable that many a one to whom "what is his" is awarded justly, but in a manner irksome to him, will be conscious only of the power before which he must bow, and not the justice.

The behavior of a man who persists in obdurate resentment makes it clear that the justice, for instance, of a judge's verdict cannot be realized by the mere execution of the verdict. The execution of the just verdict must move in the area of what is objectively tangible and cannot essentially be distinguished from the execution of an equally objective dictatorial decree. A man accepts a just judgment as just only when, in his immediate experience, he gains the certainty that that which he does receive is in truth his. The announcement and the execution of the verdict are invitations to such a reception of the truth; they cannot be more: because justice can be experienced only in freedom. The same is true with regard to the beautiful and the good. Schiller says of Greek statues, "They are stones for a vandal"; and in Pestalozzi's *Lienhard und Gertrud*, it takes a long time before the peasants of Bonnal believe in the disinterestedness of Squire Arner.

Now to be sure, the experience of objective knowledge is likewise impossible without freedom. A mind which ranges passively within the structure of natural occurrences without exercising its freedom in laying hold of the natural law operative therein cannot experience objective knowledge. But whereas the ideas of the good, the beautiful and the just, as forms of the unconditionally true, are addressed to man in his whole humanity, and therefore challenge his entire freedom, only a limited freedom, involving the intellect in its purely theoretical function, is operative in the attainment of objective knowledge.

The responsibility for the measure of goodness, of justice, of beauty and therewith of humanity, which is being realized in the social orders in which we lead our lives belongs to the individual, in his place and in line with his possibilities. There is no objective evidence of what is possible for each individual; it is left to us to affirm possibilities as possibilities; or, when we are afraid of the difficulty and the weight of a task which looms before us, to deem them impossibilities. Our human possibilities are entrusted to our own keeping—we ourselves are what we make of those possibilities. For our humanity the development of our intelligence has positive significance only insofar as it is determined by our devotion to the unconditionally true as it takes shape in the good, the beautiful and the just—determined by our love for that which makes a human life deeply meaningful and worth living. (Great intellectual accomplishments are possible even for a fiend.)

To the achievement of humanity, which is the goal of man, there are no limits. The world does not limit the Godman, the one who is unconditionally free; it cannot limit him because he is not committed to the world, he has overcome it. But the world does set limits to the freedom within which the truths of ratiocinative reason are apprehended; they are apprehended with a variable degree of certainty, and at all events without unconditional validity. When an object is seized by the intellect, consciousness is forced to accept that this object is of a certain kind and behaves in a certain way. Our reasoning *must* admit that a regular hexagon whose sides have the length of the radius of a circle can be inscribed in every circle. We cannot withdraw from the cogency of the demonstration (in the case of our example, a demonstration given *a priori*).[3] On the contrary, Raphael's Sistine Madonna, and Schubert's Unfinished Symphony do not force the one who encounters them to find them beautiful: they merely invite him to do so. The same is true in moral matters: there are men who have come to know war and who nevertheless glorify it. . . . The clarity of our knowledge in the moral domain is no guarantee against immoral action. Man's personal decisions remain free. The criminal condemned to a grievous punishment is invited to acknowledge the justice of the verdict—not only to suffer the punishment but actively to bear the inflicted suffering. The punishment is an appeal to his humanity—as likewise Raphael's Sistine Madonna, Schubert's Unfinished Symphony and, in the opposite sense, war, are such appeals. One who responds to these invitations enriches and deepens his own humanity.

However, such "invitations" leave to each individual the possibility of refusal; they are addressed to the free depth of human existence, and nobody conforms to them except in freedom. To be sure, in order that we may make the right decisions, we may receive valuable help from the structure of the community in which our life is embraced—for we do not have our personal being as mere individuals depending on ourselves alone. But all such helps are only challenges. Even where social coercion intervenes, the one hemmed in by such coercion still remains free to resist, at least inwardly, the directions in which it would point. Our situation is quite different when the decision is not one which is left to us as persons but one which is in the province of impersonal intelligence. When a scientific dispute has been decided objectively, then the man who hitherto defended the now defeated cause is forced to join his opponents. The convicted liar *must* give up his lie. Mathematical proofs are *cogent*. Every object (not excluding the objects of mathematics constructed a priori) reveals itself to the mind bent upon it as *other* than the mind itself, and it is this strangeness which coerces the human reasoning process to accept submissively the fact that it is objective. It is, moreover, impossible for the reasoning process to reach objective knowledge in any other way. Scientific researchers and technological inventors eminently manifest the freedom without which the reasoning process could not operate. It is this freedom itself which seeks what is binding and cogent, and on that account universally valid. To be sure, moral, aesthetic, juridical and pedagogic judgments of value also claim universal validity; but the fulfillment of this claim is left to the personal freedom to which those judgments appeal; only the claims of right reason coerce us to submit to them as soon as we have been able to convince ourselves, or have had to convince ourselves, that the claims are just.

Nobody will want to raise here the objection that even in the realm of morality, of art, of law and of education, he finds himself coerced into taking a specific stand, saying that when personal life has reached the height of its maturity the individual can act in only one way and that the whole breadth of life's development takes its direction from the emphases contained in those experiences. This is the case in fact. This is, however, not an objection. It would be misleading to use the term coercion to characterize such inability to act differently, for it is appropriate only when something other, something alien, comes to bear on personality, leaving it no possibility of rejection. Bacon says, *Natura parendo vincitur*: before man can become master of nature he must obey it, he must let nature be his mistress. Nature's domain over man begins by impressing him with its being thus and so, objectively. And even where man, on his part, has dominion over nature, he must will what nature wills in its very elements, he must submit to the coercion of its laws; in no other way can he realize his own purposes within nature. In the realm of the personal development of life, however, "to be unable to act differently" signifies the unconditional rejection of coercion; one who cannot act differently is in control of the situation. If the situation were in control of him, then he *could* act differently. When, in the year 1948, the Soviet government notified several Russian composers that they would have to compose differently than before—that is, to compose in such a way that the largest possible number of the mass public could take pleasure in their art—they submitted, they let themselves be coerced. They renounced freedom in their artistic talent—they found the price of self-assertion too high.

Where social coercion invades the field of endeavors concerned with ideas of the good, the beautiful, the just, there personal freedom is led into temptation. But where a personality "cannot act differently," there it maintains itself as personality, it asserts its true life with the certainty deriving from the super-empirical depths of its being, the depths over which neither the empirical existence outside the individual nor the individual's own empirical existence has any legitimate power. To keep the manifestations of this existential depth pure, even at the price of the most serious sacrifices, means to let light and love shine into the world, so that many can experience anew what the world is in truth, in unconditional truth.

The consciousness which perceives in terms of impersonal categories experiences a "coercion" exerted by objects. That very coercion turns out to be the resistance opposed to personal freedom without which freedom could not prove itself.[4] But just because this resistance in its very essence must remain insuperable, it can not reach into the depths of being-as-it-is-in-itself. It remains caught within the structure of phenomenal existence; here we are "coerced" to represent the objects the way they "throw themselves against us."[b] And our every influence upon objects must conform to their being as we know them. The "being so" of things is the revelation of their essential depth; from their being so our duties stand out.[5] In the relation to our duties there is no longer any coercion, there we are free. And as free as our moral attitude is the aesthetic attitude to phenomenal existence. It depends on us, whether and how we fulfill our duties, whether and in what ways we let nature and also the world of sense shaped by man speak its symbolic languages—the languages of music, of poetry, of painting, etc. The "coercion" exerted by objects hems us in, in the one respect that our intelligence can become aware of reality only as something outside the mind, something "objective," and must therefore move in a territory shut off from unconditional truth. The freedom of human knowledge is plainly limited; the idea of that truth which is unconditionally true cannot attain reality in the form of a knowledge of "objects."[c]

The ancient wisdom of India likewise puts absolute truth beyond every relation to objects. (The latter all belong to the dominion of Māyā.) Only beyond the world and beyond the self is truth—free from every veil in the emptiness of Nirvâna (which is not nonbeing but a blessed state, owing to the unlimitedness of that which, in a limited measure, can be experienced even by the pilgrim on earth as a liberation which yields meaning).

> 't is hard to see the nothingness of self,
> Not easy 'tis to see the truth as such.

Thus Buddhist tradition makes the sublime one say at the end of the discourses which would explain Nirvâna.[6] Our intelligence hides truth because it would let it be overshadowed by objective "truths."

The impossibility of the unlimited knowledge of objects also weighs on those other domains of life which cannot do without the service of the intelligence and are therefore dependent on the form of those services.

> Stuff would adhere for ever, strange and stranger
> To the ever glorious gift which spirit may receive.[d]

Rabindranath Tagore says: "We reach the Nirvâna which Buddha preached through love."[7] Likewise, it has been announced to the Christian West that in the world of man unconditional truth can attain reality only where the objective ties have been set at naught—only where all power has been given to a love superior to the world.

3

THE FAITH IN TRUTH
UNDER THE CHANGES OF HISTORY

Under the most manifold historical conditions, the superhistorical ideas—and through them, truth—are a challenge to human energies. In every epoch of culture, truth demands that those energies shall be exercised to the maximum of their capacity. Truth constantly puts before us the necessity of new decisions (to be sure, in an all too human view, these decisions often seem to be mere questionable possibilities, or at best possibilities left to arbitrary discretion). If the decisions are made with the freedom of the spirit, then the spiritual powers themselves assume freer forms (for wherever the bonds of the time can be broken because freedom is awakening to a higher awareness of self, there the desire for a purer representation of the ideas of the true, the beautiful, the good and the just, is uttered by science, by art, by morality, by education, by the administration of justice). But if a cultural community rejects the demands which would direct it to a newly attainable height, those supertemporal powers themselves which move history give less light and lose their resonance. Owing to the demands of the supertemporal, human life changes; and owing to them it retains its continuity.

The world of objects as such is fully immersed in time. In the order of time everything at every moment is only what it happens to be at that moment (and it is no longer what it once was). Its past no longer has any reality; subjective consciousness alone, by means of its imagination, "can follow the noble dust of Alexander till it finds it where it stops up a bung-hole." Objectively, the dust has entirely ceased to be the dust of Alexander. The Heraclitic flux will not permit an objective continuity in the sense of a preservation of the past in the present. For individuals, to be sure, and also for a community, an object can be a keepsake, a token of remembrance of a person or an event. Such objects are the supports of a continuity desired by subjective consciousness. But the old letters which the addressee reverently preserved (because for him they were more than mere objects) will be destroyed by his descendants. And if an exiled noble family has taken along into the foreign land a stone as a token of their hereditary property, that stone has no real interest for anybody else. Whatever depends merely on the evaluation of a subjective consciousness has no validity that would go beyond the continuity due to that consciousness itself. And even within that limit it remains dependent on the arbitrary decision of consciousness. A different case is that of a book marked by its former, and now famous, owner with characteristic marginals. This no longer is a matter of a mere "object." The book is such an object merely for a view which would abstract from the book's uniqueness. The fact that it was found in the estate of the great man, and, more decisively, the fact of the entries made by his hand turn the book into a witness of a life which belongs to history, and therefore into a carrier of an historical continuity anchored in the superhistorical. In its whole range, to be sure, the historical continuity rests on its objective basis. If such objects (which are more than mere objects) are destroyed, then the possibility of ascertaining the validity of their testimony vanishes: continuity becomes uncertain and eventually breaks off.

From a systematic point of view we can see a preview of human history in the history of nature, particularly of plants and animals. In the order of what can be understood biologically, there exists the continuity of a development fixed in nature. Thus every later form of an organic being is precontained in its basic traits from the very beginnings of its existence. The purposiveness (the entelechy) which works in a seed determines what can grow from it. The individual continuously leaves the past behind, but the species is caught in the past; again and again individuals come into existence having been given the direction of their biological existence in the form of an insurmountable heredity. Even a radical evolutionary transformation may not change characteristic hereditary forms; the small nummulites of the Oligocene age were preceded by the greater nummulites of the Eocene. However, the continuity of the characteristics of the species exists only for a consciousness which compares the more recent past with the more remote; the small nummulites themselves have lived their Oligocene life quite without history; their "greater" past had simply been left behind. True, in the consciousness of higher animals their own past is not fully extinguished (thus many a dog sold by its master seeks to return to him even after considerable time). Yet the continuity of life remains fixed by nature: the past attains no historical substantiality, it does not become a heritage, either the heritage which affords a proud obligation or the heritage which is a depressing weight. The past can attain such historical significance only where it is "preserved"[a] in the supertemporal—set aside because it no longer has any immediate existence in the present, yet preserved because it cannot be cast off and because it still makes demands. Every historical epoch is what it is because of its relation to what went before, a relation which is confirmed and can be experienced anew in the area of objective knowledge (and which is not merely present in a subjective consciousness). An historical epoch can rise higher only if, in the awareness of its responsibility, it surpasses the levels previously reached; it can deteriorate only by letting itself slide down from a height which previous struggles had attained. The decisions whereby historical life builds up and tears down, do leave room for human arbitrariness. But through those decisions a necessity operates which is superior to time; on the concrete basis of an historical heritage science remains directed towards the ideal of the objectively true, art towards the idea of the beautiful, morality towards the idea of truth, and law and economy towards the idea of the just. These relations remain in force no matter in what measure men neglect, or even deliberately reject, the demands which follow from them.

The superhistorical ideas, these forms of truth and laws of what is essential, appeal to responsibility; they demand faith which would prove itself by deed—not a blind faith, as perhaps an external authority might demand. From the outside, nobody can be taught to distinguish the true from the false, or the beautiful from the ugly, the good from evil, the just from the unjust. Of course, the distinctions are not to be found ready-made in the babe in arms; only jolting experiences will bring them into consciousness. But what then comes into consciousness from outside contains nothing which as such could challenge us to make those distinctions. What the outer world brings must be experienced in a human way—that is, must be experienced in its truth, and only on that account can it be related to the ideas of the true, the beautiful, the good, the just. In those ideas man does not find anything strange, but only his true self liberated from the contingencies of outward circumstances. And no timeless abstract entities determine this self; superhistorical life forces are what make comprehensible for man the truth of his self. Within the structure of this historically conditioned world, they appeal to him at every decisive moment, unlocking possibilities for him and challenging him to shoulder the responsibility for giving to those possibilities a meaningful shape, and thus letting him attain the possibility of understanding himself—of constantly understanding himself better in the course of his history. From the depth of his being arise claims made upon him by the powers of the true, the good, the beautiful and the just, bringing him the awareness that he must make decisions by means of which he will be enabled to escape the contingency of changing circumstances and the power of time. He ought not let himself be subdued by the inertia of contingency and the power of time; he ought to make his decision for the supertemporally valid; the depth of his being demands it.

Obviously these last sentences, which would attribute a "depth" to being inasmuch as it is "human," are not (objective) "science." Husserl would call them propositions of "world-view" philosophy. The sentences try to do the impossible: to give conceptual form to the consciousness of responsibility. And every further word about the "true self," about the "depth of being," would have to remain merely such an attempt.

> Whatever is cannot be said,
> What can be said is what is not.[b]

But this is not an embarrassing admission which would reduce the value of "world-view philosophy" compared with "science"; for scientific research itself works under the rule of principles

The Faith in Truth under the Changes of History

which summon the intelligence to do its work in order to force into conceptual form what is immediately experienced. These principles also determine the character of the time and of science within time. (To add to the "world-view" that truth which science must contribute is the particular task of science.) The intellectual forces which rule their own age can be called "historical ideas," and can be distinguished from the "superhistorical ideas." Science changes its directions in accordance with the change in historical ideas. The mind works at tasks set by these ideas, and the historical ideas bestow upon the tasks the unity which characterizes the cultural mentality of an age. Thus the ideas give legitimacy to the trends of each epoch's science, art, morality, education, administration of justice, and economy. Of course, the unity of culture is not rigid or unambiguous, but it always moves in relation to the often quite opposite endeavors which are characteristic of the age. The historical ideas themselves, however, have legitimacy insofar as they determine the manner of the realization of freedom which can be fruitful within the tensions of the epoch. The tasks of each time are set by the historical ideas, which in return are confirmed by those tasks if, in their accomplishment, the "awareness of freedom" increases. As long as this mutual confirmation lasts, the validity of an historical idea will last. Each one, as it approaches its end, has to struggle with existential difficulties: new contradictions turn up, and through them, new ideas come forth. It is the task of philosophy to shed light upon these intellectual currents; philosophy is always a critique of its own time. To be sure, it can tackle its task only under historical conditions; but being critical of itself, it puts its faith only in that which retains a superhistorical validity.

In the year 1785, Friedrich Heinrich Jacobi wrote, "We are all born in faith."[1] At bottom this faith is nothing but the faith in the supertemporal. Yet we are not all simply born, we are born somewhere and at some time. The faith from which we derive an intellectual vocation enters into our consciousness not in its purity but subject to historical conditions. Our certainty of the supertemporal values and of their opposites is formed with reference to particular contents. The contents of the here-and-now differ from the contents of the there-and-then; they belong to our historically conditioned environment. Not only do we become certain of the supertemporal values only as we encounter these contents, but above all, in those children of men who are still completely lacking in independence of spirit and therefore belong to their historically conditioned community by blind faith, education will often inculcate a very disastrous form of the value distinctions between true and false, beautiful and ugly, good and evil, just and unjust. (In such cases, the independent responsibility of the adult is hardly more than a fiction and in no sense a reality. One should remember the astonishment expressed by many German war criminals when they found that their obedience to criminal superiors was imputed to them as guilt.) The fight, on principle, against any defect in the historical domain can be undertaken only by philosophical reflection (which need not be in line with any philosophical school).[2] Philosophy critically relates the historical ideas to the superhistorical, to "true being," as Fichte called it.[3]

In order that conjectures shall not drift off shapelessly and meaninglessly, philosophical thoughts require concretely specific exposition. Thales would find "true being" in the mysterious amazement imparted by his observation of water. But since he was a philosopher, he did not *believe* in water with unswerving rigidity. For him, water was the ever-newly pondered problematic answer to the questions which vexed him. His faith was drawn to true *being*.

How true being could be conceptually formulated was the one question of Thales. Every answer which he may have considered had as its presupposition that faith in which he was born. And not he alone was born in this faith, but likewise Anaximander and all those who came later. The faith of Thales had a depth which reached way beyond him and was greater than his bold doctrine, if the doctrine were to be understood as nothing but an affirmative thesis. (For everyone who philosophizes, the goal which he acknowledges in its double character of confrontation and of authority over himself must have a higher value than the output of his work.) The faith in true being was shared, along with Thales, by those who well understood what he meant to say by his doctrine, yet would not be convinced by the doctrine but would try to surpass it by their independent investigations.

Philosophy can speak about the supertemporal only in time-conditioned sentences. From the most ancient times all philosophers desirous of forging ahead have accepted the fact of historical conditionality intuitively, and at first without any foreknowledge of the comprehensive significance of the conditionality. For all of them, therefore, it was a matter of course that they should confront critically the doctrines which they encountered. The history of intellectual development is marked by the constant endeavor to attain greater freedom. Philosophical doctrines make us aware of the problematic character of the time, provided we understand these doctrines philosophically (and do not turn them into a substitute for a religion). Thus we are confronted by the question of how the doctrines can be surpassed. Their claim is not to be believed, but to be met with critical endeavor.[4] With regard to the already formulated doctrines (even our own doctrines, if we are alive in our philosophizing), the critical endeavor is negative in tone but affirmatively meant; it seeks truth, it seeks true being, and therefore it will normally expound the product of its search in affirmative propositions. Only where the search results in nothing but the discovery that the doctrines which history has hitherto produced are unsatisfactory is this not the case; then such a discovery makes its own ultimate contribution in the form of negations and questions. (Yet even such negations and questions are meaningful only under the presupposition of the faith in supertemporal truth—though this faith still remains without formulation.)

In the often labyrinthine ways of the history of philosophy the imagery of faith has undergone manifold changes. And many a doctrine has been promulgated whose goal had become vague owing to the confused endeavor to make it clear, or whose goal had shifted, seen from the standpoint of the doctrine. Nevertheless, the goal remains immovable; it is the concrete fulfillment of the faith in truth—in that truth which Thales meant although he could not fix it in his doctrine. This truth can never become the prey of any systematic endeavor; but in every such serious endeavor it is present; it is supertemporal, and every philosophy which is at the height of its time has a relation to it, a relation appropriate under the historical conditions. Thus, at the height of one or other specific situation in the history of philosophy, that truth lives in the atoms of Democritus whirling in empty space; in the thoughts of Anselm about "that than which nothing greater can be conceived"; in Spinoza's substance which "is in itself and is conceived through itself"; in Fichte's "true being." An immense height separates this truth from scientific research; yet scientific research always takes it into account as a norm pointing out the right direction (even when it is denied by an unclear, self-contradictory kind of thinking). Under individually limited aspects[5] the truth appears in the revealing mode of art. When the mind is committed to morality and the desire for the realization of justice the attainment of truth appears as the highest of undertakings, never fully achieved. The supertemporal goal of philosophizing could likewise be designated as the conceptual ascertainment of the faith which is necessary to man if he is to be really human. This is the faith which protects him from the loss of himself. As reflection directed upon this faith, philosophy provides for the human spirit the critical safeguard of its rights whenever, on the basis of the heritage of the past, philosophy succeeds in attaining the height of its own time.

4

TRIALS IN THE AWARENESS OF TRUTH: TRIALS OF HUMANITY

For mankind, humanness is not a matter of course, and wherever philosophy is vague about its goals, clearness regarding the nature of being human can not be taken for granted in the works of those who philosophize. If there was a god in whom Nietzsche believed, it was Dionysos; for him Dionysos was the sacred name, impregnated with meaning by the myths, for that life whose "essence is the will for power."[1] This life has constantly assumed new forms, it has become increasingly differentiated, it has ceaselessly created for itself new difficulties. "One ought to learn anew what cruelty is and one ought to open one's eyes.... Almost everything which we call 'higher culture' rests on the spiritualization and deepening of cruelty."[2] In the second to last paragraph of *Beyond Good and Evil* Nietzsche calls himself the last disciple and initiate of the god Dionysos, whom, alternately, he calls a philosopher often pondering how he could "bring man still farther forward and make him stronger, more evil and deeper than he is." Life itself seeks possibilities for intensifying the force and ruthlessness of its thrust for power, and thereby gives occasion for the rise of new powers no longer bound by any scruples. Difficulties make man creative; life must strive to overcome them. For every life traditional morality gradually loses its efficacy; choosing the course of greatness and strength, man becomes freer and "more beautiful." In the following paragraph, the last in the book, these thoughts find an historical, partly autobiographic framework within which they turn into "truths"—they are erroneously taken for truths. And as such they cease to be young and wicked, they become "boring"; they have had their day. Life pushes on past all its "truths." This is possible for it because (as the first sections of that book pointed out) the things which pose as truth rest on "logical fictions"; it is precisely the most false of our concepts which are the most indispensable for us, and the serious question is not whether a concept is true but "in what measure it furthers life, maintains life, maintains the species, perhaps even rears the species."[3] Chapter 25 of Thomas Mann's novel *Doctor Faustus* presents the great "dialogue" between "the German composer Adrian Leverkühn" and the Devil; what the Devil expounds is Nietzschean philosophy. "I am certainly of the opinion that an untruth whose character enhances power is a match for any ineffectively virtuous truth. . . . Life is not fastidious, and it doesn't care a fig for morality."

If one abstracts from the Dionysian faith in culture, on whose ironic disregard of the purely human Nietzsche's insertion of the "truths" into the structure of historical movements rests, then this insertion was not really anything new. In a work which the twenty-five-year-old Schelling published in the last year of the eighteenth century, one can read that every philosophical system finds "the most certain touchstone of its truth in this, that . . . owing to a general shattering of what has been accepted as truth, a new kind of truth will come forth."[4] This means that whereas the overruling, supertemporal *idea* of the true affirms itself in the crises of the intellect, the specific criteria which must be satisfied by whatever would claim to be true are shaped by history. And on that account one can not foresee what attacks will yet be made upon that which has been acknowledged for a time, what fate may be in store for it.

Whatever appears to be convincing truth is what corresponds to the assumptions of personal life or of the public consensus of a given time. But, with the exception of the most general statements of formal logic, those assumptions change with the time; thus, the medieval belief in witches is no longer intelligible for us, and since the discovery of non-Euclidean geometry, even Euclidean geometry is no longer evident for us in its former sense, is no longer the only possible geometry; its very relation to the idea of the truth has changed.[5]

To be sure, Nietzsche was more radical. He spoke of "logical fictions." He made an effort to present the faith in the unconditional value of truth and the will for truth as the product of life; in his view, the logical forms themselves stem from life, which in these forms shaped its own instruments, instruments needed by the existence of a specific animal species having reached a specific phase in its evolution. These instruments of self-assertion remain subordinate to life. Not only does life adjust itself to such instruments, it endeavors to surpass them. According to a phrase in *Zarathustra*, life is "that which must always overcome itself."[6]

But the question concerning the standard by which a life is to be judged, a life which overcomes itself and rises to a higher way of being—this question is not asked, nor can it be asked within the frame of reference of Nietzsche's philosophy, because it would presuppose a scale of values superior to life. For one whose supreme faith is placed in life, life is the measure of itself. Likewise, one who has faith in God will quite logically not relate God to values which hold true independent of God; for him God himself is goodness and truth. It is precisely these values, however, which Nietzsche rejects as having no essential pertinence to life.

The self-conquest by means of which life always realizes itself afresh is a ruthless affair. "Life is essentially appropriation, violation, overpowering, hardness, imposition of its own forms, assimilation and at the least and mildest, exploitation."[7] In politics a strong man will soon be overcome by a stronger master. If the national development of one people is bought at the price of its intellectual decline, then that people's shallowness will be compensated by "the deepening of another people."[8] The measure of this deepening is no problem: "The noble kind of man feels himself as a determiner of values, he does not need any approval.... He honors everything which he recognizes in itself; such a morality is self-glorification."[9] In Nietzsche's philosophy life itself is prior to all norms; it is superior to them. In his sketches for the *Will for Power*, Nietzsche asks: "What is truth?" At first he answers with a question: "Perhaps a kind of faith which has come to be a condition for life?"[10] But immediately he goes beyond the "perhaps" and beyond the question mark. " 'Truth,' to my way of thinking, does not necessarily designate an opposite to error, but precisely when it is a matter of principle it designates only the position of different errors in relation to each other; for instance, that the one is older and deeper than the other, and perhaps ineradicable insofar as an organic being of our species could not live without it. . . ."[11] And honor is paid to "dissimulation"; dissimulation increases "in accordance with the ascending hierarchy of beings. . . . A thousandfold cunning belongs to the essence of the ascent of man."[12]

Thus life is deified: there is no truth, either in the theoretical or practical sphere, which transcends life itself. But a philosophy which would leave only a subordinate and uncertain role for truth cannot escape internal contradictions. The devaluation of truth in favor of life renders every claim to validity uncertain. With respect to truth, validity means *to be right*. If the validity of a truth is only relative, then the loss of this validity must be conceived as a breakthrough towards a purer relation to unconditional truth. Every faith which is, in the last analysis, directed to anything other than truth itself is arbitrary or contingent, and hence unworthy of our commitment.

In the sketches for the *Will for Power*[13] we read: "Among a higher species of being, knowledge, too will have new forms which are not yet necessary." It is evident that we must apply to the future as well as to the present the words from *Beyond Good and Evil*: "Behind all logic and behind the apparent authority of the movements of logic, stand evaluations. More explicitly, there stand physiological requirements for the maintenance of a given kind of life."[14] And behind such sentences stands Nietzsche's faith in a reality (the reality of life) which—untouched by the search for truth—would despise all qualitative distinctions expressing a rank among contrasting values;[15] no matter what kind of evaluations are important for "a specific kind of life" they are comprehended in the one Dionysian life and have their roots in it.

The concept of Dionysos is "the eternal 'Yes' to all things."[16] But "the fundamental faith of the metaphysician is the *faith in the contrasts of values*."[17] For these philosophers the values of the true and the good specify what *is* in the highest sense; they will not allow an equal rank to the false, to appearance, to evil. Fettered by naturalism, or more precisely by biologism, Nietzsche rejects such metaphysics as "childish nonsense."[18] "No matter what value pertains to the true, to truthfulness, to what is selfless, it might be possible that one would have to attribute a higher value to appearance, to the will for deception and to desire, a value higher and more basic for all life. It might even be possible that precisely that which constitutes the value of those good and venerated things consists in being akin to those evil and apparently opposite things, akin to them in a very insidious manner, tied to them, interwoven with them, and perhaps equal in essence."[19] Dionysos is in a position above and beyond the contrast between values. He manifests himself equally in all that men call true and all that they call illusory, in what they call good and what they call evil; he manifests himself in every way. Therefore Nietzsche can speak of him as "that great ambiguous one"[20]; and therefore the preface to *Beyond Good and Evil* can start out with the assumption that "truth is a woman" and soon proceed to ridicule the "gruesome seriousness" with which all the philosophical dogmatists have tried to approach truth: they have hoped to find only the true and the good, not the illusory and the evil!

In Nietzsche's thought the "woman" truth claims to be greater and deeper than the truth of science and of theoretical reason. The life of the spirit, according to Nietzsche, is an independent life standing over against the idea of the true (which is a fiction!) and ruling both science and theoretical knowledge. What they call "truth" is biased by being set in opposition to illusion and to what is false, and on that very account is never what it supposes itself to be. Even the "true being" of Fichte and of the many others (even those who have not given it any name) is a product of the "fundamental faith of the metaphysicians" in an ontological priority of the true over the false, of the good over the evil. Nietzsche's biologism admits no distinction of "true values" nor, therefore, of "true being." Admittedly we humans cannot disengage ourselves from the value contrasts which belong to our mental operations, but as Nietzschean "philosophers" we should be clear about the problematic essence of those contrasts—we should be aware that their validity is based not on their "truth" but only on the significance which they have for this life which is by chance ours.

The life, however, in which Nietzsche has faith is greater than our life: it is a will for power beyond good and evil, also beyond the value contrast of true and false. According to Nietzsche's doctrine, the logical forms have no ontological ground in a "true being," but only an economical ground in their significance for the life of such beings as we are. And it is precisely this ground which determines their falsehood; man is, as Zarathustra's prologue says, "a bridge," "a *transition* and an *extinction*." "To acknowledge untruth as a condition of life, this means indeed to offer resistance in a dangerous manner to the habitual value feelings."[21] Everything which constitutes our logical forms is built on insufficient presuppositions. It was the main mistake of the dogmatic philosophers, of the metaphysicians, that they surrendered naively to these questionable presuppositions. But not metaphysics alone, physics likewise is called "only a world interpretation and rearrangement, and *not* a world explanation."[22] All "insights" which logical forms can furnish have significance only within the structure of the foreground, and only there do they appear valid.

The derogatory way in which Nietzsche speaks of the efforts based on logic betrays his conviction that he possesses superior knowledge—knowledge which dwarfs the half- or quarter-truths of physics and metaphysics alike. Accordingly, after the exposition of a classic philosophical doctrine, Nietzsche introduces his critique with the words: "In truth it is quite different."[23] To be sure, the truth he has to offer is without comfort, cruel (which, of course, should be no reason for refusing it recognition); only strong spirits can bear it. Nietzsche sketches the "image of the philosophers of the future": "they will be *harder* (and perhaps not always harder upon themselves alone), harder than humane men may wish; they will have no dealings with the 'truth' for the sake of 'pleasure' or of 'uplift' or of 'enthusiasm'. On the contrary, they will have very little faith in a truth bringing with it such emotional orgies."[24]

In a very serious letter he wrote a few weeks before the end of his career, he calls himself "a genuis of *truth*."[25] And his book *Ecce Homo* contains a considerable number of passages in which he praises his personal relation to truth as quite beyond compare. (Here he speaks with less restraint than before, but the doctrine has not undergone any change.) In the section about the *Zarathustra* he says: "Till then one did not know what height is and what depth is; one knew even less what truth is. There is not a glimpse in this revelation of truth which had been anticipated, which had been guessed by any one of the great."[26]

It is impossible to mistake Zarathustra's "revelation of truth" for the methodically ferreted-out truths of scientific research—Zarathustra's "truth" which becomes revealed on "the great midday," in the "'moment of the shortest shadows." "We have abolished the true world. Which world has remained? the apparent world perhaps? . . . But no! *with the true world we have also abolished the world of appearance!*"[27] When humanity reaches its "highest point," then the faith in the contrast of values vanishes. Nietzsche greeted the new year 1882 with the resolution that "at some time in the future [he] would be one who says only yes."[28] With the doctrine of eternal return, the *Zarathustra* seemed to become the fulfillment of that great resolution. However, when in his *Ecce Homo* Nietzsche reviews his own life[29] he follows his report about the *Zarathustra* with the sentence: "After the yes-saying part of my task was solved, it was the turn of the no-saying, *no-doing*, half of the task."[30] To be sure, Zarathustra's affirmation is not to be revoked by these negations; it is rather they which are to be understood as subordinate to the affirmation and irradiated by it.[31] Wherever a negation occurs, a contrast in values is acknowledged: but for Nietzsche, negation and contrasts of values as well have no final validity—and this is what counts here. Nietzsche feels himself to be the prophet of a truth which exists with eternal power above all contrasts of values and therefore also above all negation. In the Zarathustra book he had greeted as a kin the pure deep sky before sunrise! "Together we learned everything; together we learned to rise above ourselves, and to smile cloudlessly: to smile cloudlessly down from bright eyes and out of mile-wide distance while below us coercion and purpose and guilt steam like [tropical] rain."[32] "For all things have been baptized at the spring of eternity and beyond good and evil; good and evil themselves, however, are only intermittent shadows and melancholy damp spells and rifting clouds."[33] Zarathustra gave to his soul "the right to say no like a storm, and to say yes as the open sky says yes." "Still as the light" his soul now stands and goes "through negating storms."[34]

"To be true—it is what only few *can* do! . . . Least fit for doing it, however, are the good."[35] For "to be true" means, after all, to have the courage to acknowledge that the value contrast of good and evil has no meaning which could reach into the essence of reality. This doctrine has gained great influence upon modern literature. It has produced that ironic attitude in which moral evaluations are accepted merely as phenomena. It meets them in a cool, matter-of-fact frame of mind in which it is forgotten that a truth which is no more than factual is fraught with problems and is never the ultimate truth (as Plato already knew and Kant taught emphatically). The value contrasts which Nietzsche treated as trifles have not a merely biological significance; through their inevitability human experience is directed beyond the opposition between the objective and the subjective. The inevitability is a necessity of reason; it is the means whereby we transcend the limitations of narrow-mindedness and attain self-certainty. Nietzsche's biologism would deny the essential validity of the value contrast of good and evil because "life" is unaware of it. Yet life is human only when it is aware of the contrast—when, in making this value distinction, it seeks new knowledge of itself and finds itself. Nietzsche would have us believe that man's life is only a point of transition on the way to the extinction of the present species man. Even were this so, the necessity of reason would nevertheless defy those evolutionary developments. For the value contrast between good and evil has a deeper ground than the whole of biology; it is in this contrast that man awakens to the certainty of the unconditional.

In the *Ecce Homo* Nietzsche boasts that there is nothing which surpasses his *Twilight of the Idols* in malevolence.[36] "What the title page calls *Idol* is simply that which hitherto was called truth." "A great wind blows between the trees and everywhere fruits fall down—truths. . . . But the result in hand is no longer anything questionable, it is decisions. *I* first have in hand the measure for 'truths', *I* first *can* decide. It is as if *a second consciousness* had grown in me, as if in me 'the will' had lit a light above the *inclined* track on which hitherto it ran downward. . . . The *inclined* track—they called it the way to 'truth'. . . . Now there is an end to all 'dark urge,' it was precisely the *good* man who was least aware of the right way."[37] Freed from the faith in value contrasts, the love for life alone has to decide, and it is the will for power which gives it light. The surety of this way is that "second consciousness" which ignited itself high above the consciousness rooted in the faith in the value contrasts.

Nietzsche's designation of himself as a "genius of *truth*" must be understood in the light of the sentences we have quoted. He "*can* decide." The decisions whereby he blows away "the truths" of old are affirmations of the harsh necessity of the Dionysian life. In that life they have their justification, and to that life belongs Nietzsche's religiously attuned faith. This life, however, could not be called the "true being," for such a designation would amount to a recognition of the contrast of a "true" with a "not-true" being. According to Nietzsche's doctrine, reality in its depths is the ruthless innocence of life. Life is innocent in its freedom from the opposition between values; it is cruel as it restlessly seeks self-realization through the dynamism of the conflict within itself. Of course, a philosophy which sacrifices the validity of the value contrast of true and false for the sake of the decisions of the will of a life which desires power cannot be thought through consistently. True, Nietzsche is obedient to the "light" which the will has lit for him, but he despises the "immaculate cognition" which is free of desire and rebukes those who profess their faith in it as "sentimental hypocrites."[38] Hence truth, in his doctrines, is characterized by a certain vagueness and instability.

In this way an unruly voluntarism has been prejudicial to the credit of truth; but truth has also been downgraded by an intellectualistic misunderstanding. There is a widely held thesis that one can speak of truth only with reference to statements, and that even when the word truth seems to be used in a different sense its point of reference is nevertheless a statement. One might read, with regard to this, what Leibniz says at the end of chapter 5 of the fourth book of his *Nouveaux Essais*. The thesis would deny the presupposition of an ontological truth which makes possible the very activity of judging and making statements. However, if God himself were imagined as a mind forming judgments, then it would seem as if the substantial foundations of the function of judgment were given in God. (In this respect the chapter of

Leibniz which we have mentioned is very significant—and chapter 11 is still more so, although it does not quite harmonize with chapter 5.) However, for a God who forms judgments the world is an *object*; he is quite obviously represented in the image of man. But such a representation is, of course, mythical. Judgments are the products of finite consciousness; they are clouded by obscurities which render the nature of judgment itself problematic. To look at the original significance of truth in the light of the contingent activity of man means to start by assigning to the truth a secondary role. For in that way it would be made to depend in its very essence on the existence of finite intelligences, on an empirical set of facts, on what Leibnitz calls *vérité de fait*, "a truth of mere fact." (Leibniz escaped this consequence by means of modifying the bearing of his early expositions. In the eleventh chapter just mentioned he appeals to Augustine in order to obtain an ontological substructure. Incidentally, Augustine's basic thought—that the logical has its principle not in itself but in God—already can be found in the *Eudemian Ethics*.[39])

Paracelsus spoke of the knowledge immanent in nature; the pear tree *knows* when and how to bud and bloom, when and how to ripen its fruits.[40] The expression of this thought is bold; one who does not have the good will to understand it the way it is meant will reject it as fantastic. But all essential thinking has been in need of bold formulations; the depth of the truth does not fit into the form of cautious prose; in human statements it can be intimated only symbolically. Continuing the bold thought of his great kinsman in the spirit, Schelling formulated: "Nature does not know through systematic knowledge but through its own essence."[41] Not through systematic knowledge; nature does not judge, but its creative activity is proof of the truth living in it. The *secret* of nature (which begins where nature is seen as more than "the existence of things insofar as determinable by universal laws"[42]) cannot be inferred by our judgments. True enough, what manifests itself in our judgments is their indissoluble relation to truth, yet it is manifest in such a way that truth becomes for us the object of a never-completed undertaking. Every act of judgment presupposes truth as its goal. The striving for knowledge or for communication is an attempt to satisfy the presupposition.

(This is the case even when the will of the individual would subject truth to itself and so deny it outright; the liar knows the truth, but he is not at one with himself: what he says does not conform with his insight.) In the life of nature truth is not presupposed but represented—in an unfree representation, to be sure. Nature has no independence from truth and therefore it has no trouble in conforming with truth; it is fixed in truth—in the divine nature of the true. For neither does God himself form judgments; he is himself the truth, as Augustine saw clearly and many times said. God has neither a mere relation to truth, the way man has, nor is he fixed in it, as nature is.

Only the structure of art, and of mythology in particular, permits us to make God "talk like a man"[a] and therefore to present him as forming judgments (just as nature, too, appears in these contexts as humanized in representational forms). In a human way God comes *close* to man. But only if a living truth is at work in mythology can the being which men encounter from behind the mythological masks be *God* and not an idol, not a fiction of the imagination nourished from dubious and subterranean sources. Only then does a living truth lay hold upon the human spirit, a truth for whose attainment the functions of judgment are of course indispensable, even though they can bring man to no substantial knowledge of the depths of his being. Wherever this substantial knowledge comes about, *all* man's mental functions are attuned in unity. Paracelsus recognized in his patients God himself, appealing to Paracelsus' medical art through their illnesses.[43] For Paracelsus Christian doctrine was not a system of assertions to be "believed" as a system (with theoretical reason holding sway over the personal workings of the life of the spirit). The content of Paracelsus' faith was humanity certain of its inexhaustible source in truth. "In the same way in which the angel came to Mary and said, 'You are full of grace,' . . . so grace is bestowed upon us secretly, and each of us is to hold fast the gift which God has sent him—to one this is sent, to another something else—and each is to take it as an angelic greeting which is the very same as the gift."[44] And "he who is of good faith is a doer of the works of God."[45]

Nietzsche deified the will of life desirous of power; it was this will which ignited Nietzsche. Paracelsus expects all "light" from the Holy Spirit.[46] Only by the Spirit is he able to recognize that it is the voice of God which speaks to him through the patient. It does not speak in statements. Nor does it address itself merely to the intelligence. It speaks to the whole man, to the humanity of man. God is truth. And his voice, which manifests his presence in the specific situation, reveals what the situation is in truth.

Whenever the whole man is called and understands the call, reasoning always has its part to play. Rational argument has often been decried, especially by people who prefer religious illusion to sober thought. However, ratiocination has its undeniable rights. A weak man may submit to arguments to the extent of abjuring his better insights; the ratiocinative truth nevertheless remains valid. However, it extends only to the objective order, and only to what it is capable of comprehending in that order. Its very forms contain problems. Ratiocination is incapable of expressing insights which are unconditionally true. For unconditional truth can be found only in "true being," and not among objects. As a matter of course, the human mind, in its search for insight into the real, has a relation to truth. But just because this valid relation is a matter of course man has often failed to recognize that there is always a tension between the truth which must be taken for granted and the explicit content which can be grasped within the forms of knowledge, and that therefore truth is a mystery for the human mind. It has been mistakenly assumed that man had grasped pure truth in the statements which he found convincing; but this was to overlook the fact that what seemed to be a matter of course (but actually contains obscurities, nay, impossibilities) requires a legitimation which establishes the conditions of its validity. We can expect to find such a legitimation only in a dominant order of reality. Those metaphysicians who hoped to obtain unconditional truth in the form of judgments, supposing that only thus could truth be established, overestimated the reach of the intellect, and in so doing compromised the intellect and with it truth itself. Regarded superficially and from an unhistorical point of view, the situation of philosophy could seem from early times like an endless strife between confused theories. Nietzsche had considerable acquaintance with the facts of history, yet—in line with his love for the Greek sophists—his thinking was unhistorical, and he drew the inference that the value contrast of true and false was without ultimate validity. "The courage to take risks: this is the oldest nobility in the world," one reads in the *Zarathustra*.[47] Yet the acknowledgment of this nobility could be demanded only in the name of truth, and a philosophy which has sacrificed unconditional truth on the altar of the god Dionysos has no title to such a demand. Life's will for power can make decisions only by power, and therefore only in matters of power. It may be able to decide whether a truth is to have the opportunity of propagating itself. But even a forbidden truth is still truth, and the question of its validity is not one to be decided by a will for power.

The tendency to make little distinction between might and right showed itself in Nietzsche quite early. (In this respect, indeed, Nietzsche had within his own nature the same inclinations which later helped to pave the way for National Socialism; the latter, of course, proceeded for its part to an active disregard for truth and humanity—and all the Nietzschean "noble morality" into the bargain.) The first of Nietzsche's *Essays out of Time* (1873) reproaches David Strauss for failing "boldly to derive the rules of morality from the *bellum omnium contra omnes* ("war of all against all") and from the prerogative of the stronger."[48] This means nothing but that the will for power, whenever it carries the day, is right, even in matters of morality. In accordance with this view, values are always to be taken only as means for attaining power, and they are to attain their own form as values in line with the goals of power, and in fact do conform to those goals. The autonomy of values must be understood as an illusion which, under certain circumstances, can be useful for life. (Hitler's crown jurist-counselor, Carl Schmitt, being of the same opinion, tried to subject the ideal values to the claims of politics: "As long as it exists at all, the political unity is always the decisive unity, it is total and sovereign."[49]) If one were to look at Nietzsche's own work from this point of view, one could gain the impression that in his writings he was fundamentally engaged in a fight for power—though a fight faithful to Nietzsche's own command: "Write with blood and you will learn that blood is spirit."[50] To be sure, spirit which would persuade but could not convince: "Oh my soul, I taught you to persuade in such a way that you persuade the reasons themselves to give in to you."[51] Yet even persuasion has as its presupposition the acknowledgment of truth. And if one explains truth as fiction, as a means of power used by a spirit striving for nothing but life, then even this explanation presupposes the acknowledgment of truth—the acknowledgment of that truth which is not a fiction and which can be in no way identical with a "truth" created by a will which would use it as a means for tying together all contrasts in a new unity,[52] a will which claims to redeem all things "from the servitude under purposes"[53]—that is, from a binding eternal truth.

In Nietzsche's philosophy the spirit of man sets itself up in opposition to its own creatureliness: it is unwilling to admit any truth above itself; truth is seen as the work of man, and this work decides that "the old truth has come to an end."[54] But this very decision rests on a presupposition. All argumentation, all explanation, all prophecy and all reception of revelation presupposes the unconditional acknowledgment of truth. Only empty words can deny that the distinction between the true as valuable and the false as the negation of value is unconditionally true. The distinction is so necessary for the human mind that only by means of it can the mind obtain awareness of itself and find itself. All self-understanding, all communicating-with-others, rests on the unconditionality of this contrast of values. As we make the distinction between true and false, we merely confirm for our own person the necessity by which we prove ourselves as beings endowed with reason—a necessity which has its ground not in us but in reason itself. We do not make the distinction arbitrarily, to please ourselves, but because reason has us make it: the distinction belongs to reason. There is necessity in our own being, and it is the necessity of reason. And in the shaping of an individual's personal life, reason will determine the specific form which this development takes insofar as the individual seeks to understand this necessity of his nature and is able to retain his hold on it. Precisely because for the individual this necessity involves values, it has its binding force in a superindividual authority of reason.

The very possibility of shaping existence in a way worthy of human life is damaged at the core when the validity of the value contrast of true and false is rendered conditional, whether through the seduction of a sophist world-view or the violent intervention of a power seeking to establish its ideology by force. Mankind becomes human only by way of truth, and for our humanity truth is binding as a matter of course. Nietzsche's aim was to lift us beyond the truth, to teach us the truth about truth. This is as odd as it sounds. Nietzsche handles truth like an object. Of course every particular truth, once it is conceived, has its object. But truth in itself, like God, cannot be known as an object; there can be no truth about truth. Like the meaning of the word "God," the meaning of the word "truth" can only be experienced. To be sure, it is possible to talk about experience as if it were something like an object. In this regard Fichte spoke of a "looking-at, thinking-of"; but, he says, "through the looking-at, freedom is lost."[55] The truth looked-at, thought-of, is no longer living, is no longer truth itself. It is the corpse of a life which has vanished, and like every corpse it is an empirical fact. Grammarians and the practitioners of formal and symbolic logic endeavor to dissect the fact. Such endeavors are not without interest; yet they become questionable when we fail to recognize their origin and their secondary rank.[56] The task of philosophy is to give the account which the life of the intellect must give of itself (of course, under the conditions which any given age affords for the account). In such self-reflection, objectifications are inevitable, but they remain auxiliary constructions about whose limited significance there should be no doubt. Criteria are never in what can be objectively shown but in the free assent of free humanity.

5

DIONYSOS AND APOLLO

From the very beginning of his great public career, Nietzsche paid homage to the god Dionysos. Looking back to the *Birth of Tragedy*, he says in *The Twilight of the Idols* (the last book which he himself saw through the press): "I was the first who took seriously that marvelous phenomenon which bears the name of Dionysos, for I wanted to understand the early Hellenic instinct when it was still rich, nay overflowing." And he says: "In the Dionysian mysteries, in the psychology of the Dionysiac rapture, is expressed the *fundamental fact* of the Hellenic instinct—its 'Will for Life.' What did the Greek want these mysteries to guarantee? Life *eternal*, the eternal return of life; the future promised by the past, and consecrated; the triumphant affirmation of life, in spite of death and change."[1] In the Greeks' faith in Dionysos Nietzsche found the interpretation of his own desire for life and for the depth of life. He did not want to take that faith for truth in the old sense of the word truth, but for a principle of evaluation which makes the highest claims on life, an evaluation demanded by the strong and noble will. (To be sure, for a time he was looking for a scientific basis for his notion of an eternal return, but that was owing to the lack of clearness in his views. In the sphere of logic one cannot oppose oneself to truth without presupposing it.) In his sketches for the *Will for Power* he writes: "We must become aware of the degree to which we are the *creators* of our feelings of value and, therefore, are capable of making 'sense' of history. In us, this belief in truth comes to its ultimate consistent conclusion that, if anything at all must be adored, adoration is due to *appearances* (*Schein*), and that it is the lie—and not the truth—which is divine!" "Truth is ugly."[2] In this passage, the word "truth" retains its own honest ring: for

Dionysos and Apollo

it is impossible to adhere strictly to the project of reducing truth to something produced by creative will. The ugliness which Nietzsche attributes to truth is, however, to be vanquished by the "decisions" of the Dionysian will. In honor of these "decisions" the same Nietzsche who was so sensitive and so perceptive in his feelings forced himself to articulate the many cruel pronouncements which abound in his later writings, spreading almost like a cancer.

In the *Birth of Tragedy*, that early work of genius, Nietzsche had contrasted the "Apollonian" with the "Dionysian" which he had met again, in modern form, in the musical dramas of Richard Wagner. These dramas, nourished by the metaphysical biologism of Schopenhauer, had already celebrated a liberty without awe and reverence, a liberty which acknowledges no law at all. The god [Wotan] yields, even with joy, to him who hacks in twain the "eternal spear," to the "boldest boy" who no longer reveres the god—to the youth for whom eternal norms exist no more and for whom, if once the final inferences ripen, there will surely be no more eternal truth. It was not Wagner's concern to bring those inferences into consciousness; that became the task of Nietzsche's later works. In the *Birth of Tragedy*, Apollo is the god of beautiful appearances, of proportion, of what is limited by law, what has individualized form. But this Apollonian illusion meets with truth which comes forth under the sign of Dionysos, the truth of tragedy, of the tragic myth. For the disciple of Schopenhauer, the individual forms of existence were the "works of Maya." Apollonian art will transfigure that work, and the logicians will fit it into conceptual order. And whosoever is under the spell of logic will take these "cultural illusions" (*Bildungsillusionen*)[3] for the truth.

Nietzsche says that the intellectualist takes up arms against Dionysian wisdom and art, and endeavors to dissolve myth.[4] He understands no truth but a truth which submits to the intellect. He would find a scientific basis for life, and let science become the leader of life. A few years after the *Birth of Tragedy*, it looked as if the scientific kind of thinking was to become the guide of Nietzsche's own thought, in fact as if it had taken over entirely. Richard Wagner, among others, is surely in the back of Nietzsche's mind when he writes in the first volume of his book *Human, All-*

Too-Human: "We owe to Christianity, to the philosophers, the poets, the musicians a plenitude of deeply moving experiences. To prevent these experiences from taking hold in us like a tumor, we must conjure up the spirit of science whose overall effect is to make us a bit colder and more sceptical and, above all, to cool off the fiery stream of faith in final and ultimately valid truths."[5] Nietzsche no longer affirms the pessimistic doctrine of Schopenhauer as if it were knowledge of absolute truth. Such truth is not attainable at all. In its place the demand for truthfulness takes precedence. And it is precisely truthfulness which urges us to turn away from unanswerable questions. He who has experienced the power of "cathartic knowledge" will find the "most desirable condition" in a "free and fearless hovering above men, customs, laws and traditional evaluations of things."[6] The book starts with a section entitled "Chemistry of Concepts and Feelings." Moral, religious, and aesthetic images and feelings are to be investigated by the method of natural science, with the result that "even in this area the most glorious colors are made out of lowly, nay out of despised materials." The same theme is pursued even more penetratingly, a few years later, in *The Gay Science*, this time under the heading "Hail, Physics!" Nietzsche sees no need for a critical discussion of his presupposition that "our opinions, evaluations and scales of values" are ruled by a "law of their mechanism." To avoid remaining passive products of circumstances in making our evaluations, and in order to be able to create our own scale of values, "we must become the best learners and discoverers of everything which is a matter of law and necessity in the world. We must be *physicists* in order to be *creators* in an original sense. Yet, hitherto, all evaluations and ideals were constructed on a fundamental ignorance of physics, or else in *contradiction* to physics. Therefore: Hail, physics! Nay, hail that which *forces* us into physics—our honesty!"[7] Another passage stresses the interrelationship of the most exacting precision and a relativistic humility: "As far as it is in any way possible, we want all sciences to be penetrated by the subtlety and rigor of mathematics; not indeed in the belief that in this way we shall know things, but in order to ascertain our human relations to things."[8]

To be sure, the exaltation of honesty and truthfulness, which fires Nietzsche's enthusiasm for strict science, also carries him beyond the standpoint determined by science alone. It anticipates the "noble morality" which, in *The Gay Science* and in the later works, endows a new metaphysics and a philosophy of culture with the power of expression meaningful even in our time. The superimposed rationalism could not smother the essential content of the *Birth of Tragedy*. True enough, Nietzsche had turned away from Schopenhauer. He could not know how much of Schopenhauer's biologism was a permanent element of his own thought, for he was unable to see what was pre-Kantian and obsolete in Schopenhauer's philosophy. Yet, not without reason did Nietzsche retain an affection for the work of his youth. As in the *Birth of Tragedy*, so even in Nietzsche's latest sketches, we find the expression of his conviction that cultural life needs both the "will for proportion, for simplicity, for subordination under rule and concept" and the "reach beyond the person, beyond daily routine, society, reality." Beyond "the abyss of annihilation" (*des Vergehens*) it needs the "unifying sense of the necessity of creation and destruction."[9] The former, the Apollonian, after all, is but deceptive appearance, the lie of life; the truth is with Dionysos.

Nietzsche was not the first to discover, for modern culture, the contrast between the two Greek divinities of art. To be sure, there is no doubt that he taught us a re-evaluation of the Dionysian. But the contrast as such is taken for granted, as already familiar in Goethe's poem "German Parnassus" of 1798. Later, Schelling absorbed the contrast into his philosophy, at first from an aesthetic interest, though even then from the standpoint of its widest ramifications. In everything creative, Schelling sees the tension between the blind urge to produce and the disciplined will to give form by setting clear limits. He knows works of art in which the productive power dominates: the form seems to fall short of the content; the content overwhelms the form. In other works the form predominates; fullness of content is lacking. "The secret of true poetry is to be both drunk and sober, not in consecutive moments, but simultaneously. This secret distinguishes Apollonian enthusiasm from the mere Dionysian. It is the highest task of art to present a non-finite content—a content which as such resists form and seems to annihilate form—and to present such a non-finite content in the most perfect, that is, in the most finite form." Moreover, God's creation shows him as artist; in his creation everything is a symbol; even the lowest, the most limited, the most finite form has non-finite content.[10]

Schelling's evaluation of the contrast differs from Nietzsche's. In Nietzsche's philosophy of culture, both powers, the Dionysian and the Apollonian, are indispensable because man could not endure the truth as such if it were to manifest itself in isolation. "The Greek knew and sensed the terrors and horrors of existence; he had to hide them behind the screen image of the Olympians, the radiant offspring of dreams, in order to be able to live at all."[11] Man needs deceptive appearance and error, because life demands such alleviations. In Nietzsche's biologistic philosophy, life is the highest value. For Schelling, too, both aspects of the contrast are necessary, but in his case the idea of truth is sovereign even in the philosophy of culture; seen in the light of this idea the contrast becomes intelligible for him as the tension between content and form. The Dionysian of itself would remain chaotic, and therefore would not permit any insight into its significance; and the Apollonian, taken by itself, would lack a deeper content. Whatever, in the life of culture, takes its origin from the lawless and primitive is still lacking in any clear relation to the idea of truth. Whether or not it can withstand the scrutiny of the idea can be known only when the content has found its own necessity, in consciousness, and thus has found its appropriate form.

Restless times, times attuned to renewal—the period of *Sturm und Drang*, the Romantic Movement, our own days, for example —have brought forth much resistance to form. Form is the relationship which gathers the elements of content into unity, presenting that unity as meaningful and therefore legitimate. But times of renewal will no longer accept the meaning and the legitimacy of tradition. Therefore they rebel against the traditional forms. In the sphere of art,[12] of society, of the personal life, form is alleged to be unnatural. And what is unnatural is at the same time a denial of truth! In Schiller's drama *The Robbers*, Karl Moor exclaims: "They repress healthy nature with insipid conventions. . . . What, I should bind my body in a corset, lace

Dionysos and Apollo

my will with laws! Law has brought low, to the pace of a snail, what would have been the flight of an eagle. Never yet has law shaped a great man, but liberty breeds giants and extremes." Form obstructs freedom and thus prevents the realization of whatever is true. To be sure, this obstruction is never the pure form itself, which is beyond the vicissitudes of history; it is always only a form caught up in historical change, whether a form determined by an historical idea now outmoded, having lost its freshness and its former validity, or a form which is no more than contingent and arbitrary. But there is a wild, imprudent urge to attack everything which would impose restraint, every law, every form. Such an urge, says Schelling, is animated by "mere Dionysian enthusiasm"; in terms of a limpid humanism, he presents the Apollonian enthusiasm as, by contrast, the higher, though quietly reminding us of the danger which may lurk along the Apollonian way—poverty of content.

For the Greeks, Apollo was a deity: the form worthy of his name cannot derive from the accident of human convention. The very essence of truth demands the adequate form which manifests truth as truth; it demands its own necessary form. Necessary form never imposes an impediment to freedom. However, an historical form has necessity only as long as the historical idea to which it belongs has the power of demonstrating its validity with reference to the problems of the time. Epochs of transition (and in some measure every epoch is one of transition) will always be productive of a lack of precision precisely where clarity is called for. The uncertainty of unresolved conflicts marks such eras. Not everything which boasts of being new, and therefore superior to the old, has a legitimate claim to validity within a superhistorical frame of reference.[a] When its claim is valid, it demonstrates the fact by opening up new depths for human thought, new possibilities for the attainment of real humanity. Yet even a claim thus demonstrated will be rejected by many at first.

Even the former understanding of freedom and humanity will at times obstruct the ready recognition of the legitimacy which the new interpretation may have. For in its earliest manifestations it often lacks clarity and therefore may attract corrupt protagonists and confused followers; on that account it cannot be readily appreciated by those who understand freedom in the traditional way. Jerusalem—and not only Jerusalem—has killed its prophets (Matt. 23:37) although their proclamations offered only what "the Law" itself signified in its very depths: "progress in the consciousness of freedom."[b] In a passage dealing with the history of Israel, Schelling says: "Prophecy as such was already a force directed in principle against the law. It could be called the Dionysian element in the Old Testament."[13] What became manifest in prophecy was Revelation which pointed beyond the formerly revealed Law. The fixed forms of the Law could determine man's relation to God only in an outward manner. The prophets point to a future when the external bonds will become interior. (Jeremiah [31:33f.] announces that God will write his law on men's hearts.) But even the guardians of the Law honor the words of the prophets, and such words can already be heard in the history of the Law. In Deuteronomy 30:11-14 we can read: "For this commandment which I command you this day is not too hard for you, neither is it far off. It is not in heaven, that you should say, 'Who will go up for us to heaven, and bring it to us, that we may hear it and do it?' Neither is it beyond the sea, that you should say, 'Who will go over the sea for us, and bring it to us, that we may hear it and do it?' But the word is very near you; it is in your mouth and in your heart, so that you can do it.")[14]

There is no need to labor the point that Schelling surpasses Nietzsche in conceptual clarity. One must nevertheless keep in mind that unavoidably the later period will present new demands, and hence, inevitably, later generations will neglect many things which were given due value in the thought of their predecessors. In his contrast of the Dionysian and the Apollonian, Nietzsche did not incorporate the distinction between content and form. In an endeavor to relate the two pairs of terms, one may perhaps say that by the Dionysian in art and life Nietzsche meant a definite predominance of the content; and by the Apollonian, the harmony of content and form, an equilibrium necessarily achieved at the cost of a surrender of depth and by a certain aesthetic tendentiousness. Nietzsche's era turns away from classicism with its high esteem for form because his is a period which no longer shares the idealistic faith that the forms which the mind imposes on the content of consciousness can keep us in harmony with the universe in its depths and can reconcile us with those depths.

Hegel had expressed that faith in the strongest terms. His doctrine was that though the content of consciousness "at first does not appear in the form of thought but in feeling, vision, imagination," yet "the true content of our consciousness is put in its proper light only through the translation into the form of thought and of concept."[15] Standing closer to Kant and being less convinced of the reach of the form of human thought, yet all the more alive to the significance of artistic form, Schiller had stated: "What we have sensed here as beauty will meet us in the beyond as truth."[16] The verse expresses the conviction that the beauty of art reveals a depth of reality which remains hidden for the forms of consciousness which constitute knowledge. Measured against the words of Schiller, Hegel almost looks like a follower of Leibniz, who would have artistic experience understood as the confused cognition of an object.[17] To be sure, Hegel would go further than Leibniz; he claims that the "form of thought and of the concept" is capable of absorbing all truth. "The hidden essence of the universe has no power in itself which could resist the bold thrust of the knowing intellect, it must open itself and unfold its wealth and its depth before the eyes of knowledge, and let knowledge enjoy them."[18] The whole content of art and religion is conceptually penetrated by philosophy. In its own history, the intellect of man has reached the freedom of thought whereby the form of art has ceased to be the highest need.[19] What in Schiller's verse appeared as the tension between the earthly limitation of man and the unconditional, becomes for Hegel a past already transcended: even now, in the nineteenth century, the content of the beautiful can be translated into conceptual form in which its truth can be recognized as such!

A remarkable sentence of Goethe's would admit two religions as true: "one which gives to the holy which dwells in and around us an acknowledgment and a worship which is quite without form; and the other, which employs the most beautiful form."[20] This dictum can only just be reconciled with the verse of Schiller, but with the doctrine of Hegel not at all. To be sure, our intellectual life is never "quite without form"; yet, for the sake of the highest truth, it can refuse to believe in its forms. Thus far Goethe is right in his dictum. Human thinking can direct itself to the unconditional, with unconditional certainty, and thus it can rise above the forms of the rational process; still, it never wholly rids itself of these forms, and they remain a restriction. If life does not want to lose its hold on what it is, it must retain faith in what is superior to those forms—faith in the eternal mystery which man never dispels, faith in "true being." No matter how this faith is interpreted, it is a force which turns human history into something better than a mere struggle for utility—notwithstanding the fact that we can read in Nietzsche's *Twilight of the Idols*: "The 'true' world—an idea no longer good for anything, not even for binding us to an intellectual task—a useless idea, now superfluous, therefore a disproven idea: let us do away with it!"[21]

In the sketches for *The Will for Power*, Nietzsche calls "Schopenhauer's interpretation of 'reality-as-such' as will" an essential step in the movement away from idealistic faith.[22] And in another passage of those sketches, he declares: "The world which concerns us is false, i.e. it is not a fact but a fiction and a roof over a meager sum of observations; it is 'in flux,' as something in the making, as a ceaselessly shifting falsehood, which never approaches truth since there is no 'truth.'"[23] It is an old story that the "world which concerns us" is in perpetual flux, and that, just because it concerns us, it is subject to our active interference and likewise posits tasks for scientific investigation, tasks which induce ever new formulations of the respective concepts of objects. As for these concepts "never approaching truth," Goethe's Faust bewailed the fact: "I am not higher by a hair's breadth, I am no closer to the infinite."[c] And the mathematical image of a movement which retains its direction towards a goal in infinity, if applied to cultural history, would yield an inference less unbearable; the inference that, though we never get nearer the infinite, we always get beyond the limits of our finiteness, and ought to get beyond them. However, the second half of the nineteenth century sought to devaluate the forms of the intellect. Nietzsche, the strongest representative of the trend, justifies it with his axiom: "There is no 'truth'." The very form of this sentence—"there is"—takes truth for granted, and the sentence is self-contradictory.

Nevertheless its aim is to do away with the ground and the goal of the forms of consciousness; only in the wildness and terror of the Dionysian are we to experience the depth of the world.

It may not be superfluous to focus on the fact that, in this context of devaluation, the depth of the world *must* be interpreted biologistically; for Nietzsche this means that the essence of the world is the will for power. It was with Schopenhauer's metaphysics, infected with biologism, or (what amounts to the same thing) bent upon the dethronement of truth as a reality of valid meanings, that the slide towards these consequences began. To be sure, truth as a spiritual reality was never honestly respected by a low stratum of society whose poverty of soul was due to the excessive regard which they cultivated for its natural and economic basis. Similar social conditions have long been documented—by the struggle against sophist demagogy on the part of Socrates and Plato, by Kant's insistence on human dignity, or by Fichte's fight against those for whom "their individual person is the ultimate purpose of their action, and therefore also the limit of their clear thinking." "Reason exists in order to promote this person in the world."[24] These last words are used to describe an instrumentalistic biologism, and they try to put it in its place. Only, at their time, in 1797, this biologism or instrumentalism had not yet become aware of its own nature; it existed only in the passive consciousness of common men without intellectual interests, and perhaps in some popular philosophy now forgotten. Since then, under different names, biologism and instrumentalism have pushed their way into the front ranks of culture. But the spirit of sovereign truth is eternal, and one of the insights of this spirit, already fairly old in the consciousness of maturing humanity, tells us that it is impossible for scandals not to occur: *impossibile est ut non veniant scandala*. And this would be the proper reply to the devil in Thomas Mann's *Doctor Faustus*, when he defends the presence of poisons active in a culture "which does not live from home-made bread alone."[25] In the time to come, power is promised by the devil for the ice-cold music of Leverkühn: "We guarantee the living efficacy of whatever you produce with our help. You will lead, you will furnish the drum beats for the future. . . . Do you understand? You will not only break through the paralyzing difficulties of the age, you will break through the age itself, through this cultural epoch; that is, you will break up the epoch of culture, and break its cult, and you will dare to construct the barbaric, which will be a twofold barbarism because it will be founded on the corruption of the humane and will come after true humanity." This is the dialectic of a life as naturalism understands it, not of human life, life for which the relation to truth is law.

6
TRUE KNOWLEDGE OF GOD

Like Schelling, yet three hundred years before Schelling, Paracelsus found the *content* of truth in the Dionysian and, at the same time, recognized the need of a *form* which prepares a human abode for the content among men and preserves it. True, Paracelsus used neither the words "content" and "form" nor the ancient names of the gods Dionysos and Apollo.

Paracelsus was a younger contemporary of Luther and Zwingli, and he too was caught up in the spirit of reform. He was clearly aware of the evils which afflicted the old Church and criticized them without mercy. He felt that he was the Samaritan whom priests and Levites despised as one adhering to the wrong faith, yet whom the Christian truth filled to the point where his own medical calling became in itself the service of God which he gave to the sick. "It is a great and lofty mystery that God shows us such sufferers, and that they are Himself."[1] This is the deep truth revealed to him as a physician: in his patients he meets God. Yet every calling affords the possibility of such a meeting.[2]

To be sure, there is no logical proof for the presence of God of which Paracelsus became aware when he was standing before his patients. Nor is this presence to be accepted like some esoteric priestly doctrine. The way to an understanding of its ontological truth is a life of dedication, a life which holds itself open to the spirit of God. The spirit of God is not contained by any ecclesiastical order; it is a freely flowing life. "The church is a wall," Paracelsus jots down,[3] and he does not mean only the old Church but the Reformation churches as well. The Pope, Zwingli, Luther —"they judge themselves by condemning each other";[4] they are right in their condemnations and therefore wrong, all of them. In fact, in an unpublished paper, Paracelsus encourages Pope

Clement VII, of whose rule he does not approve, to keep up his resistance to his enemies as an act well done, for, if he did not resist them, they would become even worse than himself.[5] The attacks of Paracelsus on the Church are often violent; they are directed against the all-too-human failings found in it; but Paracelsus never became a renegade. Although he exalts the divine Spirit over tonsure and chasuble,[6] he well knows that it is necessary to have a stable order, binding laws and forms. Even the wall of the church comes from God: it need not impede the life of the spirit. "We should build two temples for the life of beatitude: one for teaching—and this is a structure of walls—and the other for the fulfillment of the teaching—and that we ourselves are, in our hearts."[7]

The distinction he makes between the inward and the outward, between the spirit whose outpouring in acts of love cannot be hindered and the unchanging letter of the law which binds us externally, is Paracelsus' final word on the question of truth. For him, as for so many others, it has become identical with the question concerning God, and for him this was always more than an academic one. Like those thinkers who, when they concern themselves with reality in its deepest implications, evoke the deities Dionysos and Apollo in their contrast, Paracelsus too is aware of the discrepancy and unresolved tension in human existence. He is aware of the shortcomings of the endeavor to reach a final clarification of the problem of the truth which must necessarily be *one*. Yet, despite the riddles which true being presents to inquiring reason, genuine love fills the mind with the certainty of God.

One of the most important philosophical works of our century, Henri Bergson's *The Two Sources of Morality and Religion* (1932), indicates by its title how it belongs in the present context. Bergson opposes to the "static" religion which is kept in bonds by superstition a "dynamic" religion. But he looks for truth in the latter alone. In this he differs from Paracelsus and seems more akin to Nietzsche, who likewise acknowledged the existence of truth in the dynamic alone. Nevertheless Bergson's world-view connects him more closely with Paracelsus—and even more especially with Schelling—than with the author of the *Birth of Tragedy*. Still, as for Nietzsche so for Bergson, the static religion is a product of the "fable-making function" (which also produces the novel and the drama).[8] Dynamic religion, on the other hand, reaches its height in the mystical union in which the will yields entirely to the godhead which fills it, so that human freedom coincides with the action of God.[9] Thus there is nothing but truth in the dynamic religion. One who has been favored by the joining of his will to God—"il a senti la vérité couler en lui de sa source comme une force agissante": he has felt the truth flow from its source into him as an active power.[10]

In distinction from Schelling, Bergson deems the *form* of our experience of truth superfluous, nay almost an interference;[11] at bottom, the experience of absolute truth bursts the bonds of human limitations. It is bestowed only upon the "privileged ones"[12] who are more than merely human; they are an extension of the action of God.[13] By principle Bergson's dualism keeps God and man separate, and this is the ground for his low evaluation of form and his distance from the position of Schelling. For Bergson, the mystical experience appears only as a rare and exceptional cancellation of the essential separation between God and man. For Schelling, on the other hand, the dualistic separation of man from God has its ground merely in the consciousness of a philosophically untutored man whose notions of reality are therefore ruled by an intelligence which is incapable of giving an account of man's true relation to God. An intelligence "which moves only by way of contrasts"[14] can conceive of God only by conceiving itself in contrast to God, and thus to *unconditional* truth! And this conception misses God altogether, for God is not an "object"[a] and therefore is not at all accessible to intelligence, whose concepts can grasp only relative, only conditional truths. Nevertheless its presupposition is ontological truth, the idea of the unconditionally true, which calls forth intelligence itself and is perpetually present to it as its measure. Only with this idea as a standard can intelligence recognize progress as such, in the search for knowledge. But it cannot realize the idea itself, which does not belong to intelligence: the unconditionally true is without contrasts. Yet what is without contrasts projects itself into the world of consciousness by means of superindividual reason which contains intelligence and guarantees it.

In a supplement to his *Letters about the Doctrine of Spinoza*, in

1789, Jacobi had raised the question: "Does man have reason, or does reason have man?"[15] With a new awareness of the significance of the question, Schelling borrowed Jacobi's formulation. Continuing in the steps of Kant and thus going beyond Kant, Schelling says: "Reason is not an endowment, not a tool, nor can it be used: there is no reason at all which we have, but only a reason which has us."[16] It is "not an affirmation of the One, affirmed from a stand taken outside the One, but a knowledge of God which is itself in God."[17]

Regardless of whether distinctions and contrasts are affirmed within an individual consciousness or affirmed in respect to the relation of such a consciousness to that of another individual, all acts of distinguishing and contrasting belong to the domain of intelligence. Every individual by himself has for himself the knowledge which his intelligence affords, including the unsatisfactory concepts which he forms for himself concerning God. This is why Schelling can say: "Not we, not you or I, know about God."[18] Only where individual particularity has no bearing can there be knowledge of God. Its presupposition is reason, which we do not have but which has us—reason which is not a characteristic of distinction between individuals, but which unites us all, of which we are all aware as the certainty of unconditional truth, although what is individual in us may be loath to acknowledge reason.[19]

Individual man has the liberty to make his own decisions, arbitrarily, and many of them are determined by motives of a very contingent, onesided kind: there is no assurance that the functions of our mental life will work in harmony, no certainty that our personal humanity will be an unsplintered whole. Only one who experiences his own reality within the structure of social relationships which environs him and strives unceasingly to do justice to them—only he, in fact, who has a deep capacity for love—can in some degree make sure of the integrity, the truth, of his own person. Yet it is precisely these social structures, with the demands they make on the individual, which can pose a persistent threat to personal unity, especially in the case of those who are still immature. And what is true for the individual is equally true for the superindividual collectives; reason holds them as an overruling authority, but at the same time leaves them with the possibility of deciding irresponsibly, motivated by chance happenings. Ultimate responsibility always rests with the individual person; yet human life is possible only in a community. Wherever there is no joint bearing of responsibilities, marriages break up, education suffers, and nations confront each other with an enmity they would fain deny though it is a fact and at times manifests itself openly. The reason which is sovereign in our lives exerts no external force; it gives freedom. It leads its faithful, those who revere it, to the unworldly freedom of true love; it even nourishes in those who despise reason the freedom of that subjectivity which, though it is a phenomenon without essence, yet ever summons the subject to a concentration on his own substantial reality.

Our intelligence does not have us, we have it—we, within the narrow limits of our conditional existence. For what our intelligence allows us to conclude and accept as true does not depend alone on its logical cogency. What is logically cogent is indeed a binding necessity which shows that intelligence is no mere psychological peculiarity but has its ground in reason. But the truths which intelligence affords depends on the logical necessities only in their refracted aspect seen through the individual abilities which we brought into the world with us as equipment and which open the avenues of knowledge to us as individuals in very different measures. It likewise depends on the educational opportunities which have been made available to us. It depends furthermore on the passions which we have permitted to develop in ourselves, which are often productive of a selective blindness or a bias with respect to the things which attract and those which repel and hence make their contribution to a subjective coloration of our world-view which is all too human. In short, it depends on an immense variety of factors peculiar to our own existence. We are conditioned beings, and our reasoning processes are entangled in the conditionality which varies from one individual to another. Hence different things present themselves as true to different men. Wherever the insights of science touch upon the affective side of human consciousness, they invariably meet with violent resistance on the part of those who feel that their individual conditionality is being attacked. In the sixteenth and seventeenth centuries, the limitation produced by religious dogmas prevented many a scholar from seeing that the Ptolemaic picture of the world had become obsolete. In our century, antisemitism has kept many from seeing the legitimacy of Einstein's theory of relativity. True, one who loves truth more than the contingency of his own existence can loosen the fetters of circumstances which hold him, and he can even break some of them by himself. But even in the case of the most fortunate, the accomplishments of intelligence as such do not lose their bonds of contingency in the context of intellectual history. The intellectual contests themselves are conducted by forces which are unable to determine their own limitations. The highest which intelligence can attain is a partial enhancement of the scientific consciousness of its own time. The horizon is limited by the unknown, and never can the claim be made that knowledge considered proven will not undergo a new revolution.

Our intelligence is what *we* have, and each one has his own. But reason has *us*: we are held fast and supported by its super-individual necessity. We *must* distinguish between true and false, we cannot but hold the true as valid and valuable, and reject the false as worthless; here individuals no longer differ and their liberty is at an end.[20] For, in this contrast of values, the very reason which contains and dominates the reasoning process asserts itself. Reason furnishes ratiocination with the inescapable orientation towards the idea of what is true, what is unconditionally true, an orientation which constitutes the very life of the intellect. Subjectivistic interpretation of the idea of truth is nothing but empty rhetoric.[21] For, such interpretation, in order to pose even as theory, must appeal to a criterion which unites all individuals. However, as soon as we ask, with regard to any specific thesis, what the value contrast of true and false signifies specifically, we cannot but turn to our intelligence. And now the specific conditions of human individuals enter into play and even such sublime intellects as those of Schelling and Bergson are no longer of the same opinion: every philosophical, every scientific achievement, as the work of intelligence, depends on the historical conditions of its origins.

But the truth for which the human spirit asks is not merely the truth of intelligence. The lover knows of a reality to which logic has no proper access but which determines the meaning of our existence. Just as the necessity of distinguishing between true and false is superior to our arbitrary will, so also do the value contrasts of good and evil, beautiful and ugly, just and unjust have their ground in that reason which possesses us and over which we have no power. In those contrasts man discovers himself as a "rational being";[b] it is they which make his existence meaningful. The religions give hints of this meaningfulness in symbolic words. For the impersonal intelligence such words sound hollow, but they yield their meaning to a personality mature enough to experience the human community, with the will to make necessary sacrifices. In the story "Sainte Oliverie et Sainte Liberette," Anatole France has St. Bertauld announce the message of the Gospel to a heathen people with the words: "The God whom I am teaching you is the only true God. He is one in three persons, and his son is born from a virgin." In this ironic formulation one may see scintillating charm, maybe even some relative correctness; yet certainly it does not convey any true knowledge of God. Nevertheless, even those two sentences could express such knowledge provided that their context made clear that the Christian dogma recognizes the presence of the godhead (which cannot be seized by logical formulations) in that love which manifests itself as love, in every decision and in every fate, even in the most dreadful fate.

Antecedent to all human thinking and acting, existence refers to meaning. The certainty of this meaningfulness keeps the enigma of death free from the terrors with which superstitious anxiety has surrounded it. A life lived in relation to meaning, a life related to the supertemporal, cannot acquiesce in the opinion that "death ends everything." True enough, negative sentences demand affirmative supplements. But death is a mystery, and even the question whether there is a life "after death" cannot be asked by a philosophy which knows its own limits. If it were to take for granted the metaphysical validity of time, it would step beyond the sphere of its own possibilities.

7

ABOUT THE MYSTERY OF THE NON-FINITE

In history our intelligence finds the task of advancing in knowledge, though without ever achieving the completion of its undertaking; a termination is impossible in principle. Again and again a new day entices us with the view of new shores. Insights are made secure by means of the contexts in which they hold true. But these contexts are never conclusive, and the security they afford is but temporary. Whatever intelligence is able to grasp remains within the conditional, the finite. Yet the constitutive concepts of the conditional and finite itself point beyond it and demand the acknowledgment of the mystery of non-finiteness and of unconditional truth. The insights which rest on those concepts never bring an end to questions; on the contrary, these very insights open the way for further questions. Thus the mere fact that the very accomplishments of our intelligence ceaselessly point beyond themselves shows how much the "truth" which such insights afford is in need of completion, how limited it is, how conditional, how problematic.

An epistemologically untutored mind is wont to consider the theorems of Euclidean geometry as paradigms of absolute truth. Yet take the simplest example! Imagine a straight line intersected by another. Take any point on the second line, other than the intersection point, and let the line turn around the chosen point. Revolve it in such a way that its angle with the first line becomes always more acute, so that the point of intersection moves farther and farther away on the first line. Since both lines must be conceived as infinite, the abstract inference would follow that the point of intersection keeps moving away endlessly. Yet, in the concrete world, the amazing event takes place that the revolution of the second line suddenly makes the two lines parallel, so that they no longer intersect. And as the second line keeps revolving, a new point of intersection appears on the opposite "end" of the first line! Rationally, this is absolutely unintelligible. To ignore this unintelligibility means to have faith in the Euclidean axiom of parallels, the very axiom on which rests the theorem that the sum of the angles of a triangle is equal to two right angles. Although this theorem presents itself with apparently lucid cogency, it cannot be fully understood without the proviso of that unintelligible condition. Consequently the theorem cannot be taken for absolute truth.

We make events intelligible by reducing them to their causes. But such a reduction would be fully satisfactory only if it were not a reduction to some unknown. Therefore the cause must be reduced in like manner, and its cause in turn . . . Must the reduction go back to the beginning of the entire chain of causes? Or go on, into infinity? Yet both alternatives escape the grasp of conceptual requirements. If we require fully comprehensive concepts, the alternatives appear as inevitable yet insoluble problems. What is meant by causation, ultimately, could be known, and our causal explanation would be unproblematic, only if there were no such enigma as the first cause, or as the non-existence of a first link of the chain of causes: that is, only if our knowledge were not the result of finite intelligence. But the intelligence is bent on the finite, which is not "true being," or which, in the view of ultimate truth, "*is*" not! Owing to its very structure of inherent necessity, intelligence keeps us locked in insoluble riddles. Our causal explanations are indispensable, but they confine us to a sphere in which ultimate truth can not be found. The truth value of these explanations is only relative, only conditional. On the other hand, we must admit that we can speak meaningfully of conditional truth only because we know what the word "truth" means in its unconditional significance, and because we acknowledge this truth. We could not attribute even as much as conditional truth to our causal explanations if their relative validity were not confirmed (and at the same time exposed as completely unsatisfactory) when measured against the idea of unconditional truth.

In the long run, all the principles of objective knowledge lead into obscurity, for they demand non-finiteness, yet are incapable of positively anchoring in the non-finite the very relations within which they have their validity, incapable of deriving the finite from the non-finite. Rabindranath Tagore put it this way: "The water in the vessel is light; the water in the ocean is dark. The small truth has words which are clear and transparent; the great truth has unfathomable silence."[1] Yet the great truth embraces the little ones, and its unfathomableness is in them too. Space, time, the number series, the linking up of cause and effect—these are principles of intellectual clarification as long as they refer to objects, to finite entities. They are the principles of the world which intelligence endeavors to conceive by putting the factors together the way they belong together objectively. That they do belong together can often be ascertained only by a detour of a scientific investigation of causes. Even the awareness that the sound of an explosion (which reaches the ear several seconds after the optical perception) originated in the explosion presupposes a knowledge of a causal process: the transmission of sound. In the coordination of what objectively belongs together, the applicability of the principles of knowledge manifests itself. But these principles themselves are not "objects," they are functions of subjective acts of the intellect; therefore they can not be known "objectively," i.e. as objects. As soon as these principles of intellectual clarification are subjected to the clarifying analysis of intelligence they prove to be opaque, unthinkable. The *Critique of Pure Reason* undertook to demonstrate this in a comprehensive systematic way. Beginnings in that direction had been made long before. Augustine had said: "What is time? If nobody asks me, I know; but if I want to explain it to anyone who asks, I do not know."[2]

As formerly, so in the most recent times, yet now on the basis of insights matured during the last decades, positivistic thinking has arrived at the same result, namely, that our fundamental principles lack transparency and are therefore questionable. Positivism is inadequate as a philosophical doctrine; hence it is often afflicted with considerable blindness to problems. However, one must agree with the kind of assertions which P. W. Bridgman makes when he writes that, in mathematics, one cannot find "that mystic certainty and necessity" which one is commonly supposed to find in it; for there is no safeguard against the possibility of a devaluation of the concepts with which mathematics operates, be they acknowledged as generally "as the circle or the number system."[3] In the same book, in another context, Bridgman says that the concepts of space, time and causality have "only limited validity."[4] In the electron he sees the lowest limit for any discussion of space, but it would be meaningless to talk about "space inside the electron."[5] If specific qualities of the electron are conceived in terms of space, such images are parables but not objective knowledge.[6]

The question of the universal truth of the principles of knowledge[7] has been raised, but the formulation is not unambiguous. In its ultimate sense, the principle of causality, understood without regard to the very different ways in which it has been understood in intellectual history, has universal truth insofar as it can be applied to all objective relationships. Yet it is not absolutely true. It is true only within the objective order which must be investigated by the intelligence. This order, however, points to the incomprehensible. And therefore that principle of knowledge itself is of merely problematic truth; it holds within the finite, but it turns into an enigma loaded with contradictions if, tentatively, it is extended to the unconditional. In the same way, the mathematical concept of "set" which is unambiguous in finite relationships (being the simplest form of the synthesis of a manifold) becomes impossible if extended to the infinite; the well-known question whether "the set of sets" contains itself as an element is, at best, play with an amusing toy.

In his *Doctor Faustus*, when the choir has sung its last word, Thomas Mann lets the symphonic cantata "Doctor Faust's Lamentation" end in an orchestral passage "which sounds like God's lamentation over the perdition of his world." Mann describes this ending as "above reason" and as touching the emotions "with the eloquent unspoken expressiveness which music alone has." And "the soul listens still" after the last chord has ceased to reverberate. The ending transforms the meaning of the work, light begins to shine in the night.[8] It is a choral work with a voluminous text that ends in this manner, giving God the last word, which is no longer a word of spoken language. Spoken language is subject to reason, and is within the power of human logic. The truth of God is beyond language; it may be at work in the language, yet it does not yield itself up to it.

The fundamental principles of objective thought lead intelligence into an area where there are no paths, and thus they render problematic all the insights which depend upon them. Fichte is quoted as having said at Jena, in the opening lecture of a course in logic: "Man, or we men, are active, thinking creatures who know something merely by taking as their starting point obscure and indefinite notions and tying to them concepts which are clear and definite—in short, by tying the known to the unknown." The student who, in these words, reports what he believed Fichte said, had already spent several semesters in serious philosophical study, when, on this occasion, he heard Fichte for the first time. He continues his report by saying: "In my ears, Fichte's proposition was a blasphemy not only against all philosophy but also against sound human sense. What—I could have cried out loud—our knowledge comes about only by tying the known to the unknown? The principles of knowledge, therefore, are the unknown? Marvelous philosophy! . . . While every other philosophy finds its foundation not only in the known but in the most clearly ascertained, in the most certain and, starting from there, endeavors to investigate the unknown and to make it certain for human knowledge, you, Fichte, must do the very opposite. . . . So you know of no fact of consciousness, no principle of contradiction, etc., as the highest and most fully confirmed principle in philosophy? Nor do you seem to be acquainted with the fact that ordinary human sense starts only with what is most familiar in its knowledge and from there proceeds only to what is less familiar?"[9] This report gives a vivid account of the impression made by the impact of criticism upon dogmatism. The reporting student who believed in the power of his dogmas needed a considerable time before he could admit that the abstract principle of contradiction affords no possibility at all of taking concrete representations in tow, and that obscurities may be contained in whatever common sense (quite legitimately) takes for what is most fully known.

The ultimate insight intelligence can reach about itself is that for it there is no end of questioning and of going further. Thus,

About the Mystery of the Non-Finite

for ratiocination, the non-finite turns into a negative concept, [the infinite]. *For ratiocination*, but not *for us*; man is not identical with his intelligence, nor with the fact that he is a finite being, and man's certainty of self is greater than the certainty of his finiteness. In Greek, even the word truth ἀλήθεια, has a negative form; its first syllable is the privative alpha.[a] Goethe's Mephisto says "I tell you modest truth," and the negative word would suit him well since according to his own confession he is "thrust out into darkness."[b] The negative word may also suit that ancient language, that is, insofar as Nietzsche was at all historically right when he felt a regret in suppressing his own wishful opinion that the culture of the Greeks could and should have been "baptized in the name of its teachers, the Sophists."[10] However, our certainty of truth tolerates no limitation; the structural necessities under whose sway the insights of our reasoning must remain can make no claim to limit truth itself, the idea of the true. We become aware of our finiteness as such when we measure ourselves against reason's idea of the non-finite. That idea, too, lives in us. And it takes the appearance of something negative only when intelligence tries to take hold of it. We must bear with the short-range endeavors of our intelligence, which is not a strange employee whom we can dismiss because of unsatisfactory services. Our intelligence is our fate, and we are inevitably drawn into the domain of the riddles and the questionability of its principles of knowledge. For us, those principles are not "problems" but "mysteries," to borrow the lucid terminology of Gabriel Marcel. "A problem is something which we encounter and which bars our way. It is entirely in front of me. In contrast, mystery is something in which I find myself engaged, and whose essence therefore is not entirely in front of me. As it were, in this zone the distinction between *in me* and *in front of me* has lost its significance."[11]

Space too holds a "mystery," for, as beings who themselves occupy space, we do not have the riddle of space entirely *in front* of us.

8
THE PROBLEMATIC NATURE OF THE CERTAINTY OF SELF

Gabriel Marcel has also shown[1] that one cannot conceive of one's own body as simply non-existent; since it is my body it is no mere object for me.[2] Every living body is inseparable from the individual existence which lives in it. Objects can change their owner; even a country can be taken away from the people who have endowed it with its form and its culture, and another nation can take possession of it; but a living body belongs unexchangeably to *that* life which manifests itself in it. Individual existence experiences itself in that body. The Platonic notion of a spirit withdrawn into itself and separated from the body does not refer to any reality; it is meaningful as an abstraction, but strictly only as an abstraction. We have our reality in our bodily self, as Hobbes already stressed in opposition to the idealism of the *Meditations* of Descartes—admittedly, with Hobbesian overemphasis. What I do and have done, my body does and has done. On account of the inseparable unity of living body and animating selfhood, the question-inducing riddle of space is a riddle and a question with regard to our own existence, and it is no mere object for an intellectual inquiry outward bound.

In the contexts in which we can use it, the theorem about the sum of the angles of the triangle retains its validity unfailingly. The realm of geometric validity includes all spatially extended existence and therefore includes our own bodily existence. Yet this validity has the fateful character of resting on convincing insights which are irredeemably mortgaged, as it were; although we cannot but acknowledge the axiom of parallels, yet we cannot but admit the implied and mysterious exclusion of the respective claims of geometric reasoning![a] To be sure, we are not immediately aware

The Problematic Nature of the Certainty of Self

of this exclusion which becomes explicit in our consciousness only owing to an explicit act of reflection. As soon as we engage in this reflection, and are thus no longer naive with regard to the axiom, we can no longer claim, with a clear conscience, that judgments which refer to spatial existence as such have unconditional truth. Although the axiomatic basis of our understanding of spatial existence is evident with regard to finite forms of space, it has no unconditional truth. There is profound reason for the doctrine of old Parmenides that the world of the manifold and of becoming, the world in which we too have our being, has its place below the sphere of "trustworthy speaking and thinking about truth."[b] However, we are beings inclined to assert our selfhood unconditionally and we are wont to interpret that doctrine in a way which gives the illusion that our existence is not of a questionable character.

The truth which is unconditionally true is the ideal goal and the ultimate norm of all intellectual activity. In it are the roots of logical certainty, granted to us by the "reason which has us," and thereby of the certainty concerning ourselves. But this certainty is fused with the mystery of space. "I think, therefore I am," Descartes proclaimed, as indubitable truth. He let the self-certainty pertain to the thinking self which he sharply distinguished from bodily existence. Leibniz understood Descartes' sentence the same way; however, he remarked that its certainty is merely empirical,[3] and Kant concurred.[4] Yet, insofar as the "thinking self" is a person who occupies space and who simply cannot conceive of anything as existing without relating it to the body,[5] the self is tied to the odd mystery owing to which all spatial existence resists being resolved in conceptual necessity. And further elaboration of this statement is inevitable: Our existence and, with it, our certainty of selfhood is tied not only into the concept-resistant nature of space, but also into the ultimately unthinkable causal relationship which can be conceived neither as without beginning nor as having ever begun, and in general is tied into every riddle which, in principle, is the mark of external existence. Since, with regard to the body which inseparably belongs to our self, the distinction between external and immediate existence has only an abstract meaning, those rationally inexhaustible riddles amount to a load which weighs on the Cartesian "I think, I am" and extract from that formula the question "Who am I?" In what measure am I my own self at all, rather than an existence shaped from without?

Self-certainty, the certainty which I, this person, have of myself, is not pure knowledge. My knowledge of my existence calls for clarification. What is the precise meaning of this kind of knowing? How comprehensive is it? Though I do know I exist, I am asking how I find my way in this dark existence, and what I am to seek in it. On the one hand, I know myself as I, and as such I am bent upon unconditional truth; yet, on the other hand, I also experience myself as tied into the impenetrable confusion of the world, and as a tiny piece of it. The proposition "I think, I am," signifies not only the contingency of individual existence to which Liebniz and Kant referred; what is more, the proposition makes us feel the uncertainty of the assertion of ourselves. How can I assert myself in this world which treats me as a being that simply belongs to the world and is coerced into contexts whose alien and incomprehensible nature I feel even in the certainty which, nevertheless, I have of myself?

There is no answer which could dispose of the question unambiguously, for, to reach the certainty of our self is a task, a task which determines our whole life. What Descartes stated is but abstract form. Real self-certainty can be found only where true humanity can test its own content. It is evident that this certainty does not include the unconditional certainty of specific contents of knowledge, for instance of innate absolute truths. On the contrary, the precariousness (*Bedrängnis*) which the existence of the world and our existence in the world signify for the certainty of ourselves indicates that man's mind is denied the grasp of absolute truth. Our mind cannot resolve the enigma of existence. True enough, the insights which mind can attain are forced into the final form of a judgment, but the formal finality deceptively hides the need of further completion, a need ever present in the insights. Conditional insights demand explanations; yet these in turn can be given only in conditional judgments. The path of scientific inquiry points to infinity, and thus documents our insatiable relation to truth. Hegel says: "This infinity is the

The Problematic Nature of the Certainty of Self 89

bad or negative infinity, for it is nothing but the negation of the finite, and since the finite arises again even in the negation, it has also *not* been done away with."[6] For the very humanity of man, intelligence is indispensable. But inhumanity uses it too. Its validity is neutral. It serves humanity only where humanity takes intelligence into its own service and thus lends it a significance which goes beyond the boundaries of mere finiteness and conditionality. *The unconditionality of which we are certain is the unconditionality of the human task.*

Man is human only through his faith in truth. Without that faith, his existence would stay within the contingency of animal reality. Even if man's relation to truth is conceived in the most cautious, limitative terms, his knowledge of truth still retains its inherent reference to unconditionality. Within the certainty which I, as subject of the awareness of truth, have of myself, there arises the unconditionality of the human task, in contrast with the oppression and uncertainty of my real situation. And I know that the unconditional task is *above* me, the mere individual; yet I experience it *in* me, as decisive for my own humanity. Even deficient certainty of self knows that it refers to unconditional self-certainty, which is norm, or abstract demand. Man must demand of himself that, in the situations of an existence which is not only obscure but uncanny, he must not surrender, must not lose himself in what is alien and impenetrable and inimical to the self-certainty of his human task. He *ought* to be certain of himself; he *ought* to do justice to the situations in which reality meets him; in those situations he *ought* to do what reality, *in truth,* asks of his capabilities. This is the answer to that question: what am I to seek in this odd world of riddles?[7]

The human task of every man has the measure of his own possibilities. To a considerable extent, these possibilities depend on the favor of circumstances, and above all on the human attitude of those with whom the individual lives and perhaps must live. Insofar as the world fetters the individual by the natural and the social structures into which his life is inserted, he is estranged from his own depths, and his relation to the truth is no longer clear, less clear even than that limited clearness which is the fate of mankind in general. The thought that God is the truth was no mere thought but the most serious matter of fact for Augustine, who recognized that God is the deepest inwardness of human existence. That time in Augustine's own past when he sought God in external existence was now, for him, a time of self-estrangement. "Where was I when I was seeking Thee? I had run away from myself and I could not find myself: how much less could I find Thee!" "Late did I begin to love Thee! . . . And behold: Thou wert within me, and I was outside and wanted to seek Thee out there. And, myself deformed, I invaded the beautiful forms Thou hadst created. Thou wert with me, and I was not with Thee."[8] The very significant word "self-estrangement" signifies not only that the self is lost (in the world) but has lost itself. Thus it signifies that the self remains, as the *subject* of the loss, even in the extreme and hardest case, the case of the most inhuman criminal. The self is simultaneously subject and object. And as subject it is immediate formal certainty of the truth, the truth which summons it to take its own stand, to defend its self-identity. Wherever the self becomes estranged from itself, it has not merely suffered a loss of substance, the loss also constitutes its guilt.

Self-estrangement manifests itself in two ways: as unbridled natural drives, and as slavish subjection to the forces of social life. In both cases fettering urges prevent the individual from taking the stand which would be in line with the demands man must make upon himself, as the subject which is conscious of the truth. In the first case, he lets himself be guided by the natural basis of individual existence, in the second the goals of his behavior are determined by historically conditioned forms of social existence. In this second case, the self-estrangement, that is, the lagging behind the demands made by self-identity, is always the same, on principle, no matter whether manifest as cowardly acquiescence, as convenient collaborating, as sly pushing, or as aggressive domineering; the social fetters always work through the urges of individual nature, whose individual structure determines the *kind* of goals granted power over an individual life. Even in the most restricted circles of community life the seductive power of the social pattern can manifest itself. Wherever the husband and father behaves as the tyrant of the house; wherever the mother insists on always being right, or where the child would lie in order to appear better than he is; wherever a pupil lets someone correct his assignments before he hands them to the teacher, or, in school, copies from his neighbor: in all these cases behavior is directed towards goals which would place outward glory in a limited society higher in the scale of values than the demands made by the self which is conscious of truth. Such false glory, or even the desire for it, estranges man from the depths of his being and destroys the unity of his personal essence. Where truth retains its rights, man wants to amount only to what he truly is.

In the world of man, the rights of truth can be realized only when persons or groups of persons freely acknowledge them and disdain to shape their own existence by sheer selfishness. Selfishness does not respect the limits demanded by truth. However, human affairs are so very closely intertwined that any victory won by the violent eruption of self-will will cause, in ever widening circles, a loss of the conditions favorable to an untroubled development of true humanity. Bad educators spoil the character of the children entrusted to them, and these children carry the seeds of deterioration into their own life environments where they may germinate and become new centers of harmful influence, especially if these children come into possession of the means of economic power. More disastrous yet, if the violent will to power is that of the leaders of great states, its influence can spread beyond the confines of those states for a long time, and thus promote self-estrangement everywhere. If, finally, violence meets with violence, we have confirmation of the old adage that war, though it kills many men, makes many more men evil.

He alone can be certain of himself who knows what, in truth, he is to do. But in order to know it he needs an environment he can trust. This is true with regard to every single person, and it is no less true with regard to every state. Where there is no true trust, in the simple sense of that word, there is no true community of men. The outward appearance of community may be preserved, the appearance of human relations, an appearance which is cherished because of the desire to inhibit too overt violations of humanity. For the sake of a more or less dubious peace one is willing to condone some, perhaps much, self-estrangement. This seems to be the most acceptable way out, and in evil circumstances it may indeed be so. Yet it is not unintelligible that Richard Dehmel, in a poem of August 1914, could welcome the "honest war"; it seemed to him that truth was demanding its rights, after a long period of poisonous suspicion. It seemed to him that the time of compromise was over, when dishonesty had been tolerated and human dignity violated and self-certainty thus had been damaged. What new vicissitudes were going to replace the old ones was then a matter of the still hidden future.

In such conflicts, the individual as such is powerless. He does have responsibility, but he is responsible as a member of society, and the remedy lies in collective action. War is a collective, though a desperate, action. A more appealing collective action, which historiography cannot ignore, is called non-cooperation; but this action is blocked if the conditions of life are dominated by an inhuman power which denies the truth and propagates self-estrangement. To be sure, such a power could hardly ever be attained without cooperation. It is the curse of the evil action of those who cooperate that it becomes effective as temptation for other, and again other men, and also as coercion upon the co-operators to commit further evil actions.

What is needed is the recognition of the task of social education. Fichte voices an age-old insight in his doctrine that man can be man only among men and therefore needs education by others. But if men tolerate what is inhuman, then their educational influence upon those who grow up under their guidance can not be good—and Fichte has said that too.[9]

The task of initiating growth towards true humanity is difficult enough. It is the consequence of the demands implied in formal self-certainty. Everyone is called to contribute his share to the fulfillment of the task, everyone in any way capable of shouldering responsibility. But the individual does not engage in this undertaking as an individual, nor even as a member of his nation; for if he did not look beyond the nation or feel for more than his nation, he would do his work badly. He does the work simply as a man, as a member of mankind which comes from a past much longer than men can remember, and which goes on into a future much farther than we can see. The task itself is much more comprehensive than anything that could be accomplished by means of educational institutions, though these are very important. Even the most perfect of such institutions would furnish only a weak protection against the temptations which face precisely those who are beyond school age, those fit for military service and entitled to political rights. Though the temptations may not come from neglected corners of one's own community, they can come from afar, and will come from there in the long run. Humanity is always threatened by inhumanity, and culture by anti-culture. In any nation it can happen that movements develop which work as a corrosive on the nation's humanity. In such a case, many men may be willing to make any conceivable sacrifice, yet owing to the infectious power of new ideas, the significance of the sacrifice is lost and cannot change the collective action essentially. What was formerly held in high esteem and greatly valued was characteristic of the community, but it is now considered obsolete by those who fancy that they are the bearers of a new life, while actually they are bringing about the ruin of the community. What is needed is the cooperation of a genuine community of peoples and states, ready to restrict immediately, and thus to deprive of their effect, those areas where evil is breeding and threatening to erupt. The task is endless. True humanity is never safe. In practice this simply means that wherever the values of humanity are appreciated, the duty exists to assist, with the totality of the available resources, the fulfillment of the demands made by humanity. At every new epoch the demands assume new forms. Likewise the dangers which threaten humanity are ever new. The dangers and the demands concern everyone who has awakened to the consciousness of himself.

Society changes, depending on the currents and undercurrents which determine whether, in one way or another, the tasks of the time are understood and worked on—or neglected. Wherever there is human society there is history with its inherent possibilities, though the changes be slow and hardly perceptible. And the individual, too, has his history, since he cannot live but as a member of society. If the cultural level is high, the individual belongs to manifold social formations which may overlap or can interfere with each other. Thus the demands his history makes upon him may point in different directions and make his situation awkward and even painful. Yet they all appeal to him to take his own stand and to build a human existence for himself by making decisions. He cannot simply surrender to the fact that he happens to exist. The biological fact that he is alive is not all. His human existence is characterized by the fact that he becomes aware of being in his own charge. Reason, which he does not have but which has him, brings unrest into his relation to reality. Let him do as he desires, act well or badly, be diligent or lazy, he is shaping his existence, his own and the existence outside of him, both simultaneously, for they go together indissolubly. The certainty he has of his own existence is the certainty of a life which has its own history and which unfolds itself in a surrounding history, a life charged with responsibility. His responsibility links him with the tensions of his time and makes him co-responsible for the future.

Reason does not let us ignore the distinction between true and false, valuable and worthless. We have already stressed that these distinctions are no mere matter of logic but concern the whole mental life. How the individual will make his decisions depends on the cultural possibilities which his historically conditioned existence offers, and it depends on the energy he devotes, or neglects to devote, to maintaining his personal identity at the very height of his own possibilities.

A human life cannot stay locked in itself. With manifold manifestations it issues into the public sphere. Even what we would want to keep for ourselves becomes manifest in indirect effects. In our common public existence our own claims, actions, works meet with others which may be akin to ours or antagonistic, and the result is strife. Since we cannot permanently evade reason, human strife inevitably finds its orientations in the necessity of reason, though reason will not accommodate us with the guarantee that our decisions will be reasonable. But both, criticism and defense, are under the control of the same criteria, and therefore the truth content of the mutually opposed claims, actions, and works can find nothing but clarification through intellectual contests—provided, of course, that the strife has really become a concern of the intellect.

Some have considered it blameworthy that philosophers are

inclined to defend their doctrines to the last. Their attitude has been denounced as intellectual imperialism. But the philosopher must serve truth, and how could he do it better or, as the case may be, how could he do it at all, if he did not try to refute every objection he meets? Certainly not by conciliatory compliance. As long as there are different points of view whose exponents can defend themselves against each other, the situation is not yet sufficiently clarified, and the knowledge of truth is furthered by polemics—which need not lack dignity. Polemic must not be mistaken for power politics, for the arguments of polemic can appeal to no other authority than the convincing power of truth. Even one who—as the head of a school, for instance—should happen to have a kind of social and political power cannot use it in the area of philosophy. No, for the attainment of philosophical clarification, it is irrelevant what motives may induce a man to fight. If he should be motivated by a will for power, then Hegel's dictum proves to be true: the purposes of reason thrive on the strife of the passions which wear each other out.[10] Or, to put it in the words of Dominique Parodi: The "inherent causality of the ideas" puts those in the wrong who would regard the phenomena of intellectual history from the standpoint of the "pure politician."[11] In the domain of the intellect there is no struggle for power. Only this much is to be admitted: that outward power, which decides nothing in the realm of truth, can endanger the *social* life; it can happen that the discussions which call for an intellectual decision are deprived of the possibility of being genuinely intellectual. And since man becomes really man only through education, and since the interferences of external force are liable to give decisive direction to an educational system, it is possible that in those domains in which men will submit to obstacles put in the path of their outward freedom, those obstacles can cause cultural catastrophes.

Cultural catastrophes are demonic suppressions of the truth. They render obscure and deny expression to that which would make attainable the height of the possibilities given to any specific time. As a consequence of such catastrophes, the possibilities which derived from antecedent history and gave promise of a richer content cease to be possibilities. They are reduced to impotent dreams in the minds of those who have kept the promises of the past in their hearts. In situations which are dominated by demonic powers there is no longer any height of possibilities at all. In those situations action is poisoned at its source. And the word which Hebbel puts into the mouth of his Margrave Rüdeger attains unqualified validity: "Whatever I do and whatever I leave undone, I am doing evil."[e] Where demons rule as princes of the world it is beyond the power of man to provide a sanctuary for the truth. Paul Tillich says: "There is no way one could conceive by which the spiritual and social demonism can be overcome. . . . The demonic power is broken only by confrontation with divinity, possession releases its hold in face of the holy, destructive fate in face of redeeming fate."[12] But when, in the life of the community, the power of responsibility is strong and the life is accordingly healthy, then the danger is proportionately smaller that life might succumb to the overwhelming pressure of the powers of darkness. For it is the self-alienation of men which is the soil in which the powers of darkness thrive. Where there is genuine community, intellectual contests take their bearings from the idea of the true, and thus are protected against the demonic forces of untruth. However, in the current of historical events there always remains the threat of a destruction coming from without.

9

THE ROLE OF THE INTELLIGENCE IN THE LIFE OF THE SPIRIT

The intellectual function of the life of the spirit is not as such involved in self-alienation, in the loss of the substance of personal existence (a loss which can occur in many degrees), the loss of the power of resistance in a person called to defend personal dignity under pressure from natural urges or the demands of society. The intellectual function of the human spirit is impersonal. Stupidity is not a phenomenon of self-alienation; on the contrary, a deep-reaching self-alienation is possible (and not infrequent) even when the intellectual performance is well above the average. However, this impersonal function of the mind is indispensable for personal life, and it is the task of the educator to include intellectual education when he wants to help an adolescent in his endeavor to understand himself and therefore to have a real understanding of the environment which claims him. Nevertheless, intellectual education can proffer only auxiliary services towards shaping a life in a human way. The immediate concern of intellectual education is only that side of the shaping of life which is neutral with regard to the demands of humanity. (Truths of a purely intellectual kind can be made the very sturdy foundation of the very worst untruths.) But where humanity is concerned, the *idea of truth* is in no way neutral. Nor does the idea of truth culminate in the sphere of interest of mere intelligence. All domains of the life of the spirit direct their autonomous orders towards the idea of truth. Only under the norm of that idea can they find a conclusive confirmation of their meaning, a confirmation which casts out every doubt.

Truth has a depth of being which excludes the prose of scientific knowledge as well as the prose of everyday, but which can be experienced in the revelations of art. And without relation to the idea of truth the very word "revelation" would be meaningless. Further: the conduct of life demands a kind of action which takes the situations with which it deals as that which they are in truth; wherever our urges dominate, we see the situation differently from what it is: its import manifests itself only to the ethical will, which alone can see the demands that are to be fulfilled. Thus again the word "truth" has a meaning which goes beyond what can be grasped by sheer intelligence. And further, the familiar formula for what is just, "to everyone his own," demands that those for whose sake the formula is invoked should receive what is their due, often in deliberate contrast to what exists in fact, or to what may be feared. All the realms in which the life of the human spirit unfolds receive their deepest confirmation of validity from the idea of truth.[1] As a fact, this idea appears so very much in the foreground of the sphere of intelligence that men came to believe that intelligence alone governed the idea. Yet this belief in itself afforded no comprehension of the substance of the idea, the substance which demands that we commit the personal functions of our mind. Such a personal putting of ourselves at stake is needed to attain what is possible in principle, and only at the point of that attainment does the substance of the idea manifest itself as that goal which we "rightly" seek. Even for our purely intellectual quest of knowledge, "rightly" refers to that truth which is unconditionally true.[2]

The intelligence has the prerogative of being the most universal and comparatively the most independent function of the mind. Quite of itself, starting from sense data, it arrives at its impersonal, neutral insights. The other functions of the mind depend on its services, and the intelligence furnishes such services regardless of the goals involved. It always serves, whether the goal is the creation of art or of trash, whether the will is bent on what is good or what is criminal, whether true justice is sought or justice is made a farce. With the help of the intelligence the life of men obtains the kind of knowledge which is needed for reaching the goal of the moment.

It is quite evident that we need intelligence when, in the interests of systematic knowledge, we investigate those superhistorical forces (*Lebensmächte*) which sustain personal culture, as they in their turn can be fostered only by personal accomplishments. The work of the historian of music is accomplished by the labor of intelligence, although the undertaking requires of him a living, sensitive response to music. In their proper meaning, his insights can be communicated only to those who are likewise musical and sensitive. However, like all cases which are methodologically similar, this example of musical historiography shows that the formulations of the intellect, whose concepts fall short of living reality, always state either too little or too much—the latter by way of a conceptualization which is deceptively clear-cut and definite in view of the fact that the fullness of living experience cannot be contained in it. Thus the services of conceptual thought must be considered a necessary evil. Its formulations are ordered towards an unambiguous precision which characterizes the abstract structures of theoretical knowledge but not the goal in reality which is desired, for this goal lies where the non-finite, the inexhaustible, is manifest in the finite. So it comes about that although in seeking the highest level of its attainment the human mind finds the efforts towards intellectual clarification indispensable in the labor devoted to understanding cultural matters, these efforts cannot here produce the same degree of consensus which they produce in the objective research of mathematics and the natural sciences.

In cultural studies intelligence is even divisive; for here it is not independent, not free. It is given the task of furnishing reasons for trends which have already taken the direction of some given world-view; here ratiocination serves up arguments on every side. To be sure, an unspoiled mind will not agree with such arguments merely because it cannot disprove them; only an intellectualist lacks the reservations of the unspoiled. Whatever the trends are which need the services of intelligence, it will serve the demands of any view of life manifest in any specific trend. It serves all trends and thereby deepens the enmity between them. Through its own form, intelligence determines the logical meaning of propositions, but its work does not produce decisions about the essence which the propositions are meant to express. The judgment concerning essence must be made in immediate experience

—for instance, in listening to a musical performance. Experience seeks to reach through intellectual discipline (*Wissenschaft*) a clarification which would establish the legitimacy of its immediate judgments. Yet the conceptual order of intelligence never penetrates into the sphere of what is essential and hence affords no test of the essence of anything. Hence it is always possible for the various disciplines of cultural studies to talk at cross purposes with each other. Only if the scholar writes the winged words of the poet, letting his expression transcend the sphere of the logical form so that it comes closer to its theme than could mere prose, does the power of the expression to convince go deeper, and therefore minimize the divisive effect of ratiocination. In this sense, Schelling spoke of "historical art," meaning the art of the historiographer.[3]

In the religious area, the tensions which separate denominations and theological schools rest largely on the fact that the labor bent upon formulating dogmas and explaining dogmas cannot always make use of the artistic expression of religious experience. In the inwardness of their piety the different denominations are much closer to each other than in their dogmas and in the intellectual experience they involve. Denominations cannot evade the need for dogmas. But one who is committed to dogmas restricts the life-view which is at home in his denomination. He mistakes the formulations of the sect for the life itself. He should regard the dogmas as historically conditioned endeavors to give an account of the religious certainty manifest in the consciousness of the respective community, but these endeavors account for it by the inexpedient means of logic.

Like the denominational dogmas, doctrinal theorems of aesthetics, too, harbor the seductive tendency to rob life of its original freedom. An unbiased approach to works of art should constantly give one occasion to investigate the merely relative validity of aesthetic dogmas. If, instead, a man's enjoyment of art is dependent on aesthetic dogmas, he is in permanent danger of making unjust judgments about artistic movements with which the aesthetic authority he acknowledges cannot cope. This is no objection to aesthetics as a discipline, just as it is no objection to the dogmas of religious denominations nor, in general, to the discipline of cultural studies as such. Yet it must be said that, in all these matters, the role of the intellect is less significant than it appears in the immediate awareness of the intelligence itself. The intellectual process itself cannot decide between the claims which are being discussed. On the contrary, wherever in cultural life factions confront each other, the intellectual labor performed within them brings their differences into sharper relief. If a reconciliation is reached between the points of view (nowadays those who love Bruckner are wont no longer to object to the music of Brahms), it springs from incentives derived from immediate life, and the clarification furnished by theoretical knowledge has only a very mediate influence upon those incentives. Still, no matter how inexpedient and how questionable are the accomplishments of the theoretical process, they remain indispensable for the life of the intellect. Their impersonal service flows into the vast cultural structures and continual re-examinations produced by the problems of our changing life which makes ever new demands for the investment of our personal convictions.

Something similar is true of all philosophy. The different schools which, since Parmenides and Heraclitus, have been at war with each other are ultimately differences in world-view seeking clarity with regard to themselves and therefore having good reason to take themselves to task very severely. This practical motivation gives them all a common cause, in spite of all theoretic differences. Yet the intellectual undertaking involved in the construction of a philosophical system can be understood only with difficulty by a thinker who is anchored in another world-view, and can be understood only in some degree of approximation to the way it is meant to be understood, in its hidden foundation—namely, as a justification of that way of life which is not congenial to the opponent. An antagonist will let the system influence him only in its objective form and without its life ground, and will seek to evaluate it without that ground. Presumably the author of the systematic work did in fact look for a linguistic form which would compel mentalities of all different kinds to acknowledge the universal validity which his arguments claimed. Yet their fate is almost certainly to be met with manifold misunderstandings, and to be rejected as subtleties lacking substance, as entirely uninteresting quibblings, or as exercises of an academic mind caught in false formulations of the problems at issue—in short, as not worth the trouble of reading. Such verdicts have been made even about the greatest thinkers, and not only by contemporaries as yet below the thinker's level; the verdicts are repeated in a scarcely milder form generations later. And quite serious men are caught in the pitfalls of such misunderstandings which, again and again, document the fact that the most earnest endeavors of the intelligence come up against the incomprehensibility of that truth which is beyond its reach. Nevertheless its labor is not in vain. Not only does the one who undertakes the labor need it for the sake of reaching the highest level of his own life, and for the sake of helping similarly attuned minds a stretch along the way to themselves; the opponent also advances his cause if he wrestles with arguments which would never have occurred to him. In a modest measure it also happens once in a while that through such efforts of study, something of the humanity of one's fellow-man becomes patent, and that thus one's own intellectual life becomes freer by understanding, from the depth of one's own humanity, the alien mode of expression which at first seemed so unintelligible.

In December of 1798 the Helvetian government sent Pestalozzi to Stans, where he was to care for the many children orphaned by the bloody events of the ninth of September.[a] The fervently Catholic population did not like to see him come. But in a letter which he wrote about the time he spent in Stans he could say: "Friend, can you believe it, I found the heartiest welcome for my work among the Capuchins and the nuns."[4] True, Pestalozzi did not operate in Stans with rational argumentation. In dealing with the children he set the rule for himself to introduce only at the very last, and to use most sparingly, "the dangerous symbols of good and evil, words."[5] Arguments which express not merely abstract matters but touch upon the concerns of life itself contribute to the dissolution rather than to the strengthening of cordial relations, when the arguments clash with theses in the intellect of the listener or the reader with which they are irreconcilable. And if, moreover, those who argue are philosophers, then even abstractly formulated thoughts will be interpreted as symbols of a life, and will easily disturb formerly cordial relations. Fichte and Schelling, Schelling and Hegel had been friends; their philosophizing brought about unpleasant divisions. They had assumed the friend would acknowledge their arguments, and they would not admit his right to be of a differently attuned mind when he in turn expressed himself in his own way. Not understanding the difference in his philosophical stance, whose very possibility they did not see, they would interpret this difference as a sign of narrower, nay, less valuable humanity. Pestalozzi, however, knew from the very beginning that his activity in Stans had to speak for itself and was not to be accomplished by any conceptual justification, even in the form in which Pestalozzi had already published his principles of education, in the third and fourth part of the first edition of *Lienhard and Gertrude*, to which he refers at the beginning of the letter mentioned.

For Hegel and for many a thinker who took his starting point from Hegel, religion appears as a preparatory stage of philosophy and is to be dissolved in philosophy.[6] Religion furnishes pictures, symbols of truth, and philosophy is to bring the truth itself, the truth in its necessary, its adequately articulate form. One will readily concede that in things holy for religion, the depth of truth is expressed only in symbols. But philosophy on its part articulates itself through the work of the intelligence, which is always historically conditioned and therefore always demands new formulations. The relation of philosophy to religion is similar to the relation of the science of literature to its realm of interest. Just as the science of literature is possible only on the ground of poetic experience, so philosophy presupposes experience, an experience which can never be comprehensive enough or deep enough for the aims of philosophy. The expression of philosophical insights is determined by the intelligence in such a way, however, that our understanding does not remain a matter of sheer abstraction but appeals to the norms of the sphere of human experience in its comprehensive domain. But while poetic art (*Dichtung*) awakens the forces of experience and enhances them, and while the science of literature has its highest task in assisting the power of poetry to evoke and enhance experience, enabling it to attain an efficacy unrestricted by the limits of place and time, philosophy endeavors to attain a critical clarification of the experience which it must presuppose, and in this endeavor it relates the experience to the idea of what is true—a relation which is to be established only by a methodically strict discipline. Now, there is no danger of a dissolution of art by the science of art, no danger that the work of the historian of literature should ever make superfluous the works of Dante, Shakespeare, Goethe. Neither do those who know what help philosophy offers, and what can be expected of philosophy as such, ever expect that their religious experience will vanish if it is confronted by philosophy. To be sure, the discipline of literary studies can be fruitfully fostered only by those who are receptive of the language of literature, and can benefit only those who are equally receptive. Similarly, the problems of the philosophy of religion can be understood only by those who have seen those problems in the depth of religious experience. Yet others whose own experience rejects religion also feel the attraction of dialectical inquiries into such problems.

10
PERSONAL WHOLENESS

The insights of the intelligence as such are indifferent with regard to man's role in the world. They often serve ends unworthy of man. And many a time a man will enlist rational arguments deliberately in order to attain an evil goal. One who spends his efforts on the attainment of evil ends diminishes the substance of his own personality. Instead of becoming a more substantial self, he loses substance. What he loses will seem to enhance either his mere nature or his society, though in truth neither will benefit. Weakness of character benefits neither a man's nature nor his society. And genuine humanity suffers wherever the accidents of individual urges and social trends gain undue influence on the way in which we become aware of the true, the just, the beautiful. Wherever a human life lets itself be forced into its decisions, personal integrity dissolves into *contingency* and often into subjective uncertainty.

True enough, one can say of every home environment that it is contingent compared with the certitude a finite mind requires. Lessing lets his Sultan Saladin speak of the "contingency of birth." Yet Saladin meets with an answer which points out what is unsatisfactory in his formulation.[a] "Home" is something contingent only for the kind of reasoning which is incapable of comprehending, in its categories, the real meaning of "home." The service a man gives to his "home" has not at all the effect of a dissolved integrity. On the contrary, through such service a person attains an essential content and increases the substance of his certainty of self. To be sure, it must be *true* service, rendered out of a conviction of responsibility. For it is responsible conviction which makes a man's "home" into something quite different from a contingent place of origin; he belongs to his "home" in the very depth of his existence, in that depth where his consciousness finds obligation in the autonomous orders of the true, the good, the just, the beautiful. Nor can he furnish *true* service to his "home" except under the norm of these ideas.

Undeniably, the history of mankind, right into our own time, shows only too many examples of brave men who had to suffer martyrdom because powerful trends had arisen in opposition to the supertemporal ideas, trends which, on account of their enmity to ideas, inevitably aimed at the ruin of man's "home." The trend of the time might make subjective opinions prevail, opinions which would borrow high-sounding phraseology, would praise the ruination as reconstruction (*Aufbau*)[b], and would thus try to prevent those willing to yield to the trend from becoming aware of their bad conscience. "Home" is something specifically human. Used with regard to the life of animals or plants, the word loses the intense and binding sense which is all that matters here. The devotion which one's "home" requires can be provided only by genuine humanity, and when humanity is under duress, that circumstance may induce those who are committed to humanity to seek "home" far from the place where, for the sake of God and justice, it should be.

Man is entitled to be at home with his human task in every country, and in every country this task demands citizenship. In the *West-Eastern Divan*[c] we read: "My heritage, how glorious, far and wide! Time is my property, my field is time." There are no final boundaries of one's home field, either in time or in space. Wherever men seek and find the possibility of living and working for the true, the good, the just, the beautiful, there our earth becomes home. Everywhere we are surrounded by that which intellectual abstraction can esteem only as something shaped by the contingencies of nature or of history. But everywhere we have the task of turning contingency into necessity: into *that* necessity which we have in ourselves, necessity as consciousness of the autonomous orders. Thus we plow the field into which fate has put us.

The task is never entirely done, contingency is never finally overcome. Schelling says of the "I am" of Descartes that it expresses only a doubtful being, though indubitable to him who voices it, yet questionable as such.[1] Impersonal intelligence which, owing to its impersonality, is universally valid, cannot but call my existence and my fate contingent. Moreover, it is precisely the personal functions of the life of my spirit which furnish the further comment that even the measure in which *these* functions fulfill what is demanded of man never attains necessity, but falls short in the face of the human task. Nevertheless *for me* my existence has necessity; the situations which confront me objectively put me again and again before tasks which are *necessary for me*, tasks in whose necessity I become aware of myself as a *personal* self, tasks which I could shirk only as a deserter. No matter how contingent my existence may appear to the intelligence, *I myself* experience its relation to necessity. What I thus experience is my personal self-certainty. Its measure, the measure of my personal being, is entrusted to myself. The personal stand I take, with regard to the seemingly contingent appearances which yet make their appeal to my certainty of supertemporal necessity, decides the very essence of myself. Man never becomes a "necessary being"; yet he can become aware of the truth of Schelling's exquisite phrase that man is a "nature turned towards God,"[d] and that we are so constituted that "God is *in* our consciousness, in the same sense in which we say of a man that a virtue is in him, or more often yet a vice, meaning that it is not objective for him, is not something he wants, nor even something he knows."[2]

"God's is the orient, God's is the occident."[e] Yet this acknowledgement of ubiquity is only a human thought, an endeavor to push forward, and to enter symbolically into that which is transcendent and no longer comprehensible. Human experience is already taxed to its limits, nay overtaxed, when it attempts an adjustment to the conditions of a foreign culture. He who must seek his home away from the place where he was born and grew up must suffer damage to the roots of his physical and intellectual existence which reach down into historical growth. Some of these roots may sprout again, in a foreign soil; others will wither, and many an attempt at new beginnings will fail. For the very beginnings of every human life are in a large measure decisive with respect to many a trend and possibility of personal development. Through these beginnings everyone is forever connected with those from whom he heard a "thou shalt" (of course, in the specific form demanded by the particular circumstances) innumerable times before he could ever say to himself "I ought to." Even the most autonomous life begins with the decisions of others, and at first is irresistibly at the mercy of those decisions.

Our membership in an environment limits our personal possibilities, and this membership, this participation in common concerns, never ceases, even if we rebel against it. But he who understands the place to which fate and his own decisions have led him knows that the social relations which largely determine the content of his awareness of himself amount to an *obligation*. True enough, the particular "duties" which social structures (family, state, professional organizations, etc.) would impose on an individual are not always identical with that which, in truth, is his duty. The identity could exist only if society were throughout what it ought to be. But society will contain many an insufficiency and, therefore, will make claims on an individual in furtherance of the very insufficiency. Such claims may be masked in some enticing ideology. Confronted with them, the individual needs independence of conscience in order to recognize his true duty, the true call of the situation; he needs certainty of the unconditional. Not as if an individual's conscience were the voice of God without admixture; what is experienced as the concrete call of conscience is only too often determined by the fetters which weigh upon the life of society, fetters which are put upon the immature quite early. Nevertheless each individual conscience is induced to take a critical stand by the very *form* of the individual's activity. Human activity involves welding the contents of manifold data into a characteristically meaningful unity, and this is the personal form of human action. Alien contents may have imposed themselves on the individual's conscience, or may try to impose themselves on it; yet that form will make the conscience critical of such impositions. From its deepest necessity, conscience strives for its independence, its freedom, and the individual whose striving is sincere is on the way to the highest possible course which his life can take.

Society does have a claim upon its members. However, since the social forms are interdependent in many ways and are never entirely pure, this means for each member of society that he, in his place and in the measure of his possibilities, is responsible for society. And this responsibility can be undertaken in a truly human way only in the liberating awareness of the unconditional. True enough, the unconditional is not meant to be turned into a simple reality since it cannot be made merely real: the ideals do not fit into reality as it is; but they must point the direction in which we are to move in order to take the responsibility for society; the direction cannot be found in the mere conditions of a given situation. The shortcomings of social conditions must be taken quite as they are; we can never know them with sufficient accuracy. Through these conditions the intellectually independent person, sure of the unconditional, recognizes his task. He will cull everything possible from the very shortcomings of the situation. The intelligence, in the service of conscience, must ascertain what is possible in each case, and how it is to be realized. Here, too, politics is the art of the possible.

"Weeds, I find, one does not eradicate; one is lucky if only the wheat grows taller," says Grillparzer's Bishop Gregory.[f] The danger of self-estrangement always threatens, it threatens every man and every society. Self-estrangement brings darkness down over life, it makes us blind to the substantial depth of reality and renders reality's demands unrecognizable. A man may have lost his personal integrity, being caught up in the urges which are every man's tie with impersonal nature or in the trends of social life. Such a man still knows very well what movements he is making, with which persons and objects he is concerned; his consciousness is still fit to grasp universally valid insights, though it be but foreground vision; but what he is doing in truth is hidden from him. He may be quite clear about the connection of his own actions with what he himself or what others have done or suffered before; yet he does not know his relation to the unconditional truth.

In his book *Overcoming Hatred*,[3] Friedrich Siegmund-Schultze writes: "He who hates does not see reality correctly, nor does he correctly arrange his world. . . . The teacher who hates a pupil will not do him justice. The German who hates will neither see the hated Jew correctly nor treat him justly. Reciprocated hatred will be as little able to give a faithful portrait of the German, nor will it be able to furnish a just judgment concerning the guilt of the German people." One who hates—indeed, one who acts under the obsession of any passion—misapprehends what his own act is in truth. Some natural urge dominates him, and his action is determined by that urge; he is unfree, estranged from the depths of his self. His reasoning may be quite clear. The word "self-estrangement" does not refer to the impersonal intelligence, nor to an abstract, general I, it refers to the personal self. And the human task of achieving self-certainty is set for the same personal self. Every endeavor to do justice to that task does need rational inquiry and uses intelligence for the purposes of personal life. Yet for the intelligence as such, reality is accessible only insofar as our knowledge of it rests on sense perception. He who works at his human task will not grant to the intellect alone any right to an independent determination of the shape our existence is to take. To live with certainty of oneself means to gather one's various functions into a higher unity and thus prevent each separate function from coming to bear on our existence separately.

Rousseau in his time demanded that education should be concerned with the unified wholeness which man ought to have. He demanded "that things which ought to go together should not be separated, and that man who, at each moment of his life, is a whole entity, should not at one point be made whole by only one of his faculties and at other points by the others."[4] Pestalozzi translated this significant thought into reality. One of the most important aspects of his philosophy of education (*Pädagogik*) is the fact that he has seen the danger of the *disunity* with which mental life is threatened during the school years, and has taken the danger into account. "Should my father or my mother say to me: 'Child, pay attention to this or that!' my whole soul is engaged. Likewise when the requirements of their home draw my attention to ten, to twenty, to a hundred objects, this attention cultivates the powers of my soul coherently and purely and in proper relation. In the child's upbringing in the home, the intellect and the heart, memory and judgment, imagination and reason collaborate, alongside each other and within each other, and thus

Personal Wholeness

these powers grow in mutual harmony. Actually I learn with my whole united humanity. In school it is quite different; there the learner is now my reasoning, then my memory, and again the imagination, but seldom the human being. Therefore if the school is at work alone, without the security afforded by a solid upbringing in the home, education is often at the expense of my very humanity."[5] Thus he spoke in a memorial address in the summer of 1802. And in the New Year's address of 1809 to the pupils entrusted to him he said: "Among us you do not suffer the misfortune of seeing your whole being, your entire humanity, subjected and sacrificed to the development of one single power of your being, one single aspect of your nature. . . . People around us acknowledge that in our activities we set as the ultimate goal of our efforts your humanity, not your intelligence nor your skill."[6]

During our school years we are subject to the particular temptation of detaching intelligence from the unity in which it is bound up with the other functions of our conscious life and of letting it pose as the only legitimate representative of the mind since its particular task is to know truth. Thus the horizon of our life closes in; the movement of our human existence towards the unconditional slackens, becomes indistinct, problematic; the word "non-finite" seems to have only a negative meaning; the goals of life are sought where the grasp of rational inquiry can reach, perhaps within the sphere of the useful or the agreeable, and not in the order of ever renewed invitation to harmony which freedom demands.

In order to prevent such a fragmentation of the personal life, it is not enough to cultivate the other human potentialities alongside intelligence. The decisive task is to interrelate all our potentialities within a living interdependence, in a personal unity which contains them all: one and the same personality is to have its being in all of them. Science, art, morality, law, all differ according to their respective ends. But the elementary *human* task is to let the powers of the spirit work together in building a unified life, although each one of these powers has a different history and receives its impulses from a specific sector of cultural life.

For the individual, the task has a personal meaning which concerns him in accordance with the kind and measure of his individual potentialities. But it also confronts the large social structures; they too differ owing to their particular potentialities. The task can be immediately experienced only by individuals, yet the experience does not concern them as mere individuals, but as responsible members of the social structure. The educational community has taken still immature human beings into its fold and given them their initial contact with the values which spirit implies. If the social structure in which the individual is anchored is sound, the values become powers and it provides a solid foundation for the continual development of the humane aspects of life; it opens up new possibilities for a yet higher level of humanity, springing from the soil of the old heritage, so that, under normal conditions, one who awakens to the awareness of his responsibility can find the content and frame of reference for his self-certainty in the manifold movements of the cultural life which surrounds him. However, if the powers of destruction have grown so strong that the fight against them is beyond the strength of the individual,[7] then in that kind of society, which no longer furnishes true duties, even the immature are ensnared in the web of guilt wherein the functions of personal life become disordered. Only impersonal intelligence can in some degree take a stand against the cultural catastrophe, and in the long run, even this rational function is threatened. It persists for a while, in somewhat the way that hair and nails continue to grow on a corpse. Yet, Pestalozzi asks, "What good is all the outward light of truth when we lack the inner light of humanity?"[8] We are all responsible not alone for our own person but for all those with whom we have some relationship, directly or indirectly; if we carry out this responsibility inadequately, we draw others into the spiritual misery of our own existence. Then the task of atoning for the guilt which poisons the life of the community inevitably faces those also who are not responsible for the fact that it is a degenerate environment in which they came to the awareness of their own existence. Just as glorious deeds done long ago still fill later generations with a collective pride, so collective guilt can become hereditary; it belongs to the same logical category as national pride. The evil which has been done cannot be undone, but it cries out to be assumed as a responsibility, and an honest acknowledgement of the guilt which calls for atonement would open up new possibilities for a life certain of itself. Certitude is rediscovered in the concrete awareness of the link between the recognition of guilt and the responsibility man has of being fully human.

If life is to be certain of itself, if the life of a culture is to be lived at the highest level of its possibilities, its representatives will not be onesided specialists in science, art, morality, law. Even the genuine humanity of the individual calls for a redressing of the balance in this respect and an unremitting effort to resist the fragmentation of personal existence. And the same requirement issues from the responsibility of the individual for the culture of his community and, within that culture, for the humanity of others. Only genuine humanness is equal to man's cultural undertaking. The culture of a people, whether it is felicitous or disconcerting in its expression, is always a characteristic form of what is human. And it is a high culture precisely insofar as, instead of producing "inverted cripples"—learned barbarians, sour moralists, and the like—it produces the truly human by interrelating, in its own way, man's functions in the various domains of his creativeness. These different spheres of activity are not ends in themselves; they exist because a genuine humanity needs them. And it needs them in very different measures and in ever different manners, depending on historical change. Whenever social conditions are such that they force the worker to withdraw from society if he is to satisfy the claims which a rich human heritage would make on his human essence—for instance, where the painter or the poet is condemned to a bohemian existence—the very existence of the man of this type is an indictment of the nation's culture.

Still worse than the miseries of a onesided culture is that deprivation of culture which results when overwhelming social circumstances force a broad class of people to be exclusively concerned with sheer economic survival, so that science and art, though available to them in ersatz products, are inaccessible at a level worthy of human dignity. Then the pressure of life's miseries brings into being a class bent upon the satisfaction of only the most indispensable needs. The aesthete, the intellectualist, the moralist, and even the practitioner of an arid legalism would at least receive the orientation of their lives from ideas through which *the truth* points beyond an existence which is one of passive vegetation. But where human existence is forced to expend itself in the struggle for what should never be *more than a basis* for a truly human development, then from the very depth of its essence such an existence cries out, whether consciously or unconsciously, for salvation.

11
ABOUT THE SUPER-OBJECTIVE

The imperative which summons the person who would be genuinely alive to gather into a living and integrated unity the various functions of the mind contains no implication that the proper role of any of these functions should be curtailed. Most particularly it should be noted that this imperative has no relation to that kind of pusillanimity which would rein the intelligence for fear that it should imprudently bring up for discussion any of those plain, blunt propositions of science which would challenge the equanimity with which some of our most treasured and revered conceptions are entertained. Such discussions can turn out to be very necessary. Once we become aware of intellectual difficulties in any area, the unity of our personal life is breached by their hypocritical repression. Our intelligence requires freedom in its own domain; there it is autonomous. It cannot take orders from another authority as to what it must acknowledge as true; what must not be thought—or at least not be mentioned. It is true that it is ever in danger of error, but the endeavor of self-correction likewise is constant. Especially in the sphere of science, intelligence imposes the most rigorous standards upon itself as a matter of principle.

Notwithstanding this rigor, there is a typical error which often becomes an unresolved temptation, hindering—indeed making impossible—a personal synthesis of the totality of the mind's functions. This is the error with regard to the sphere in which the intellectual process exercises authority. Legitimately this domain comprehends everything which can become an object of knowledge; and here the word *object* has its precise sense: the relation to a consciousness confronted by an object in such a way that for the mind of the knower a multiplicity of images (*Vorstellungen*) is united in the object in a unity which claims objective validity. Kant says: "We know the object if we have established a synthetic unity in the manifold of the imagination."[1] (On the borderline of such knowledge stands the case of the concept of which no image can be formed—namely, of an "object as such," the "transcendental object.")[2] Every object is determined conceptually as the unity of a multiplicity; it is therefore finite and cannot be otherwise. What is infinite[a] is incapable of determination as a unity, of being made an "object." Thus, in another of Kant's formulations, the universe is not "an object knowable in accordance with the laws of experience."[3] Another error, one which persists in face of frequent refutations, is the tendency of intelligence to treat the non-finite as if it were finite, even to the point of constructing a scientific "world-view" (*Weltanschauung*), especially a view based on natural science. But one who has seen clearly that every causal connection is embraced in mystery[4] knows that this form of knowing cannot be taken for a constitutive element of a view of the *universe*, although the significance of causal connection is undeniable in the comprehension of *objective* structures.

The findings of intelligence have validity only within the sphere of the finite. If this fact is misunderstood, the misapprehension may creep into our thinking on religious matters, where it comes to flower in the form of fantastic dogmatic speculations. In the works of Christian dogmatists one can find information about the "attributes of God," or one can explore the question of whether the punishments of hell must be of endless duration because the guilt of the damned, consisting in an offense against God's infinite majesty, is in its turn infinite.

It is only proper to add, with regard to this kind of theological opinion, that every faith requires some mythological symbolization of its religious experience, a symbolization in which logical analysis has a role. Furthermore, on the higher levels of culture, any religion organized in a church must give to the doctrinal content of the myths a fixed form consisting in a science, namely dogmatics. The labor of conceptual thought is essential; but if intelligence makes religion the matter of its *independent* concern, then the discrepancy between the logical forms and the living

About the Super-Objective

content of religion will be increased by the activity of conceptual thought even to the point of absurdity. From being merely inadequate, the forms of this knowledge will proceed to becoming an uncomfortable burden, and even one which is felt as unbearable, on the cultural consciousness, thus threatening the unity of the spiritual life. It is perfectly true that intelligence is autonomous, but its autonomy is restricted to the domain of objects. If dogmatics makes use of intelligence, it does so legitimately only for the purpose of ordering its images in such a way as to bring them into line with the requirements of the intellectual life of the given time. It cannot use intelligence to produce new religious insights. Religious imagery must be understood as symbolic hints at what is superobjective. What the images seek to convey, their relevant meaning, does not lie in the domain in which intelligence, owing to its autonomy, is sovereign. If it is aware of its proper role, it cannot endeavor to analyze the contents of those images and synthesize new concepts from the elements such analysis gains. Religious symbols are not susceptible of rationalistic analysis; the ground of their validity is not within the sphere of the objective. From the realm of the objective they have only borrowed the logical form which is indispensable to the human mind in its search for truth. Their content, which is nonobjective, is unobtainable through merely intellectual endeavor. If objectivistic thinking gains the ascendancy in the sphere of religion, then spirituality loses its direction, its depth and its inwardness; it inclines towards an inhuman rigidity and is incapable of fusion with the genuine needs of the culture. The sole task of the intellect with respect to religious experience is to ensure that the words in which the experience is conveyed insofar as it can be conveyed in words at all—the words which would give an account of the experience—are words whose sense is at the highest level of the time.

This is an undertaking which serves not religious insight but only the interpretative ordering of the words whose meaning is symbolical; it can be carried out only when, in the case of a given individual, the intensity of his life has integrated the different mental functions in a personal unity. Then the intelligence, having its proper place in that unity, is no longer tempted to insist on its own autonomy. Its legitimate desire for intellectual unity, no longer confined within the narrow limits of intellectualism and individualism but liberated by true humanity, finds its proper function in a life bent upon universal peace.

Christian theologians speak of the *personal* God. For polytheism the personality of every god is self-evident. So far as Christianity is concerned, it was above all the struggle against pantheistic dilution of the concept of God which made an emphasis on the personal necessary. To be sure, this brings with it the danger that God may become a "Somebody," and consequently a finite being. The art of painting has made its own contribution to this misapprehension, since owing to its representations people tend to conceive of the Trinity tritheistically. Whoever is somebody has his personal qualities based on his individual constitution, and this constitution can be objectively ascertained. The emphasis on the personality of God in Christianity, however, should not lead the mind to a serious conception of God as an object of anthropomorphic imagination. Mythology may make God seem human; but faith seeks God not in the myths but in the comprehension of the myths, behind the myths—and before the myths.[5] Presupposing faith, theology makes use of mythological concepts only in the knowledge that they are not to be taken literally. God is not somebody. But personality can be attributed to God because this word derives its meaning from our experience of values which transcend all that is attained and attainable by man.

Man never comes to the end of the possibilities which he ought to realize owing to the challenge he finds in his personal relation to values. Albert Schweitzer speaks of the "responsibility which, extensively and intensively, leads us into the domain of the endless" and of a "frighteningly unlimited responsibility."[6] But intelligence is impersonal; hence no one is a "personality" merely on account of his intelligence. If men were nothing but intelligences, the thought of personality would never have occurred to them, nor the thought of goodness. A human being is a personality owing to the persevering will, by whose shaping power he has gathered the given possibilities in his nature into a unity characteristic of him as an individual though never finally achieved. Through this unity he brings his personal possibilities to bear on the life of society.

About the Super-Objective

Everything that is in the strictest sense personal comes to man in such a way that he cannot by right call himself its creator. New thoughts whose rightness and immense implications are unquestionable *arise in him* spontaneously, conferring uniqueness on his existence as they become his own.[b] The images of desirable goals just *come to him.* Here the contrast of active and passive, so important for the intelligence, does not apply. The word *receptive* gives a hint of this unfathomable occurrence, which is impressively manifested in the many accomplishments of genius but no less unaccountable where the quiet maturation of ordinary human efficiency is concerned.

Man is sorely tempted to reckon as merit whatever gives him eminence. The small-minded are vain even about the elegant way of life afforded them by inherited wealth. How much greater will be the sense of personal worth derived from the quite genuine knowledge that without the effort of one's own will the possibilities represented by one's "talents" would have evaporated! Nevertheless the ground of our human being, from which the possibilities of our personal growth derive, is not in ourselves. We become aware, in the depths of self, of this reality from which we live, and those who know that they are only receiving speak in terms of Grace and of God's love. And since that which they receive is precisely the content of their sense of *personal* worth, they acknowledge the ground which is its source as the *non-finite* personality of God.

Admittedly there are demonic seducers who are "personalities" too—one thinks of a Mussolini, a Hermann Göring; the word has no unambiguous reference to supertemporal values. The power of man's will whereby he is able to coin himself as a personality of one kind or another can work to his detriment. Yet even when the shaping power of the will takes wrong directions, these directions still depend on man's relation to the supertemporal; for, should he merely give in to his natural urges he would become a wretched sort of drifter, never a "personality." Those whose course is evil are deprived of the joy of that revelation which comes even in the most modest circumstances to a man who finds his own unique, self-directed way of realizing values. Those who bring evil into the world close their minds to the supertemporal ideas which are the norm of value; hence for them only counterfeit values appear, and in a false radiance; values which have no attraction for those who have achieved intellectual clarity in their personal lives. The world is not enriched by what is false, nor does it contribute worth or humanness to the life of society. In the demonic personality of the evildoer there is no characteristic which would make intelligible the transfer of the word "personal" to God.

The non-finite ground of the personal has no objective aspect. In this regard those epistemological reflections which deny metaphysical rank to all that is objective become significant. The reflections of Gregory of Nyssa in the fourth century were in this vein,[7] and with Kant and Fichte this epistemology has attained sufficient clarity and precision to justify its admission into cultural consciousness. What is ultimately real does not consist in objects. The concept of God cannot signify an object. Jesus of Nazareth, like every man, had an objective existence; but as a Second Person of the Trinity "in heaven" he would render inconceivable the unity of God as *one* if he—the Son eternally begotten of the Father, through Whom all things are made—were to retain objective attributes in his supertemporal being. In contrast to the modern accent on the personality of God, an emphasis which usually evokes only the thought of God the Father, the ancient Trinitarian concept has the advantage of forcing even the naive believer to place the notion of God in a higher order than what is consolidated objectively. Assuredly every human word which would designate God by an attribute is inadequate—inadequate, yes, but it springs from an unavoidable need.

Wherever goals of knowledge can be understood as having objective significance, the intelligence is capable of consolidating our relations to those goals in terms of abstractions, be they ever so lifeless—for instance, in numbers. Our intelligence can be sure that its results are applicable to the objects in question. But if, for instance, a juridical kind of argumentation should insert itself between God and mankind, for the ostensible purpose of making intelligible the relation of man to God and perhaps also to the Devil, such an undertaking would not deserve even to be called an "experiment on the wrong object." For the very concept of object could not be used literally, but only figuratively, as a token.

About the Super-Objective

Abstract expositions cannot shed light on religious reality. Hegel says that crass reasoning, undaunted by the fact that its forms are finite, will make heaven finite, "since it makes no difference to the intelligence whether or not its distinctions are valid in this area, whether or not the finite has any validity here. Hence those meaningless questions and the endeavors to answer them. Though flawless in abstract logic, it is meaningless, detestable, and tasteless to drag the distinctions of mere intelligence into an area where they have no place at all."[8] Intelligence mistakes its proper role if it tries to construct formulas which can have no meaning outside the range of the objective. For in the non-objective sphere the true sense is addressed not to the intelligence in isolation but to the unity of the whole human being, a unity whose objective manifestation is characterized by the mystery of non-finiteness. If the intention which induces the intelligence to trespass beyond its own realm is that of apologetics, the result will be embarrassing, fantastic, even contradictory. The Christian doctrine of salvation offers impressive examples of this in the reversals which are part of the history of dogma. But if the intention is polemical, then the attempted reduction of reality to the dimensions of the intelligence will contract the horizon of the whole spiritual life.

In both cases the intellectualistic attitude will work to the detriment of the very causes it is meant to serve. For in one thing, religion and culture coincide: they are the concern of the whole man. Accomplishments which are in themselves onesided can have salutary effects only if they are absorbed into larger structures in which their onesidedness is eliminated. We have an ugly confirmation of this in the no longer deniable fact that the immense achievement of intelligence which has brought about the astounding development of technology has been in no way productive of the more human conditions of existence which should have resulted in view of the fact that much stultifying labor has been rendered superfluous by machines. We do not, of course, mean to detract from technology's real achievements. Yet this bears stressing: we have thus far lacked, and are still lacking in, those "larger structures" within which man, matured to the point of unity of his personal being—the whole man—is able to control the technical possibilities conferred upon him by his intelligence.

The word *intellectualism* is not, however, unambiguous. Where, like many other "ism," it indicates the excess of a tendency legitimate within its own limits, it signifies that intellectual attitude which exaggerates the claim of intelligence to autonomy. This overemphasis is due to the unwillingness to acknowledge the incongruity—indeed, the meaninglessness—of any attempt to establish a relation between finite forms of knowing and the nonfinite. For this kind of intellectualism, the intelligence becomes the primary principle in the formation of one's life. Now, every man becomes aware of the autonomy of his thinking in terms of his *individual* existence, and often in opposition to the thought of other individuals. That kind of intellectualism would therefore establish him within his individual frame of reference to such an extent that all his being and doing would center on his *individual* thinking, which would seem to constitute the sole judge and censor. In Schelling, however, we can read that "Descartes' *I* think, *I* am is the basic fallacy in all knowledge since his time." With good reason Schelling saw in Kant the one who "more than merely a second Descartes" has lifted us wholly above and beyond "that entire position" which Descartes himself held, and above and beyond the metaphysics Descartes meant to refute as well—the position in which ratiocination is sovereign.[9] Schelling saw subjectivistic skepticism as the almost inevitable consequence of the movement whch started with Descartes and which Kant transcended.[10] Schelling's insight is confirmed by the fact that those who have not in principle moved beyond the position of medieval metaphysics tend to find subjectivism and skepticism in Kant even today. But Kant said that he had done away with knowledge in order to make room for faith.[11] The "knowledge" he left behind was the knowledge of mere intelligence. Kant makes it clear that rationalism is questionable in its very principles and hence cannot lead to ultimate truth: it is not adapted to "proving" what has been termed "the existence of God." For Kant, "faith" is faith in reason (which contains intelligence and confirms its specific rights). Schelling praises Kant for having succeeded in "bringing reason back to itself, out of its estrangement in a merely natural, i.e. unfree, kind of knowledge"—namely, the knowledge of an intelligence unaware of its own merely conditional character.

Kant's success was limited by the fact that he conceived even of reason as "subservient," as "instrumental."[12] Schelling's own doctrine, enunciated long before the time of the passages just quoted, was that "reason is not a tool, it does not let itself be used."[13]

What Kant had set forth in the *Critique of Pure Reason* had not been made clear enough in the Critique's "transcendental dialectic" with regard to the cultural bearing of critical thought and its final implications.[14] It is consequently in order to say more explicitly what was meant by Kant's doing away with "knowledge" in favor of "faith." As the continuation of the basic trend of the *Critique of Pure Reason* and of the two subsequent Critiques, it was the subjugation of intellectualism. The ambiguousness of the latter word becomes evident as soon as one recalls the meaning it had in medieval times as compared with its modern meaning. We see in the very first place that in medieval use the word *intellectus* does not have the restricted connotations of *Verstand*, or intelligence, as we find this word used in Kantian and post-Kantian philosophy. Instead, *intellectus* has much the same meaning as *reason* in Kantian and post-Kantian thought and should be translated in German as *Vernunft* or occasionally as *Geist* (spirit). There is, however, this distinction: as a faculty, the intellect can be used as a tool in demonstrations, or "proofs," particularly of the existence of God or the immortality of the soul. In this respect it is fair enough to speak of the "intellectualism" of a Thomas Aquinas, whose philosophy attributes to man the power to proceed with cogently demonstrative arguments even so far as "objects" like these.

However, since it is truth which enters our consciousness, Thomas regarded knowledge as a grace, a feeling which is strongly expressed in his writings wherever he probes more deeply into the nature of knowledge. Every truth, even the most trivial, can be apprehended by the mind of man only because he is elevated over every creature that lacks reason. Every truth is in the likeness of the first truth (*similitudo primae veritatis*). The fact that we can recognize truth is a confirmation of the Old Testament revelation that we are made in the image of God. "From the truth of the divine intellect as exemplary cause, our intellect knows the truth of the first principles, according to which we make all our judgments"—"a veritate intellectus divini exemplariter procedit in intellectum nostrum veritas primorum principiorum, secundum quam de omnibus iudicamus."[15] True, our judgments do not allow us to know the real as God knows it—he in whom essence and being are identical, whose essence is unmediated awareness of the real: *Bewusst-sein*, i.e. identity of being and awareness. We know only by way of analogy with the knowledge of God—and that does not amount to very much; even not-being is conceived by analogy with being. What is of great import in Aquinas' dictum is that human knowledge as well as divine is worthy of being called science (*scientia*) inasmuch as the mind of the creature follows a path indicated by the creator: our knowledge of the first principles is unerring.[16]

The profound distinction between this kind of intellectualism and the kind which is an evil in our present culture is unmistakable. Thomas did not intend that human life should be based on the activity of a single faculty on which, taken in isolation, all its certitudes should depend. What he did mean is that human life, owing to the gift of reason whereby the human intellect has a distant but real resemblance to the divine, is related to the divine sphere in such a way as to receive from this source certain knowledge which is unconditional. Kant's "doing away" with knowledge has its foundation in an insight which rests on the "first principles" of judging. The analysis of these principles in the light of themselves demonstrated the incompetence of mere intelligence wherever it would trespass beyond the domain of "phenomena." Intelligence by itself is restricted to the sphere of *objective knowledge*, to the knowledge of *finite* objects.[17] As critique, the *Critique of Pure Reason* is concerned with the modern view of intelligence as a distinct function of the mind. But there is a broader foundation for Kant's critical concept which restricts intelligence within its proper limits. These limits exist in fact. They designate a specific way of knowing, the way of all objective intelligence. And no epistemology can do without Kant's critical concept. Therefore Kant's determination of the limits also amounts to a critique of medieval intellectualism.[c]

12

CONCERNING THE TRUTH OF FAITH

Kant did away with knowledge in favor of faith. Here "faith" must be understood in the sense in which the word means to enhance knowledge by seeing it from a more comprehensive view. We speak of the objects of knowledge. But when we speak of our "faith in" something, it would be a mistake to imply that that something is some "object." We have faith in our freedom, but freedom is not an objective property like the color of our eyes or the weight of our body. To objectify freedom, to turn it into an *object* of conceptual knowledge, would mean to classify it among the phenomena,[1] and it is precisely as a phenomenon that freedom can never be ascertained; it can, therefore, have no "objective" proof. "To give expression to our faith," says Kant, "means to express the firmness of our subjective confidence."[2] So, too, will the concept of God be misapprehended if its objectification, though proper in the sphere of mythology, is turned into the content of faith. Faith in God cannot be proved objectively because God is not an "object"; he is not any "thing." The correct form in which genuine faith expresses itself is not "It is morally certain" but "I am morally certain."[3]

Genuine faith is something quite different from believing in the truth of a given mythology. Faith is an *immediate* certainty, and the subject of faith is the whole man. Our thinking can detach us from the ground of our existence; indeed, the exigencies of life almost incessantly enforce that detachment whose very nature is abstraction. But the *reality* of man rests on the existential ground which is present in his being and which sets him ever anew the task of constructing a *unified* personal life out of the multiplicity of his talents.[4] One who is torn by inward divisions is unfit for real faith; only the man whose self-shaping is centered in the conviction of responsibility which keeps him mindful of the profound meaningfulness of his existence is beyond the danger of such fragmentation. A life can attain unity only if it is ruled out of its own depths, if its wellspring is the very being of truth. For it is these depths which constitute life in its reality; from them life can be separated only in abstraction; through them it becomes a call to the attainment of true humanity. From out of these depths all our life activities are directed towards their true freedom. The commitment to the unconditionality of truth lays our subjectivity open to the supermundane self-affirmation of faith.

In whatever sense one is using the word faith, the concept of faith cannot be separated from its relation to truth. If the faith is concerned with objective matters (I believe it will rain tomorrow, and the like), then that relation is laden with some uncertainty and the word faith, or belief, does not signify a satisfying degree of knowing but only a subjectively accepted probability. One who believes in something which was or is or will be in the objective world would like to have the certainty of knowledge, but at least for the moment it is beyond his reach. But if faith bears upon the superobjective content of personal life, then its certainty cannot be doubted. It is immediate; it refers to something manifest in one's own experience, not to something foreign, and as foreign exposed to doubt. The certainty of faith has its content in life itself; however, this content manifests itself in different depths of being (*Wesenstiefen*).

The form of unity of the I, "the mere apperception: I think,"[5] is constitutive of every knowing consciousness. But since this formal I is without content, one cannot very well speak of a "faith" in the I. Yet, to be a man means to fight, to strive for meaning and content in life, and one who prevails in this struggle is a fighter for faith. The content of life never consists in the purely intellectual, although the service of the intellect in attaining this content is indispensable. The agent in the struggle for the conquest of life is no single function of our developing powers, it is the concrete personality. And whenever the reward of our victory is obtained in a greater or lesser measure of self-affirmation, the form of the I becomes the vehicle of a faith in some way attuned to the essential being of the supertemporal ideas. In them the I finds the content of what is purely human. Outward circumstances may tempt the I to lose itself; but when it prevails in the struggle it is absorbed by a manifestation of the supermundane reality of the true, the good, the just, the beautiful. It finds faith in the supertemporal ideas, and the clear content of this faith is the immediate certainty of human freedom.

To speak, or even to think, of immediate certainty means to objectify it, to rob it of its immediacy. This is invariably true of the ideas we have just mentioned, and it is even more true with regard to the ultimate depths of experience they open. Whenever immediate certainty becomes the content of knowledge or of communication, it is converted into a representation, veiled in imagery (*Vorstellungen*) which belongs to the objective order and hence is no longer immediate but mediated. And this mythologizing veil prevents the original certainty from being immediately experienced; thus the mythological representation can render doubtful—even unbelievable—the content of faith, even while the fact remains that the superobjective can be neither retained in consciousness nor expressed without the representation. And only by being expressed can the superobjective establish a community. As Kant puts it, the veil "really turns into a phenomenon that which cannot be the object of experience."[6]

During the era of experimental psychology, the existence or non-existence of the freedom of the human will was supposed to be ascertainable by experiments. Similarly, wherever people search in the objective order for reasons for faith in God, or, having looked in vain for such confirmations of the transcendent, wherever unbelief supposes itself to be on firm ground, we find an equally naive and fantastic transformation. That which cannot be an object of experience becomes a mere phenomenon. The transformation drags the issue down into the conditions of the finite.

In mythology this is inevitable. But in mythology the finite form of the historical report affects only the objective sense of the report, as intelligence would apprehend it. The truth of the myth, however, demands to be experienced in the rapt assent to the challenge made by the report. It is a challenge to the whole person and thus transcends the sphere of intelligence. The heights of human life are determined by the superobjective; one *must* talk about it, and that is why myths are necessary. When intellectual freedom has been attained for the life which is determined by superobjective reality, the mythological veil will be taken for what it is; the veil will be distinguished from the veiled content of faith. However, if our conscious life is tyrannized by the sense of objectivity and thus unable to make this distinction, mythology will separate men and tend to sow enmity among them. It will fetter men's minds. When mythology is understood as what it is, however, it gives not only depth to the intellectual life but breadth and freedom.

There can be no unconditional certainty about the kind of objective thinking which would give superobjective experience the fixed form of a mental image—no unconditional certainty about mythology. Most of the people who are passionately inclined to deny this fact have only a "certainty" which is conditioned by fear and by hope. If the report that Jesus fed five thousand human beings with five barley loaves and two fish, and that what was left over filled twelve baskets (John 6:1-13), is accepted as objective truth, those who believe the account do so on the word of an external authority to which they are bound. Such a tie can last a lifetime, and as long as it lasts it rules out the critical attitude with which the historian approaches any report. If necessary, an appeal will be made to the fear of hell, in the effort to make sure that the belief remains unaffected by any doubt. "We have received a letter from God. It is an unforgivable sin to doubt the authority of this letter."[7] But all intellectual freedom is attained by finding a way through doubt. Admittedly the road to freedom leads along the edge of the abyss. Along that road pedagogical tasks await us—tasks whose hour has come when, for our intellectual conscience, doubts have condensed into certainties.

If, in the name of the old faith, those who desire intellectual freedom are denounced as unbelievers, then the community is in the process of disintegration. The danger of this can be prevented only if those in charge of the immature will refrain from feeding them any intellectual sustenance which would force them into a deliberate opposition to the demands of a serious search for truth. Some may lack the courage to see this educational task because they are not equipped to tackle it. This is ominous. If doubts already in the air are repressed, then the human integrity of which the quest of truth is an inalienable part must suffer; intellectual freedom is inhibited, and without such freedom man cannot be "whole." Mature spiritual freedom includes the certainty of faith—a certainty no longer enmeshed in mythological trappings nor confused by them. Intellectual freedom leaves the interpretation of the *objective* meaning of sacred (as well as profane) tradition to the domain of historical criticism, which prevents the false conflicts that arise from the timebound presuppositions of the myths and thus renders the supertemporal content of the myth accessible under the conditions of the new age. If the task is recognized too late, it can become very difficult. For the linguistic formulation of the myths, often enhanced by pictorial art, belongs to an order which is determined by the objectifying functions of the intelligence and which is also historically conditioned. These historical conditions may easily lead a biased imagination to a distorted image of the mythological figures. What was once the proclamation of deep experience has become a prison for intellectual freedom. And the situation has dire possibilities; for if enlightenment breaks these bonds, a new danger looms up—that the truth of faith can no longer be apprehended in any formulation and that its ancient witness meets with contempt.

The word faith also has reference to men and to mankind. To have faith in a man ("to put one's hand in the fire for him") means, like faith in freedom or faith in God, a "subjective firmness of confidence"; it means more than "taking something as probable." Men live in a world which is for them an object of knowledge but which does not absorb them. One who has faith in another man sees in the ordering of this man's life the sovereignty of the superobjective: "Faith in man is implicitly faith in God."[8] To be sure, faith in a specific man can have no immediate certainty and hence is not secure against disappointments. Yet such faith is not exclusively concerned with the other man outside us, for the capacity to have such faith is rooted in the reality of one's own innermost being. From the profoundest depths of our being emerges the immediate and unconditional certainty of our task of being fully human[9] in its universal connections, with all the superindividual obligations it involves. To have faith in another man always means at the same time to have faith in oneself, or at least the desire to find faith in oneself justifiable.

We can put our faith in specific men, but likewise we may put it in human undertakings such as those of science or art—in the mechanistic explanation of physical reality, for example, or cubism —in technology, the state, or some technological or political principle. Whenever we have a faith commitment in these areas our subjective confidence in them attains a degree of firmness which casts out doubt. It is hardly necessary to say that political faith can meet with disappointment. But it must be said explicitly that the weakness of any such faith does not arise merely from the fact that the things believed in have their existence independently from the believer and therefore exclude an immediate certainty. Furthermore the uncertainty often depends on the fact that such a faith rests only on some particular function or functions of the mind and not on the totality of the agent's personal life in its inner multiplicity. Of course such onesidedness occurs not only in the sphere of politics, it can also occur in science, in art, in the field of morality, in law, in technology. The opposition between specific functions brings a tension into our lives, and the integration of our powers into a living unity becomes difficult. This spiritual struggle confers a greater breadth and depth upon our realization of the purely human, but where the goal of life is determined by a onesided inclination the resolution of serious tensions is unlikely. It may be that conflict between the different directions in which our life may move will become permanent. In that case the striving for self-assertion will stay clear of the deeper problems of life. The growth of our human reality will be stunted as a consequence and our personal hold on it will be precarious.

Nevertheless we must be aware in principle of a fundamental distinction. Insofar as faith is concerned with the ontological depth of the superhistorical idea—a depth which reveals itself in science, in art, and so on—the commitment is in no way precarious. For these spiritual forces constantly manifest the supertemporal depths in man. It may look as if such a faith were committed to the operation of a single function, but the unconditional validity of these ideas springs from the fact that they represent substantial truth; hence in their supertemporal reality they cannot be separated from each other.

One who is committed to the truth of science and art in their depth is committed to their human reality; indeed his faith in them is faith in God. If, on the contrary, science is understood in a purely intellectualist way as nothing but science, and art in an aestheticizing way as nothing but art, then faith in them has only a conditional validity; for science which is nothing but the product of an intellectual effort and art which is nothing but the play of imagination (supported by the intelligence) exist only as cultural effects unworthy of "faith." As for mere movements—for example, mechanism in the scientific sphere or cubism in pictorial art— they have only a time-conditioned validity, and this validity is further relativized by movements in the opposite direction. Having "faith" in such trends involves only the recognition that in the historically given situation it is an advantage for science or art that the trends should be allowed to develop. Only then can intellectual freedom be preserved. And then, such a faith is nothing more than the commitment involved in a personal point of view whose validity depends on the degree of education of the one who holds it. If this cultural level is low, the point of view is often fanatical. The fanatic, lacking an understanding of the foundations of the movement he would defend, is incapable of appraising it realistically; he is unable to grasp how conditional the validity of the movement is in relation to the absolutely true. Fanaticism raises to what is ostensibly the level of an absolute something which may have validity within a limited context, whereas true humanity tries to determine the place in which the partial truth has its relative validity.

Rabindranath Tagore accused the West of having neglected genuine humanity owing to an excessive regard for vocational activity.[10] We should have the same kind of commitment to our vocation in life that we have with respect to scientific or artistic movements: our vocation has its legitimate rights within a social structure by which it is regulated; it calls for our working in a specific direction. But we shall misapprehend our vocation and treat ourselves as what we are not if we do not bring to it our whole personal humanity. To understand one's work only objectively and evaluate it only in terms of objective accomplishments means to prevent it from bringing the satisfaction it could provide if the demands it makes on our humanity were fully acknowledged; for our life work comes into being as part of the effort to give human shape to our existence. Every vocation has a side which involves human relationships, but one who does not bring his humanity into his work will hardly learn to respect those relationships which belong to it. Pestalozzi says, "You are in the first place a child, a human being, and only then an apprentice in your vocation," and he calls for a permanent subordination of all professional training under the primary concern for what is human. The recognition of the necessity for this is, for Pestalozzi, a truth found "in the innermost essence" of ourselves, a "universal human truth," a "truth which unites dissidents with each other."[11] In fact, being human has a unifying power, and in the first place it renders the individual at one with himself.

If a faith commitment is onesided, if it is restricted to concerns of the intellect, of morality or aesthetics, not in their ontological depths but as ends in themselves, our humanity remains under a strain. Genuine faith is the expression of the unity of our personal being; it makes its demands on the whole man. If the interrelationship of our various powers is defective and this deficiency determines the goals of faith, then faith lacks certainty. For the goal which supplies the deepest meaning of those functions is not implicit in them as separate functions: the goal is humanness. One who lives in a really human way lives in harmony with himself,[12] a harmony which reaches down into the ultimate depths of his being and has its ground there. Marc de Munnynck called this ground the "unification of the totality of life under a divine principle."[13]

SECOND PART
THE REALM OF TRUTH

1

ON BEING AT ONE WITH ONESELF

Hegel found the philosophical concept of truth in the "consistency of a content within itself."[1] The first edition of his collected works, edited by Leopold von Henning on the basis of lecture notes, contains some important elucidations of this "deeper meaning of truth." Referring to the ordinary ways of speech, Hegel says: "Thus, for instance, one speaks of a *true* friend, meaning one whose behavior is in conformity with the concept of friendship. Similarly, one speaks of a *true* work of art. In the same sense, untrue means bad, inappropriate in itself. A bad state is accordingly an untrue state, and the specific meaning of bad and untrue consists in the contradiction found between the essence, or idea[a], of an object and its existence. It is possible for us to have a correct image of such a bad object, but the content of this image is something inherently untrue. Our minds can accommodate many such correct images which are at the same time untruths. God alone is the truthful conformity of the idea and the reality. All finite things involve untruth to some extent: there is the idea of them and their existence, but the latter does not conform to the idea."[2]

Historically, these propositions are directly connected with Fichte. The doctrine that truth and falsehood have their precise meaning only with reference to statements[3] undoubtedly expresses a striving for conceptual neatness. Nevertheless the doctrine is unsatisfactory, for truth can be contained in statements only in a limited sense.[4] Our certainty of truth goes beyond this, involving the whole life of mind and will. Even as our power of judgment is trained on truth it points beyond itself. If, along with the "deeper meaning of truth," we reject the ontological question—the question concerning "true being"[5]—and accordingly relate the idea of truth exclusively to what is stated, then our desire for truth would seem to pertain exclusively to logic and the positive sciences. Insofar as aesthetics, ethics and the philosophy of justice and of religion cannot be reduced to positive sciences, they appear in a wavering light: they would seem to take their origin from the needs of the mind and from social conventions which are the product of historical change. And in fact such evaluations of the values of life are quite widespread.

Assuredly the problem of truth is tied in with logic, and Hegel was aware of it. Immediately after the sentences quoted above he declares: "The contemplation of truth in the sense here explained, as conformity to itself, constitutes the genuine interest of logical inquiry." And one will recall that in the philosophy of Hegel, and also in this particular § 24 of the *Encyclopedia* to which the sentences quoted are appended, logic coincides with metaphysics. In a similar way, the philosophy of Fichte had already absorbed metaphysics in a "science of knowledge" (*Wissenschaftslehre*). In a short 1794 publication of Fichte's (*Some lectures on: For what is the scholar meant?*) one can read: "The final destination of all finite rational beings is absolute at-one-ness, steady identity, full harmony with oneself. . . . Not only the will is to be steadily at one with itself—which is the subject matter of moral doctrine— but all the powers of man, being basically but one power and distinguishable only in their application to distinct objects, are to be attuned to perfect identity, and are to agree among themselves."[6] The attainment of the ultimate goal of this demand, which aligns man with the universal structure of life, requires his influence upon things: "Man must endeavor to modify them and bring them into agreement with the pure form of his *I*."[7] "To subject to himself everything which lacks reason, and to rule it freely, in accordance with his own law, is the final destination of man, a destination never fully attainable. And it must remain eternally unattainable if man is not to cease to be man, if he is not to become God. The very concept of man implies that his ultimate goal is unattainable, and his way toward it infinite."[8] These sentences imply an ever present relation to the truth. Fichte takes it for granted and does not voice it. Hegel makes it explicit. He could have made use of an explicit phrase already coined by Fichte, who speaks of the "highest, truest man."[9] The bold superlative is significant. We shall see that it points to what is quite specifically new in the philosophy which has absorbed Kant's *Critique of Judgment*.

The words quoted from Fichte, and more particularly those of Hegel, may recall the scholastic and neoscholastic doctrine about "ontological" or "metaphysical" truth.[10] Thomas Aquinas distinguishes between the *veritas intellectus* and the *veritas rei*. And a *thing* is true if it agrees with its idea. Hans Urs von Balthasar[11] has clearly seen the importance of this thesis. He can derive his insight from one among many statements of Thomas himself. He realized that "the last measure of the truth of reality" is "ideality which gives meaning," is what "ought to be." "It would be very naive to believe that the truth about a thing can ever be analytically extracted, like a fixed quantity, from the being of that thing—or even less from its appearance."[12] The doctrine of ontological truth has been interpreted unsatisfactorily for a long time. As recently as at the turn of the century Désiré Mercier, the professor of philosophy at the Louvain who contributed most creditably to the renewal of the medieval tradition, explained the doctrine in his *Ontologie* with examples which are rather too innocuous, too lacking in metaphysical tensions. For instance: If something looks like wine and has the taste of wine, yet does not come from the juice of the grape but from a laboratory, then it is not true wine. (In line with medieval doctrine one should say that the ontological truth of the wine has its meaning in the total context of creation.) Again, a man arrested under the suspicion of murder may have a face which seems to confirm the accusation—"une vraie figure de criminel."[13] Like Fichte and Hegel, Mercier relates what is given in experience to a norm of its truth or falsehood. He calls this norm "type idéal." However, his phrase is not meant to refer to a higher order: "The ideal, the norm of judgments about what is true, is abstracted from experience."[14] The norm for whatever we meet in experience is taken from experience itself.

But the great turn of direction in the history of philosophy which was started by the *Critique of Judgment* made possible a new content of the problem of ontological truth—or rather it restored the great content which the problem had with Thomas, and restored it in a new and epistemologically clearer way. Above any objective entity of experience ranks that entity's "final destination" (Fichte) or "what is of reason" (Hegel). For Thomas the entity of experience stood in relation to the *intellectus divinus*.[15] Experience (*Erfahrung*) proves to be an appeal to an experiencing (*Erleben*) bent upon the depth of reality which ought to be unlocked by entities of experience.

In Hegel's *Encyclopedia*, in corollary 3 to §24, we can read: "What counts in experience is the sense in which one approaches reality. Great good sense makes great experiences and sees in the motley play of appearances that which counts. The idea is present and real, it is not 'over there' nor 'back yonder.' Great good sense, as for instance the sense of a Goethe, looking into nature or into history, makes great experiences, beholds what is of reason (*das Vernünftige*) and voices it." In a devitalized Thomistic tradition which, nevertheless, continued to the present time, the interest in ontological truth, notwithstanding the fact that its formulations resemble those of the post-Kantians, has moved in a framework of what Hegel called "the *untrue being* of the objective world."[16] However, Hegel's incisive phrase must not mislead us into forgetting that the Thomistic doctrine expressed the significant insight that truth concerns the essence of *things*, not only the essence of judgments. The theses of the later Thomistic tradition retain their value. But the "truth" which these theses call ontological belongs to the realm of what is objective in the strictest sense. Since Kant, however, this realm can no longer be unhesitatingly identified with "being" as such. One could call this truth "phenomenological," if that word were not already overloaded with meanings. Thomism is not on principle inclined to separate the merely objective from the depth of reality. In an exposition of the doctrine of Thomas Aquinas, Mathias Baumgartner, putting together the empirical and the metaphysical, says: "The Aristotelian-Thomistic concept of truth and knowledge implies the conviction of the objectivity and transcendence of the object of knowledge. What is known are . . . the things outside the soul, the things in themselves."[17] And Mercier could speak of a "knowledge of ontological truth"[18] which occurs in judgments. Yet ontological truth always concerns the whole man, and the words in which ontological truth seeks its expression need the function of judgments only for the sake of communication.

Pre-Kantian philosophy assumed, as a matter of course, that the mind of man is confronted with a reality of which man becomes aware through the task of depicting (*abzubilden*) it by means of his intellectual powers. To be sure, the uncomfortable difficulty was that the correctness of the picture (*Abbildung*) cannot be verified. Protagoras brought the difficulty into the open, and he even tried to show that every assertion of a truth which is valid superindividually (and what would truth be if it did not have superindividual validity?) is an irresponsible risk: "As every thing appears to me, so it is for me; but as it appears to you so it is for you."[19] But the scruples of the great sophist were set aside by the unceasing confirmations which practical life furnishes for the correspondence of our imagery with the "real" things. The belief that the goal of judgment is the correspondence with reality of the image to be furnished for the consciousness very nearly attained the certainty of an axiom. To doubt the belief was exceptional. In his *Philosophy of Phenomena*, where he exhibits the origin of the medieval problem of universals, Heinrich Barth finds the following significant formulation for the nonchalance with which that age ignored the problem: "Species and kinds have a twofold existence, as abstract images in the understanding, and as corresponding being in things."[20]

Nevertheless the obscurity, the enigma, associated with the belief that knowledge is a copy could not be entirely ignored and forgotten. A knowledge immune to doubt would have to presuppose that the mind was immediately united with the substance of things. "Whatever ought to be perfectly known ought not to be known through another but through itself, being aware of itself immediately."[6] So said Franciscus Sanchez two hundred years before the *Critique of Pure Reason*, in the charming little book *Tract on the very noble and first universal science that nothing can be known*.[21] He did not dare to present his doctrine as knowledge—for there is no knowledge! In Kant's youth, David Hume elaborated the difficulty most impressively, finding it insoluble on the traditional basis. He found no reassurance in the fact that our imagery finds confirmation in practical life; it was a confirmation which only served to render the problem which he saw clearer and therefore more acute. He was plagued by the "curiosity" which was his "as a philosopher."[22] In pre-Kantian philosophy, which took its problems not from the lived (*erlebten*) but from the represented (*vorgestellten*) world, the old desire to penetrate the curtain of what can be experienced by the senses remained strong enough to prompt further inquiries. Yet whether, despite the obscurities, the purely theoretical processes were still credited with the power of depicting being as such or whether the obscurities were taken so seriously that "curiosity" had begun to border on "skepticism," the pre-Kantians were in agreement with respect to the affairs of daily life. Action was based on the real itself, with which one could interfere purposefully only through the activity of reasoning. What mattered was to do good and avoid evil in that reality. Furthermore, in that reality there was many a thing to be treasured as beautiful or as useful and many another to be rejected as ugly, untrustworthy, or harmful. The assumption was that the human mind, in the form of an intellectual, moral, aesthetic, and practical consciousness, was confronted by a being subsisting in itself, a being which had its own laws.

Kant recognized the problematic character of this assumption, and Fichte abandoned it. Declaring that the thing-in-itself is something superadded by thought to the contents of experience,[23] he denied it a place in metaphysics. "A truly living philosophy," he wrote, "must proceed from life to being. To go from being to life is entirely an error, and it cannot but produce a system that is erroneous in all its parts. Those who posit the absolute as a being have quite extirpated it in their own being. Nor in the sphere of knowledge can one contemplate the absolute as if it were outside of oneself, for the product is sheer phantasmagoria. On the contrary, one must be and live in the absolute in one's own person."[24] This formulation of the two possibilities which point up the greatest possible contrast—either to extirpate the absolute from one's self or to live it in one's own person—makes the superlative of "true" on page 137 above intelligible: we are responsible for the depth and fullness of our life and therefore for the measure in which it is "true life" and in which we are "true men."

Once truth is seen as something to be absorbed into personal life, the knowable truth must likewise appear in a new light and with new significance. In 1804 Fichte began to lecture again on his science of knowledge, and these lectures are rich in impressive formularies. One is: "What we truly comprehend (*einsehen*) becomes an essential part of ourselves, and if it is a truly new insight, then it means a re-creation (*Umschaffung*) of our own self."[25] Knowledge is not merely an attainment of the intellect which is preoccupied with its objects; it is a power which enhances life itself, granted only that knowledge is aware of the significance it has for giving shape to the conditions of life. And the ideal norm for raising life to the height of its possibilities can be nothing other than being wholly at one with oneself. Kant had already pointed in the same direction, when he said: "Knowledge (*Wissenschaft*) has a value as inward truth only as an organ of wisdom."[26] The power of knowing must be related to a goal which transcends the possibilities of knowledge itself. As long as the function of knowledge is nothing but itself, it can attain to only a truth of conditional value. Such truth is not an end in itself. There is a tension between the truth of systematic knowledge and that which gives such knowledge its "true value." It is a tension which will not resolve itself but which imposes on one who has dedicated himself to the pursuit of such knowledge the duty of resolving it. Kant gives to the humane goal which the values of systematic knowledge are to subserve the name of *wisdom*. In the abstract framework of theoretical speculation these values are seen only in the cold light of the intellect. Pestalozzi, too, called the value of systematic knowledge into question when he wrote, in his *Inquiries* of 1797: "Truth and justice have a real value for man only insofar as he makes truth and justice meaningful."[27] The challenge implicit in these words is not addressed to the isolated individual. The mission of knowledge is fulfilled in "uniting our forces with others" in mutual "service."[28]

Pestalozzi's reference to the life of the community in which alone "transformation" and "wisdom" can develop and prove their truth in a human way can be taken as an elucidation of the words just quoted from Fichte and Kant. Individual man has his own theoretical knowledge which he is free to use as he likes—for the adulteration of wine, if it suits him. This neutral intellectual activity, "freely hovering," as Rudolf Eucken significantly describes it, is able to recognize the "truth of things" only within the order of objective existence. Yet the life course of man does not consist in an objective process enacted in the midst of objects from among which one can select one's accommodation in terms of the purely theoretical constructs of one's own mind. From the very beginning of his existence a man depends on his community; and if he is mature enough, he is challenged by the community to become aware of the unconditioned reason (*Vernunft*) on which the community rests. Reason urges us to distinguish between true and false, good and evil, just and unjust, beautiful and ugly. The way in which each man makes these distinctions is his own affair; his historical situation merely specifies his starting point. Nevertheless the necessity of concerning himself with the distinctions cannot be evaded by anyone endowed with reason. And the more seriously he takes them and the more intensely his responsibility is experienced, the greater will be the freedom both of the individual and the community. As to the objective conditions of our existence we are coerced by necessity; so also does the freedom of the community suffer a fatal blow if our intellectual activity is put into the service of our appetites, thus intensifying the conflict of interests and aiding and abetting the thrust for power. But where a community exists which is authentically human, not only has reason superindividual authority but the life of reason is manifested in its substantial reality through its liberating effects. Through reason every community enriches the life of its members, and the more genuinely true humanity is operative in them the greater is the enrichment. Individual existence is raised to a higher level by the very fact of belonging to a community in which humanity is at a high level. But above all, since the creative tension between what has been attained and what is still to be attained never ceases to operate, the fact of belonging furnishes possibilities for the further development of the purely human; and moreover these possibilities have a greater multiplicity and involve a greater moral dignity in proportion to the extent that those basic Herculean labors have been performed which "modify" things and turn them in the direction of the goal which is the at-oneness of man with himself. It is here that the question with regard to ontological truth proves its deep significance; it is the question of what things have to tell us in the name of reason for the sake of a meaningful life. What they tell us is that from the superindividual depth of our existence we are challenged by reality. Whether we respond to the challenge is for us to decide; but if we ignore it, our personal at-oneness is abdicated.

Reality does not stand still but presents a ceaselessly changing aspect, and it is different for each individual. Natural events alter the face of reality and, even more significantly, so do human actions, reasonable or unreasonable, as they come to bear on the individual in his own situation.

It is well known that Fichte (for good reasons) scorned any rigid or binding terminology. For his philosophy it is essential to understand that the depth of reality is manifest only in ceaselessly changing experience (*Erleben*) and not in existence as the intellect represents it (*Vorgestellten*). Towards the end of his first major work Fichte summarizes his position. "If the science of knowledge should be asked, 'Just what is the constitution of things in themselves?' the answer could only be, 'What we ought to make of them.'"[29] The rather moralistic bias notwithstanding, the words of the formulary are impressive and instructive. For Fichte, "things in themselves" are done for, since they belong to a metaphysics which is no more than a construct of theoretical understanding in its timeless operations. They are struck down by the verdict of the *Critique of Pure Reason* that ontology must give way to "a mere Analytics of pure understanding."[30] This kind of ontology has, however, its prototype in the rationalism of Christian Wolff. No matter how it is formulated, there still remains the valid question of "the reality of being," of "ontological truth," and Fichte, making use of the expression for once, eleven years after his first major work, connects it with the absolute, which "one must be and live in one's own person." For any man who lives his life from the profoundest depths of reality, things have a language which powerfully communicates their meaning. All things are interrelated, and through these relations we are aware of the resonance of the supertemporal, which liberates us from the power of time, guards us against the loss of our selfhood, maintains our at-oneness with ourselves. Freedom, protection, maintenance—all these realities things can and do affirm.

Our understanding tells us, quite correctly, that a sound which nobody hears is not a sound; for in addition to the physical reality of the vibration there must be perception by the ear. Something analogous is true in the intellectual order: the truth of a "true work of art" is not truth for the uncultured but is manifest only for one who has the personal qualifications for its appreciation. The ontological truth of the order of reason cannot be acknowledged as something simply sufficient to itself; it is perceived as an enhancement of life and as a mission, just as, in the Lord's Prayer, God's Will, "as it is in heaven," is the model for what is to happen on earth.

Ontological truth is not within the grasp of the individual as such. Whenever and wherever it manifests itself, the individual comes to self-awareness as the member of a historically determined community; and this is so no matter how imperfectly the idea of community is realized therein. The truth as it concerns the individual person belongs to the community's content of freedom. (Works of art created by our contemporaries in our own environment express the content of a life which we, too, live; but if we encounter the ancient art of a people whose history is not preserved in our own—for instance, the art of the ancient Mexicans—then, if we are not to be confronted with a total enigma, we must try to gain access to that art by taking as our starting point the consciousness of the widest and most universal community—namely, the necessary consciousness of mankind, which cannot be but what it is.) Only an experience of reality which belongs to freedom permits us to speak of "ontological" truth; the first half of that word must be understood with reference to the "true being" which Fichte identified with the supertemporal life, the divine life.[31] The intellect in its purely theoretical processes can grasp only an existence which is bound up with the representational (*des Vorgestellten*); as for what is essentially real, the theoretical process grasps only its appearance (*Erscheinung*), which is, so far as our reasoning is concerned, without essence. For example, the true significance of Rembrandt's masterpieces cannot be expressed in purely in-

On Being at One with Oneself

tellectual categories. That our human existence not only became richer in an external sense but gained inwardly new possibilities for having "great experiences" owing to the fact that Rembrandt lived and left behind him a rich legacy of "true works of art"; that these manifestations of the depth of humanness opened doors to fresh knowledge of what gives meaning to life and thus altered the historical aspect of an age; that the ontological truth of human life appeared newly revealed through Rembrandt's works —these facts are not within the horizon of the purely theoretical process; they are the liberation, the grace, which comes to us through supertemporal reason.

Reason always manifests itself as the experience of the true, the good, the just, the beautiful. Men, living under historical conditions, receive these manifestations in accordance with their level of culture. But this level is never uniform in a cultural community; things never have the same meaning for all. As a rule, few are ripe for revelations which do not fit into the frame of reference which is habitual to them; yet even those who resist what is most splendid can be honest seekers for the meaning of life. When the ontological content of truth opens up in a wholly new way for anyone, the experience is a grace. For them the very life by which they are embraced, the choices which reason demands between one value and another, attain a deeper meaning. To be sure, it is precisely on account of this that the time-conditioned existence of such men can be forced into the most painful conflicts with the representatives of the prevailing order. In the Gospel of John, the high-priestly prayer concludes with Jesus' expression of his certainty that he is the bearer of God's words, beloved by God. The report of his arrest follows immediately. (The impressiveness of this sequel is lessened only by the editorial gap between chapters 17 and 18.)

Not only in the large-scale history of mankind but also in the personal history of each individual, life is determined by the decisions with regard to good and evil, the just and the unjust—and last and supremely, with regard to the true and the false. Many decisions derive from intellectual error, many from bad will. False assumptions make a situation appear different from what it actually is. The interests of an individual or a group come to becloud what is necessary according to reason. Yet, no matter how confused a given situation is, it still remains within the order of what is supertemporally necessary. Even a man who would deliberately oppose himself to that order is grasped by it all the same, since error and falsehood claim acceptance as truth, the worthless counterfeit poses as beauty, the execution of inhuman orders arrogates to itself the dignity of the fulfillment of duty, and the judicial murder the dignity of the carrying out of the law. Every form human existence takes will have a relation to the contrasts between values which are the necessities of reason: true and false, good and evil, etc. However, the relation of the values to the concrete contents derives from the historical situation, and hence changes. The circumstances of life which lead to value judgments and decisions bear the impress of their time: their specific form, and often the very possibility of their occurrence, are matters which are caught up in the great movements of history and the problems which are paramount in each situation. Though we may seldom be clearly aware of it, the stand we take with regard to reality unavoidably determines the manner in which we carry out our daily responsibilities, and this stand itself is determined by the measure in which the ontological depth of truth has become alive in us.

The grasp of truth in its depths must have as its starting point the knowledge of whatever seems to be manifestly true; it is indispensable to ascertain the truths in the foreground. To begin with, their usefulness is incontestable, nor could one contest their conditional validity within the context of culture and history. But unconditional truth illumines the structures of community life from within whenever the members are aware that they are called to participation in the development of what is human. This knowledge, this truth, is unconditionally true.

In Fichte's posthumously published lectures of 1813 we find the sentence "Is there any truth in our knowledge? Yes; not, however, in our knowledge of what is but in our knowledge of what *is to be, eternally*, through us and through our freedom; what is to be purely from the spirit, shaped and presented within the reality which is given to us; and for that alone is it given."[32] This unconditional truth absorbs the truths of discursive thinking. It needs those truths which are only conditionally valid for its own realization. The conditional truth as such has an inherent relation to the absolute as to something unrealizable; but insofar as it belongs to a superobjective structure of meaning—for instance to a structure which makes aesthetic or moral claims—we become aware that the link between the conditional and the unconditional can be made real. We discover that the true goal of discursive thought, which discursive thought itself is incapable of comprehending, nevertheless exists in an area which transcends our reasoning. Our intellectual activity is unconditionally necessary for the formation within the conditions of history of what is truly human—namely for the establishment of the perfect rule of superhistorical reason in the world. It is true that the activity of the intellectual process is onesided and beset with problems. Yet superhistorical reason, which illumines the relations between men in such a way as to give ever new expression to man's humanity, and points upward, beyond all that has yet been attained, to a freedom which is greater and purer, is a call to the transcendence of everything that is only partial. Reason lays claim to the whole man. Reason challenges him as the one called to be in harmony with himself notwithstanding the inequalities in the development of his powers and the unavoidable opposition between their disparate tendencies. The insight derived from theoretical knowledge is a necessary contribution to the edifice we are to erect.

Admittedly our understanding is an ambiguous helper, since it opens roads even for inhumanity. And often it is practiced in the art of shielding those who have taken inhumane courses against discovery and punishment—indeed in securing high honors for them in "the world." All the forces working towards the disintegration of humanity call for the acumen deriving from discursive thought. At the same time, the evolution of cultural life necessitates a constantly higher level of training in the intellectual sphere. Thus the task of education becomes increasingly more difficult. Pestalozzi says: "In order to attain harmony with himself, a man who knows a lot is more in need of guidance than any other; and the guidance will be able to rely less on nature, since it will become more of an art to harmonize his knowledge with his circumstances and to attain consonance in the growth of all his mental capacities. If the harmony is not attained, the light shed by his knowledge will be delusive."[33]

In his *Addresses to the German Nation,* Fichte says: "The only end in itself is the life of the spirit, nor can there be any other end in itself."[34] The life of the spirit as an end in itself involves overcoming everything which can put a man at odds with himself. It means to be at one with oneself. This sounds like a formula, and it must not be misunderstood. It does not mean individualism. The individual lives as a member of society. He is a "work of society"—a phrase from Pestalozzi's *Inquiries.* Nevertheless, as Pestalozzi himself emphatically stressed, his precise danger is that he might be nothing better than a mere product of society: "My social conditioning is not my full self. I cannot stop at acquiescence with my social condition, and I am just as little able to acquiesce in the mere satisfaction of my animal needs. No matter what my case, my social conditioning has maimed me: distrust, distortion, unrest have entered my soul."[35] A humanity which is genuine makes *demands* on society. And higher than these demands is the ultimate norm for them: man's at-oneness with himself; the recognition of the life of the human spirit as an exclusive end in itself—in short, the recognition of humanity as such. In his birthday address of January 12, 1818, Pestalozzi exclaims: "Man, look at yourself and inquire into the ways in which you arrive at a harmony with yourself, and the ways in which you are at odds with yourself and with humankind." And he demands that the educator shall "recognize the spiritual essence of the human organism in its depths, for this reality alone is capable of unifying the totality of our human powers and directing them, through faith and love, towards the ultimate goal of this totality, which is the freedom of the human will."[36] The word "love" indicates that being at one with oneself is conditioned by one's willingness to cooperate with others in the solution of society's problems. No one can be at one with himself unless participation in the essential concerns of his world has become for him an inner need. In particular, each individual should understand his calling in society as having its origin in this need.

On Being at One with Oneself

Whenever Pestalozzi elaborates upon the theme of man's need to be at one with himself, he writes with great emphasis, well aware of the unspeakable difficulties which confront anyone who is trying to make clear to his contemporaries what their *human* obligations are. He knew from personal experience that a man who commits his life to such undertakings tends to be mocked as a dreamer and either ignored or treated as a dangerous disturber of the peace. But just because genuine humanity is not something to which men attain as a matter of course, the kind of love is required which concerns itself with our fellow men not because of their lovable characteristics but because of their miseries. And the less aware they are of their wretchedness the more they need that love—yes, even if they are hardly conscious of their wretchedness at all. They need the assistance of those who will put their whole lives at stake without stopping to inquire as to the kinds of discomfort which might result for themselves.

Pestalozzi was filled with ardent patriotism, but he was a trial to those in the seat of government. Men who are motivated by the desire to understand their true place in society and to do justice to it are not necessarily to be found among those who happen to have risen to power in public office. Pestalozzi was aware, above all, that the desire to be at one with oneself is threatened when inhuman ordinances are issued in the name of the state. *Concerning Legislation and Infanticide*, published in 1793, is a powerful indictment of the criminal law then in force. "To strain at gnats and swallow camels is the very spirit of our legislation and our customs; if it were not, we should honor humanity above sterility, and we should not pay for childlessness with the spoliation of human lives." What is of urgent necessity is "to ennoble the legislative will and the governmental power from within."[37] Even decades later, Pestalozzi speaks in the same tone.

He recognized early that the state's inherent interest in power makes its interference with the liberty of conscience inevitable. And since the need for power belongs to the constitution of the state, the guilt of the state in failing to keep abreast of the requirements of humanity is a tragic reality. As early as 1797 Pestalozzi writes that these interests have led us to the point where "we have become nothing but public men and can no longer be private men." The state will no longer allow us an unlimited right to our own conscience; wherever the power interests of the state are at stake, it will sequestrate our conscience. Owing to this "sad truth," we have "lost the sweet word fatherland and have become subjects of the state."[38] To be sure, we may note, the word "fatherland" has kept its warm sound, and whenever a state is in the process of organizing all available resources of power and is about to recruit its citizens for unjust ends, it will not fail to usurp the "sweet name." Pestalozzi saw clearly that the evil of the "emasculation of the citizen"[39]—that is, of the lack of civil courage—cannot be immediately eliminated; hence his demands with regard to education for citizenship. In our time, which has manifested the omnipotence of the state in various forms, we may find ourselves filled with consternation when we see that there is no surer guarantee today for the rights of conscience than there was in Pestalozzi's day. Only an unconditional deference to these rights would permit man to be at one with himself—that is, would make the realization of the demands of man's humanity a possibility. Assuredly this is a fact which does not call those commandments with regard to humanity into question but, on the contrary, implies a judgment with regard to our states.

Pestalozzi stipulates that the state "has the duty to protect and to maintain the rights of individuals to be faithful to their convictions in all cases."[40] Such a claim stands superior to everything time can bring—or can enforce. Obviously one can object that men's convictions are too wholly unreliable and too much open to question to be given free exercise. There is historical prescience in Spitteler's mockery in his *Olympian Spring*: "One sole conviction in this land shall live./ Believe or die! How else could order thrive?" ("Es darf im Land nur Eine Überzeugung sein/ Glaub oder stirb! Wie könnte Ordnung sonst gedeihn?") Still, the obvious objection merely reveals the misery of an age in which the state, which should be only a means for the creative activity of human beings, has become more important than man's humanity itself. To be sure, the role of the state as a means stands out in high relief; even one who is without faith is convinced. Yet humanity is nothing but a content of faith.

Fichte too, in agreement with Pestalozzi, defined the state as "a means, a prerequisite and a framework for that which the love of the fatherland truly desires."[41] He claims that this love, "as the unconditionally highest, final and independent magistracy," must itself rule the state. The state needs such overlordship in order that there shall be "liberty, even in outward life." Liberty "is the soil in which the higher form of man can grow." And for the sake of this form legislation must leave the largest possible range for liberty, "even at the risk of a lesser degree of silent concord and with the consequence that the task of governing may be rendered a little more complex and arduous."[42]

In Max Frisch's play *The Chinese Wall*,[43] the poet Min Ko calls the victorious emperor a criminal in that he "prevents the rule of the truth." And he does so "because he knows that, in truth, he is no prince." He knows "at the very core of his despair that he is born to be a carrier of water." But "he is ashamed that this is so, and so he prefers to be a scoundrel, a knave in purple, rather than to accept his role of water carrier in the kingdom of truth. . . . He acts at odds with his knowledge." The rich possessions he calls his own, the princely gardens in which he receives his guests, do not in truth belong to him. He knows it, "and that is why he fears the advent of the rule of truth. That is, not he alone fears it! . . . A strange thing indeed, this matter of truth. All know that there is truth and that there is nothing but the truth, and one does not change it by proclaiming the opposite. . . . Nevertheless they all act contrary to the truth."

The truth makes demands. In the language of the poet, it demands its "realm." It demands it: for the role of truth could exist automatically only where there was no role for freedom of the will at all. To let Min Ko speak again: "No lie can make water flow uphill nor sparks fly downwards, and our earth revolves around the sun whether we are allowed to say so or not." But the emperor in that drama prevents the realm of truth from existing because he has power over the expressions of his subjects' wills. He can impose heavy penalties for any affirmation of the truth. He threatens to have Min Ko's head on the point of a lance.

Many have said that power is evil in itself. It is true that power gives rise to interests which are opposed to the demands of truth, to the "realm" of truth. Even the intellect (*der Geist*), says Jacob Burckhardt, "comes forward to accommodate power. . . . Literature and even philosophy become servile in their glorification of the state, and the servility of art becomes monumental; or at least, all three produce only what is admissible at court. The intellect becomes a pensioner in all kinds of ways, fawning on the 'facts.' "[44] Of course there are exceptions: wherever the human spirit is at the height of its development, where its powers are unified and oriented towards the idea of the true, it corresponds to its own necessity. But power is practiced in the ways of curtailing the human spirit's possibilities.

Plato dealt with this danger in his *Republic*. Explicitly aware that he was saying something unusual—indeed something that would jeopardize his reputation—he declared that the only remedy is to place power only in the hands of those who do not want it, who accept it only because they have grasped the fact that they are endowed with knowledge and skills for the benefit of the public, for the good of the state, and not for their personal enjoyment. "That state in which those designated to rule have least desire to rule will of necessity be governed the best, and with the least unrest. . . . But if authority is made the matter of a struggle for power, then such civil strife and warfare means the ruin of both the contestants and the state."[45] Hence Plato's often quoted demand that "philosophers become kings, or the kings and princes of this world have the spirit and power of philosophy."[46] The phrase "the kings and princes of this world" sounds the same note as is heard in Max Frisch's play when the emperor is said to be merely a carrier of water, and not a prince, in the kingdom of truth.

When Plato set down those sentences he may have had his unpleasant experiences with Dionysius, the tyrant of Syracuse, on his mind; yet there is no doubt that Greek literature as well helped to produce the image of "the kings and princes of this world." For example, Sophocles' *Antigone*, with the character of Creon. When Creon issues that order against which Antigone appeals to "the unwritten eternal law of the gods," the chorus of Theban old men—not to mention the sentinel—submit to the emperor's will. They all know the unwritten law and hence have no rejoinder to Antigone's charge that they are afraid of Creon's arbitrary power. And when Creon says to Antigone, "You are the only one in Thebes who is looking at it this way," she retorts, pointing to the chorus: "They see it too! But in your presence they hold their tongues."[47] Like the emperor in Max Frisch's play, Creon prevents the rule of truth. Even for him the voice of truth is wholly audible, but he does not want to hear it; and that is why, in the realm of truth, he is no sovereign. He is only one of "the kings and princes of this world."

2

THE FOUNDATION IN THE REALM OF TRUTH

In the preceding chapters four values were often mentioned together—the true, the beautiful, the good, the just—and of all of them it was said that they have their goal and also their unity in the truth (which is beyond the reach of mere intelligence). In the fall of 1790 Fichte, engrossed by the study of Kant's philosophy, had the intention of bringing before the public a clear presentation of the gist of the *Critique of Judgment*, the book which was meant to confirm the unity of the master's doctrine. The following year Fichte gave up his plan, and later, in 1804, he claimed that Kant's mistake had been to pursue a different absolute in each of the three Critiques, with the consequences that for Kant the clear concept of one true absolute faded into something which was no more than a common trait of all three.[1] It is not enough to state that the supertemporal values share the trait of necessity bestowed by reason. Their relation to the goal of truth—particularly the relation of the beautiful, the good and the just to truth—is not a relation to something different from their own essence: instead they are the self-realization of that goal. In these values reason itself assumes its proper form— the reason which summons us to distinguish between the true and the false, the beautiful and the ugly, good and evil, the just and the unjust.[2] The values of the true (in the narrower sense of what is true in the domain of the intelligence), of the beautiful, the good and the just need no proof of their origin in an external reason; they are not external objects of reason but reason's own immediate manifestations. Reason is at work in the history of mankind through its demand for ever renewed and novel evaluations in conformity with the four ideas. And this work of reason is comprehensive: outside its domain no activity of the spirit of man is possible at all.

The Foundation in the Realm of Truth

Reason is one and indivisible. The fourfold supertemporal values do not partition the realm of truth. All four have a claim on every act of the human spirit. Of course, the form in which a specific certainty of truth manifests itself to consciousness indicates which particular value is exercising the dominant attraction. One who reads these lines is reading them with a logical interest, concentrating critically on their content of theoretic truth. Yet one could also be applying critical standards with regard to expression, judging the lines aesthetically. And the use which the author is making of his time, as he is writing these lines, can be subjected to a moral judgment. Finally, when it comes to the just, this is a value destined to make possible the shaping of what is human in social life. In its fundamental significance the just designates not a positive value as a quality of some human accomplishment nor even a value of man himself; rather it is the proper characteristic of the basis itself on which the positive values of life—the true, the beautiful, the good—can be realized. Literary tradition usually names these as a threesome.

"To each what is his own." Wherever this demand of justice is insufficiently heeded, the realization of the immediate values of life is hindered, and the obstacles may take on insuperable proportions. An unjust social order subjects the development of great talents to the contingency of circumstances. An unjust government will call "duty" what is actually contrary to true duty. An unjust preference of a child by parents or a teacher spoils the character of the child who is slighted as well as that of the favorite.

To return to the example above, the lines before the reader: the claim of justice concerns not the author as an individual nor his individual accomplishment, but the very basis of his own existence in society. Wherever (as in Germany under Hitler or in Russia under Stalin) the work of philosophy is hampered by autocratic measures and is directed towards preconceived goals, the undertaking is deprived of the possibility of serving truth in the measure which is its due, a measure characterized by the comprehensive meaning of truth, not by the merely theoretic sense of the word truth. Whatever must be evaluated in accordance with logical, aesthetic or moral points of view has its immediate basis in the very nature of personality; the person is the vehicle of the subjective life of the spirit. The just, however, refers to the spirit as it becomes, or has become, objective reality.

The twofold foundation of human existence must be the object of unceasing concern. A healthy, efficient body is a good of great value; so is a just social order. But both are exposed to many dangers incidental to their own development and involvements; and even if both are in their optimum condition, the value of life is not yet guaranteed; what is given is only the favorable conditions for its realization. Whether it is realized will depend on the decisions made by freedom, above the level of the basis of existence. Every man, by his nature, belongs to the whole of nature and is subject to nature's laws; but by nature he is not yet his authentic self. So far as his economic means and the subjective rights connected with these means are concerned, they are held within the social movements of his time, movements which cannot be directed even by the most powerful individuals, even though they may influence them. The nature of every individual and the social order, which promotes as well as limits the capacity of every individual for shaping his own life, furnish the basis for a human life, but they are incapable of producing humanity as such. Neither, however, are their defects insuperable. Obstacles thrust into the path of humanity by nature or by society supply an occasion for humanity to demonstrate that although the basic conditions of existence can be managed to some extent but never fully mastered, the superiority of the spirit (*geistige Überlegenheit*) makes life worth living even under unfavorable circumstances. However, a human life in which the interests of basic conditions assume so essential an importance as to overthrow the dedication to personal values will turn out botched.

In the seventh canto of the *Inferno*, Dante caused the same punishment to be inflicted on spendthrifts and misers alike, who belong together owing to the very opposition of their forms of guilt—*colpa contraria*. During their lives on earth these sinners failed to see the economic goods of the social order for what they in truth are; hence they became inwardly dependent on them. And as the social foundation can hold an unfree spirit captive, so also can nature enslave him, in opposite ways, and *colpa contraria* associates the Epicurean bent on enjoyment with the wretched pessimist who sees in life an existence steeped in anxiety and bound for death. But the supertemporal offers humanity the possibility of finding that which gives value to life. The temporal, the time-bound and time-conditioned, belongs to the mere foundation of human life; hence, too, the privileges issuing from the social order of the time, and our natural powers, which grow stronger or weaker.

The just has the sphere of its effectiveness chiefly in the administration of justice, yet antecedently in education. In contrast to the other values which shape any personal life, the just is carried into effect by coercion; justice can be fulfilled only on the basis of power strong enough to break resistance. To be sure, owing to its dependence on the existing organization of power which inevitably brings forward its own claims, justice is a value weighted down with problems. One can understand (though with mental reservations) Fichte's uncomfortable feeling about "attributing justice to God; justice, which even in man's case has such a subordinate position!"[3] And one understands even better the melancholy reflection of Pestalozzi, who despite his high regard for the mission of the state, was nevertheless acutely aware of the "eternal contradiction" which exists between the demands of true humanity and the claims of the "collective existence of our human kind," claims which the state must satisfy, yet cannot satisfy without injustice.[4] Nevertheless the validity of the idea of the just is unassailable, and the task of fighting for whatever is possible in our time, in the direction pointed out by the idea of the just, remains constant. A stronger statement than the words quoted from Fichte and Pestalozzi is this dictum of Kant's: "If justice vanishes, the life of men on this earth loses its meaning."[5] Fichte and Pestalozzi point out the irrevocable precariousness of human affairs. Kant's statement, however, is a castigation of those who would undermine the very basis of humanity.

There is no way of enforcing the values which make life worth living directly; they attain reality through freedom. We use phrases like just judges, just rulers, just teachers, clearly meaning the characteristic which distinguishes them as individuals; but that is a *moral* quality which manifests itself in the free dedication with which these men come to grips with the tasks which they find at hand in the maintenance of justice. What is effective in the personality of the just judge or ruler is the idea of the good. This idea he serves in freedom. However, justice, which it is his office to fulfill, can be enforced. Nevertheless, so far as true humanity is concerned, coercion leads to no final goal: the enforcement of justice is only a stopgap so long as the right disposition (*Gesinnung*) in the recipient does not provide the complement. This cannot be enforced, and the stopgap makes plain how paltry human existence can be.

It is true that, even by way of sheer contrast, this paltriness belongs to the nobility of man, for it is left to man's freedom, which is superior to any coercion, to manifest itself as noble or ignoble. Wherever justice shows its power, it amounts to a challenge addressed to the forces of freedom. Man has forces of freedom as a *social* being. Justice appeals to his socialmindedness. He must come to an understanding with others and together with them find a common order. The meaning of such orders is to make manifest the idea of the just, to the very limit of what is possible within the temporal conditions of existence. These orders have been brought about not by blind chance but by the desire for a life worth living, a desire which, to be sure, is in frequent danger of falsification. The moving principle at work in these orders is the idea of the just which subjects to criticism any flaws in the condition attained at the time. In all organizations of common life, the idea of the just appeals to the awareness of social responsibility as it is experienced by the individual members of the community. For instance, if the state imposes taxes (provided the state has a just organization), those who are aware of the real meaning of what is asked of them will not consider the tax as a vexatious nuisance (to be shrewdly reduced as much as possible) but as a not unwelcome participation in the expensive tasks confronting the state.[a] In manifold ways the organizations of common life are the holders of the power which justice needs in order to enforce its claims, a power, assuredly, of which the authority of justice alone should dispose. Socialmindedness, in the measure of its probity, furnishes the criterion for the degree in which power really works for justice. Whether willingly affirmed or reluctantly respected, power protects the stability of what has been created. If its order is threatened or disturbed, power shows its ability to coerce.

All coercion is an *external* interference with the liberty of life; its immediate effect on a man amounts only to a restraint of his external functions. But if coercion is used in the service of justice, it is to be understood as an appeal to a man's inner attitude (*Gesinnung*). Nor can coercion as such reach the inner attitude; instead, it attempts to win over the inner attitude by appeal. Man remains interiorly free; he can ignore the appeal. If the arm of justice has apprehended a criminal, put him before the judge, and locked him in prison, it still remains an open question whether a man so roughly handled can recognize justice and is willing to acknowledge it as justice. Perhaps he recognizes only its power, which is stronger than he is. Under such power he must suffer. Yet, although his purely instinctive reaction is to repress the depths of his own being, these depths would provide him with the possibility of meeting his fate in freedom from the shackles of his individual interests and affirming it as a realization of justice. If he would thus affirm it, he would not merely suffer under it but would take it upon himself and bear it, standing inwardly above his suffering. Only if the execution of the sentence makes possible the awakening of a man's humanity in its depths and the liberating acknowledgement of justice which assigns to the guilty what is now truly his own, only then does the punishing authority give to the punished what the authority owes him—his own. If this does not come to pass, the authority must be satisfied with the guilty man's suffering—and of course this satisfaction can minister to the desire for revenge. But it is the inevitable shortcoming of our exertions on behalf of justice that in the administration of justice and in education we can give to one we want to punish—or even one we summon to furnish the contribution due from him (e.g., taxes)—that which is his own only if he accepts it as his own. No outward power can force him to accept it. What is required is the individual's capacity for rising above himself, insofar as this self is taken to mean individuality submerged in its own interests. Although one must expect that superiority in every human being, one dare not take it for granted in everyone. But the superiority is required if man is to discover in the superindividual ideas the depth which affirms the truth, and if he is to acknowledge the validity of the truth even if it condemns his own self, or summons him to make an effort. Pestalozzi said: "Prisons, houses of correction, workhouses are nothing else, nor should they be anything else, but a school which leads a man who has gone astray back onto the path and into the condition in which he would have been had he not gone astray."[6] Every good school respects in the human being the goal which is set for him, which is personal self-reliance. No good school has the intention of forming man from without.

Penal institutions have the purpose of bringing back the awareness and the acknowledgement of justice, the justice whose task it is to make the basis of social life secure, a task impossible without the power which can coerce. The meaning and the purpose of this power is not the enjoyment of power as such; power ought to serve the freedom of human self-determination. In every manifestation of power the outward coercion points beyond itself, it appeals to the forces of freedom. Of those who would keep themselves locked within the narrow confines of their poor individuality, power demands that they become aware of the essential and superindividual depths of their own being, and that they pay homage to the idea of the just. It is the necessary function of the forces which would serve the idea of the just to prevent threats to the preservation of the true, the beautiful, the good, and to repulse interferences with that concern.

The *Philosophy of Right* by Friedrich Julius Stahl[7] begins with the sentence: "The philosophy of right is the science of what is just."[b] One can make serious objections to the work of Stahl. But the unswerving desire for philosophical knowledge of the just should be the rule for every treatment of the great topic. If nevertheless the recent literature presents a quite different picture, this truly strange fact may have its explanation in the deep impression made upon modern authors by the ostensible contrast between justice and the security of legal order. Such authors no longer have the courage to make Stahl's sentence their thesis. Power, which should have helped justice to materialize, has instead subjugated it. Yet it is obvious that wherever that contrast is accepted in theory and in practice, the security of the legal order has ceased to be a security of justice, and has been transformed into the gloomy expectation that any injustice enforced in the name of the state must be raised to the dignity of a maxim. No positive law which disregards the idea of the just, whose validity is above all human arbitrariness, can deserve the name of justice.

A highly regarded man of jurisprudence—we need not name him since too many others have said similar things—has declared: "The judge who deviates from his own decision disavows himself and must necessarily be in error either in his decision or in his deviation." This is undeniable, but in the context it amounts to saying: to err is human, yet since the judge decides in the name of the state he cannot admit error. Therefore, if he has erred and has later recognized the error as such, then in every analogous case he must repeat the error and call it truth. Hence the sequel in our quotation: "A judge who deviates from the principle of the verdict of other courts (in the same community of law) thereby designates their verdict as erroneous and, by his own verdict, establishes himself as a superior court. In either case, the deviation reduces the security of the legal order, and any such reduction must be prevented by the judge, owing to his noble office (*sic!*). Thus tradition becomes a bond of restraint, regardless of the possibility that verdicts may have erred in their interpretative acceptance of the existing law." Another author of high repute says the same thing in other words: "The customary is the norm for what is right. Therefore an interpretation in line with what is customary is binding upon the judge even when, with good reason (!), he considers it erroneous because it is counter to the law or because it is unjust (!), that is, counter to just law. Some are of the opinion that such a sacrifice of the intellect (*sacrificium intellectus*) is not to be demanded of the judge. But that opinion proves too much, and therefore proves nothing at all. For the same opinion could put all obedience to the law in doubt. And he who entertains it fails to recognize the blessings bestowed by the security of the legal order. The interpretation in line with custom furnishes an end to the quarrel." Apparently it does not matter whether it is a just end, as long as justice puts in jeopardy the so-called security of the legal order. As a commentary we may quote an eminent representative of forensic medicine, who had many years of court experience. In 1937, in his treatise "Concerning the Reasons for Difficulties Encountered in Diagnosis and by Diagnostic Witnesses in Atypical Cases of Poisoning," Heinrich Zangger writes: "For me a particularly disheartening piece of information consists in the fact that even educated legal minds demand of medical men, even in uncannily difficult cases of poisoning by volatile chemicals, a quick and almost divinatory decision and, what is more, a decision which brings absolute certainty, as for instance the absolute confirmation or absolute rejection of a suspicion. It is well known how such legal minds will later cling to such premature and very nearly extorted 'decisions,' often even against later well-founded evidence."[8]

In just such cases, and in all cases where the demands of justice are disregarded, the "security of the legal order" is nothing more than the certainty that the injustice once incorporated in a verdict from the bench must keep on begetting what is unjust. Nevertheless the claim is made that that security is a "blessing"—justice or no justice. A blessing for whom? Who is the one blessed? Certainly not he who must expect—nay, who has the "security" —that, in line with the unjust "norm of right," his own just claims will be rejected and that his case will be decided against him, unjustly. Perhaps it is rather the judge who is the blessed beneficiary; his office is made easy for him. Yet no doubt that is not what was meant by the author who praises the "security of the legal order." He can have meant only a state in which the subjects of the law exist in order to obey and to keep their peace. Thus, the tendency to put "security of the legal order" above justice trained nations to tolerate injustices, and prepared the triumphs of the dictatorial endeavors of modern despots.

In the fourteenth volume of the *Enciclopedia Italiana*, in 1932, Benito Mussolini explained the doctrine of Fascism. We read sentences like the following: "For the Fascist, everything is in the state, and there is nothing human or spiritual outside the state, nor can anything have any value outside the state. In this sense Fascism is totalitarian, and the Fascist state, as the synthesis and unity of every value, interprets, develops and enhances the whole life of the people. . . . Fascism aims to reshape not the forms of human life but the content, man himself, the very character, faith.

And for this end Fascism demands discipline, and an authority which sinks into the inward depths of minds and exercises a rule which is undisputed."c In the totalitarian state the security of the legal order, in opposition to the idea of the just, has made patently manifest what had to come, once the *unconditional* acknowledgement of that idea had been sacrificed and once, in that way, the very basis of human life had been deprived of its *necessary* relation to humanity. The theory of an ostensible philosophy of right had blazed the trail. It had kept humanity from having roots in a soil which could have nourished its development, and thus it had conjured up the danger of barrenness in that soil. It had left justice in a merely contingent relation to its soil. For instance, economic interests can pose, in shameless nakedness, as the sole representative of that soil, and they can brazenly claim the ability to give "each what is his" undisturbed by the question what, in truth, is each one's own. To be sure, as long as the state is still fit to do so, it can supervise the economic dealings, it may even regulate them. Yet a state which has yielded to that pernicious theory is no longer filled by the desire for justice which Plato attributed to the sound state. The state now takes for right what it finds useful, and the difference between a state which loudly declares this stand it takes, and the state which tries to hide behind a mask is only slight.

If a nation or a civilization has tolerated the claim of conditional interests in preference to the unconditional demands of justice, it is an unmistakable sign of a cultural decline. A truly human shaping of life can attain its potential height only if the direction is pointed out by the unconditionally valid. In the *Addresses to the German Nation*, Fichte says: "Let us abide by the old criterion of greatness, which tells us that the great is only that which can apprehend ideas and find its inspiration in them, for ideas can bring only good to peoples."[9, d] Let us listen also to a contemporary author. In the beautiful book *Truth and Ideology*, Hans Barth declares: "Human existence is in its origin social existence. This means that what is immediately given, along with man, is the possibility of an order of his social existence. This order is committed to the idea of justice." Man is "the living being which has freedom. . . . His freedom implies the possibility of error and of guilt. But on that very account freedom must be preserved for him. For, every consolidation of whatever formerly was, or now is, taken for true or just, brings about the possibility of making untruth and injustice perennial. Only by moving persistently towards the ideas of justice and truth, as towards fixed stars, can man hope to steer clear of injustice and untruth—or, in case they should have solidified into a system, to overcome them and to replace that system by a new order."[10] Any administration of justice tied to precedents which have been recognized as unjust amounts to a disturbance, even to a destruction, of the basis of the social life of men; central to that basis is the demand of a life worthy of human beings.

One cannot do away with human weakness. Unjust verdicts will be pronounced again and again. Ever since the late Middle Ages, the unjust judge, and especially the venal judge, has furnished the frequent theme for literature and for popular woodcuts and engravings. In a letter dated November 27, 1909, which Leo Tolstoy addressed to a student of law in Petersburg,[11] the judge is described as standing in the service of a wide-stretched net of power which uses high-sounding words in order to hide its real intentions. Tolstoy says that what is called law, "in its relation to those in power, is their self-given permission to force men, over whom they have power, to do what is advantageous for the rulers; but in relation to the subjects what is called law is the permission to do anything they have not been forbidden to do." Tolstoy blames the "empty talk about the law" for having frequently the quite immoral purpose of "justifying the existing evil."

In the final analysis, the "existing evil" rests on the conditions of economic power whose action becomes unrestrained in the measure in which the administration of justice denies the unconditional validity of the idea of the just. Then, with fateful inevitableness, situations will come about such as Karl Marx described in his work *Capital*, in which he gave many illustrations from earlier times and especially from the period of his own life experience. "In line with its own contradictory nature, the capitalist way of production will regard as an economically efficient use of the invested capital the very waste of the life and the health of the worker and the reduction of his standard of life, counting them as a means for increasing profits. . . . Such economies comprise the crowding of workers into narrow unhealthful shops, a procedure called the economy of building investment; the crowding of dangerous machinery into the same narrow spaces, and the neglect of protective measures; the omission of precautionary measures in methods of production which by their very nature endanger health or are physically dangerous, like work in the mines."[12] One who seeks dependable reports on similar cases of capitalistic inhumanity during the last decades may consult the works of Heinrich Zangger.[13, e]

Still, the picture of social conditions drawn by Marx is false in spite of the impressiveness of the material he gathered: in reality injustices are never mere facts which must be accepted as such, since of necessity they also give offense. Such injustices do not simply fit into the social reality as its constitutive elements. Instead they appear as disturbers of the peace, disturbing those structures which are necessary for social reality and which social reality necessarily seeks. The injustices challenge true humanity, they recall into consciousness the idea of the just, and they awaken forces of resistance, forces in which the power of reason is at work, a power which ranges above everything historically conditioned and which purifies the conditions.[14]

The economic basis of human life demands persistent endeavors to keep things up to date, and these endeavors cannot ignore the norms which constitute the human spirit and which furnish the measure for the evaluation of conditions. The relation of these endeavors to the idea of the just is not imposed on them from without, it is inherent in them. Rudolf Stammler declares that justice and economy, "for the social thinker, are two necessarily connected elements of one and the same object." "Law is not a thing existing by itself, in independent contrast to social coexistence, and exerting some kind of influence upon the latter. Every legal norm always implies a regulation of the basic social economy. . . . The commands of law have meaning and content only as means of regulating the human cooperation which makes social life possible."[15] Social life as such is defective if the ruling powers effectively curtail its relation to the idea of the just. On this account injustices are never mere facts, they are always the occasion for the idea of the just to appeal to social conscience and to the forces of freedom in order that they may resist the demands of injustice.

Any theory in social science and any political ideology is inadequate if it neglects the inseparability of social reality and its relation to the idea of the just. Wherever injustice occurs, humanity hears the call to devise and follow ways for overcoming shortcomings in the existing situation. In the year 1948 a Swedish journalist, Birger Lundberg, told of mentioning to a female student in Moscow the fact that in Stockholm almost every workingman's family has its own kitchen. She retorted: "Do not imagine that I believe every fairy tale you tell about your capitalistic country."[16] The young woman had grown up behind the Iron Curtain of communist rule, and dogmatic Marxism had concealed from her, nay, it had denied, the significance which the forces of freedom have in social reality. Therefore she was convinced that, in a "capitalistic country," capitalism rules in the manner described in Marxist books, and that, accordingly, workingmen live most precariously.

Forces of freedom are not activated by causal necessity; they are appealed to. One can never foresee with certainty whether and how the appeal will find a response. If the moral freedom is limited, one may expect that an injustice suffered (even though more is involved than a submission without dignity) will evoke only revenge, and that the successful carrying out of injustice will bring only satisfaction into the limelight of consciousness. For those who understand the corrosive of injustice as it truly is, the task of social pedagogy becomes obvious, and they will endeavor to create a sphere of influence not only among those who suffer passively but also among those who want to "turn the wind-buffeted cloak of injustice inside out" (as Pestalozzi once put it) and those who enjoy the fruits of unjust acts. The hope is that such influence will evoke the awareness of freedom, so that consciousness will admit the truth even if it is discomfited by it and demand the radical change of any existence bound by insensate suffering or by passion.

The idea of the just has reference to the economic basis of

human development. The sheer needs of life will assure that this basis is not neglected. Even the quest of *just* solutions is very often a matter of course, be it only insofar as a group exploiting its predominant power will come up against postulates which may yet set the slowly grinding "mills of God" in motion. After all, every injustice somehow disturbs the coherent structure of social bonds. Nevertheless even the most justly constructed foundation falls short of making human life worth living, for that depends on what the foundation has to support. A life which is human, and human in more than a merely zoological sense, a life which develops above the economic basis which ought to be ordered according to the norms of just law, such a life has its own values, and only these values—the true, the good, the beautiful—through their realization can make human existence free and thus meaningful. In order to see clearly in this matter, one must distinguish between the *objective* attainments with respect to the social order of the basis of life and the *personal* accomplishments in the service of those goals. The personal act of putting oneself at stake belongs to the world of freedom and is subject to the norms of that world. As distinguished from it, the factor which objectively determines the possibilities of the economic sphere is the basis of the life of society and manifests itself in its own domain as coercive power, whether just or unjust. Nevertheless everything which has attained objective form in the foundations of social existence is an appeal to the forces of freedom. The appeal is made to true humanity, as a challenge to exploit the possibilities which lie open to it for the fulfillment of what is human. If the appeal meets with no response, this merely confirms the uncertainty of every undertaking which depends on human freedom. As far as *coercion* is effective there is certainty; but in affairs which call for human solutions any situation is unsatisfactory if it is coerced and if the matter rests there—that is, if the appeal implied in the situation is disregarded.

The ancient wisdom of southern China saw the use of power as wrong in principle. As late as 1930 sinologist Jean Escarra of the University of Paris, reporting in the *Bulletin de la Société de Législation comparée*[17] on the codification of Chinese law then in process, showed the West the low regard in which the coercion of law was still held in China. And even the herald of the "good European" and of the "will for power," Nietzsche, says in his *Zarathrustra*: "It is the most soundless words which bring the storm. Thoughts which come on doves' feet steer the world."[18] Nevertheless a complete renunciation of power is not possible to any administration of justice, and therefore no action serving the idea of the just can renounce power. But history shows profound differences in the use of power, and in a given case it is the way in which power was brought to bear which brings justice into question, although the idea of justice is unconditionally valid. The symbol of Justitia's office is the scales; yet no precise weighing is possible. It is, perhaps, amazing to reflect that, quite usually, the sense of justice accepts without flinching the fact that in the ordinary way punishments are meted out in fairly round numbers. There was the elementary school, for instance, in the good old days, in which petty offenders received two strokes of the rod, serious offenders six, and there was nothing in between. The fact is that exact measures cannot be created for the carrying out of justice; for no criminal can a just degree of punishment be found. Strife has broken out again between Jews and Arabs over Palestine following the Balfour declaration, and no stretch of the imagination could award to both parties, with precision, what is in truth each party's own.[19]

What bestows true meaning on those acts which are meant to serve the idea of justice objectively does not in the least lie within the reach of the objective, within the domain of whatever the use of power as such can attain. The use of power, if it is experienced within the structure of social reality, is a challenge to the forces of freedom, to true humanity. Only if it is understood in this way, as a challenge, and not seen merely as coercion, does the service it renders to the idea of justice become fully a reality. Whenever force is exercised according to the law in service of the idea of justice, it will produce in the one concerned not merely an awareness that he is undergoing coercion but a sense of his obligation to take a free stand. All that matters, so far as success in the service of the idea of the just is concerned, is that the challenged humanity comes to an awareness of itself. In criminal procedure, this awareness is to be invoked in the first place in the penalized culprit, but in the second place in everyone for whom the penalty is meant as a deterrent and everyone who might see in it merely a means of revenge. This is what really matters in the service of the idea of justice. The court should render such assistance to the culprit condemned to imprisonment that he does not ask whether by any chance the court has dictated a term a few days or months too long: the verdict merely projects into the objective realm what is due to the culprit as his deserved fate. The *objective* order demands an exact measure; but the gravity of the guilt is not an objective quantity: there is no true objective measure for it. Any measure written down in the penal code is an expression of the *subjective* judgment of the legislator. The guilty man should accept the burden put upon him and carry it with humility and fortitude. The meaning of the penalty for him lies in the expected victory over the objective burden by his essential humanity. The meaning of punishment is missed if the penalty is so light that it does not impress the penalized one in the depths of his consciousness; it is likewise missed if the penalty is too heavy and therefore crushes the culprit or pushes him into an even more pronounced opposition to society.

For the humane, the notion of penalties being suffered without any recognition of their justice is always painful. So far, at least, as the penalized one is concerned, the recognition is most likely if the penalty meted out is mild; and for the dissatisfied public the court's restraint might be an occasion for reflection. A humanitarian would rather exceed in leniency than in harshness. To his mind, whatever goes beyond what is necessary if humanity's challenge to the culprit is to be heard is cruelty, not punishment. It is for this reason that in the course of the centuries the administration of justice has again and again shortened sentences and abolished cruel punishments. A state which increases the severity of its legal code is certain to meet with the charge of barbarism. Such a state shows contempt for the endeavor to be as just as possible to those who must be punished, imposing penalties which do not exceed the measure of what in truth is due to them. In education too, disciplinary measures have become milder; in particular, corporal punishment, once considered highly effective, has lost its prestige. However, not only punishment but every other device needed for the establishment of a socially satisfactory order has its meaning in the consent given to the challenge addressed to humanity, and that consent is wholly outside the objective domain. Jews and Arabs in Palestine must come to a human consensus.

The relationship of the social order to the idea of justice is immanent in society itself.[20] This implies that all the actions connected with this idea must be understood as challenges to the forces of freedom, even if such actions are unjust—whether it is that human weakness makes men unequal to their task or that power is in the hands of the unworthy, who wantonly or hypocritically make a travesty of justice in the administration of its forms. Even the unjust act is held fast by that supersensuous order within which, as Fichte observes profoundly, the moral action infallibly succeeds while the immoral action fails.[21] The moral order makes it fail necessarily by converting unjust acts into appeals to the responsible will; thus even the unjust action is given its positive relation to the meaning of life. Of course, one who disregards the appeal made to him by the supersensuous order loses, in his own person, the proffered possibility of meaningful freedom. He may find an unreal substitute, or perhaps even a harsher servitude when the unworthy wielders of power bestow their favors on him. Wherever there is freedom, there is also the freedom to do evil. As long as the refusal to acknowledge the meaning of the appeal which issues from the depths of our being prevails among mankind, the appeal remains hidden. The meaning of human existence rises above the instability which puts all in doubt only insofar as the supertemporal values which proclaim that meaning are embraced in personal convictions and given form, in harmony with the possibilities of the time, by acts which bear witness to the humanity of man—in Pestalozzi's words, "proofholding humanity" (*probhaltender Menschlichkeit*).[22]

3

CONCERNING INJUSTICE AND THE RESISTANCE TO IT

Where unjust demands are made in the name of the power which sustains the social order, people are wont to regard obedience to such demands as of moral necessity. Molière has his Don Juan say, "All fashionable vices pass for virtues." Nevertheless one can read in Hofmannsthal (and similarly already in Aquinas[1]): "Man is a measure and is himself measured." Insofar as man is a measure it is always open to question, never the final norm, for he does not possess himself. His humanity belongs to the structure of reason—that reason which holds him fast and directs him endlessly beyond himself. He is measured by the standard of reason.

The words in which unjust demands are expressed command actions which are irreconcilable with true humanity; actions which involve a failure to accept the very reality in which they are to become operative for what it actually is. To act in these ways is incompatible with man's quest for personal integrity. Only a concern with the supersensuous order is compatible with man's humanity; that concern is the ontological truth. Thus fidelity to man's quest means the response to a call from the forces of freedom, a call which makes itself heard above the sound of those words, demanding resistance to unjust activity. One who offers himself as a means to ends against which humanity must revolt dishonors the autonomy of his moral consciousness. And since everyone bears his responsibility not as an isolated individual but, in his individual situation, as a member of the community, his duty transcends his individuality, extending to his total sphere of influence in society. If a man rendered influential by a high position acts inhumanly, the effect is detrimental to the trust which men place in what is right and in the dignity of human nature. The servility of an officer towards his superior leads those who depend on him for orders into deep insecurity and a torment of temptation. Among them his undignified submission becomes a natural motive for the surrender of their own conscience.

The idea of humanity has a supertemporal dignity. In the changes of history, it calls forth the forces of freedom with demands which are constantly becoming better defined and constantly increasing. Yet the forces of freedom can never conform to the idea with finality. Society makes the demands of humanity its own only in the measure in which the conditions of the historical situation are favorable to them. The effort to turn commandments of absolute purity into legal codes and enforce them in the social order is bound to fail.[2] For it will meet with the resistance of the power which thrives in the "fashionable vices" and can never be disregarded in matters of statecraft. Politics is the art of the possible, not of the human in its purity, not of the good in the unrestricted sense. In the year 1254 Louis IX of France—St. Louis—sought to eradicate prostitution: he succeeded only in increasing the evil.[3] Further examples, in the same field or in others, are not lacking, even to our own day. What can be done is this: one who manages to attain in his own person freedom from the disheartening stress of the circumstances under which he lives can show by his example that circumstances do not bind anyone who does not consent to be bound. Thus an individual can furnish an impressive model of life which may exercise a purifying influence on the conditions of society, especially if his collision with the historical limitations of the "world" brings him the most severe suffering, and in this very suffering the opportunity to prove himself. He becomes a saint, a martyr; his sacrifice has the deepest and most enduring significance. However, it has true significance only in those cases when the acceptance of a harsh—indeed of the harshest—fate is of strict necessity in accordance with a personal striving for integrity. The call to martyrdom belongs only to the man who would otherwise betray the mission which constitutes his very personality; one for whom the refusal of martyrdom would mean self-abdication. If his decision to step out of the framework of the historical situation were to issue from individual self-will, it would be vain and capricious. The decision must be made by one who is unable to do otherwise.

According to ancient tradition, Buddha decreed, from a deep insight, that only one who has no longer any worldly ties may be ordained a monk. Among the questions addressed to the postulant before ordination are the following: "Are you your own master? Do you owe anything to anybody? Are you free with respect to royal service? Do you have the permission of your father and mother?"[4] The secular life calls for taking into account the limitations within which the superhistorical idea of humanity is realized in the world which surrounds one. This does not in the least mean that one must behave as if he were nothing but a product of those limitations; the situation in which each individual finds himself amounts to an invitation to him to take responsibility for his era's attainment of the possible height of the time. And he can give this responsibility its due only if he endeavors to make a correct evaluation of the possibilities which actually lie within his province. In the conduct of his own life, his conscience is to rule relentlessly. If the demands he makes on his own humanity are higher and more rigorous than the culture of his time would require, these demands are *valid* for him. But the demands he makes on others' conduct of life must take into consideration, with intelligent love, those weaknesses which are the weaknesses of the age. In every true community love is the bond. To understand community and to fulfill its tasks is possible only on condition that love brings one's personality into harmony with itself.[5]

War as such is a denial of humanity. One who has made the decision to step in protest out of the objectionable framework of historically conditioned life cannot possibly enlist in a war without betraying his decision. Buddha, Jesus of Nazareth, Francis of Assisi—they simply could not have been soldiers. Nevertheless the historical conditions of human existence have again and again made going to war an inescapable duty. But it is a duty only for those who find the goals of their activity within the historical situation as such. If a monk takes up arms to defend his fatherland, he shows that he is still tied to the historically conditioned shortcomings of his century: the goal of his will is not yet detached from them. The bearing of arms can be a solemn duty for the citizens; but it is one which involves the task of changing the conditions within which alone this duty is possible. When the monk takes vows he separates himself from those conditions of his time; from the moment of his vows he should be beyond them. (If the state does not permit the monk to abstain from military service, it means that in the state's laws the secular order is making totalitarian claims.) But even the monk ought to understand the historically conditioned necessity to bear arms. Under certain conditions the monk has the obligation of encouraging a fellow man made reluctant by cowardice, of explaining to him why the citizen capable of bearing arms must respond to the call of the fatherland. However, this fatherland belongs to the world and to its secular history. When the fatherland issues a call to go out and kill, the fact that it is inescapably bound up with the imperfection of all that is historically conditioned emerges with painful clarity. One who lives his life under the conditions of history and for historical goals determined by those conditions may not withdraw from the duties which the historical hour imposes—the hour in which the fatherland can defend itself only with inhuman means against the inhumanity of an oppressor.

Historical necessity forces the fatherland to share in the inhuman characteristics of the "world." For the monk these inhuman characteristics have become an object, something he recognizes as existing outside himself. For the citizen this sharing is not an object; it is fate, which confronts him in the immediacy of his self-identity as a citizen. Nothing which concerns the destiny of the fatherland can remain external to the citizen. If, as Fichte said in his lectures *Concerning the Concept of True War*, "the freedom and independence of the nation are attacked, if the movement of the nation's development is interrupted by some outside power, if the nation is in danger of being absorbed by an expanding foreign empire, or if, as the result of this absorption, the nation's own empire is to be destroyed—or even all law is to be destroyed—"[6] then the defense of the threatened historical life becomes a valid demand upon those for whom the very meaning of existence consists in collaboration in the historical tasks of the community of which the individuals are members.

But not every war is a "true war," and many a war is just only for one of the two parties. When a nation is called upon to use outlawed weapons, then that nation would have had the duty, even in advance, to refuse obedience to those who would exact from it the employment of such unjust means. But perhaps the nation has been blind to the possibility of such a refusal; perhaps demonic powers[a] have compelled the nation's obedience; and perhaps the collective guilt reaches even beyond this nation, drawing other nations into its vortex.

Be that as it may, whenever demonic powers claim recognition, evil temptations attack the substance of community life as it has already been attained. And then only a resistance at any cost can save the soul. If the historical situation is abandoned to these evil temptations, it is exposed to decay. The agents of the decay will call the obedience they demand "duty," they will claim that it is the law. But to obey them means to surrender the possibility of being at one with oneself. That "community" for which such obedience is claimed should not exist at all. Whoever recognizes that it should not exist—and the recognition can only spring from the depths of man's being, only from the vision of real love— hears at the same time the call from the realm of truth, the call to reject the ostensible "duties" which the service of the demons would demand of him.

An opinion has been current that the demands of the state are binding on the individual even if the state summons him to participation in an unjust war. Coupled with this opinion was the view that an individual would remain morally uncompromised if, recognizing the injustice as injustice, he rejected the victorious conclusion of the war as any part of his personal aims in participating in it and omitted any effort which would go beyond the immediate commands he received from the state.[7] This opinion would make it appear that the soul of a man can retain its purity while his hands are doing the devil's work. It would offer the individual the comfort of denying his guilt of participation in unjust actions. And one would gladly permit such comfort to those who seek it, since when the demons are in power those who are bound to the historical situation cannot attain to the height of their time: to have resisted these uncanny forces would have required the strength of a martyr. Nevertheless one who would be willing to keep his own soul, his innermost will, from having the decisive word with regard to his conduct remains a house divided against itself. And this kind of existence, divided against itself, will always evoke our doubt as to the credibility of argumentation presented by that opinion. Hofmannsthal puts in the mouth of the governor of the tower the words, "I am an instrument, nothing else." But this endeavor of the governor to justify himself is rejected by the physician, who says, "Thus speaks the body; but the spirit knows its guilt."[b] The human spirit is in duty bound to truth, and if in a given state it is no longer able to recognize the "true" state, then the actual state's commands are no longer orders for it.[8] Nor are the state's commands orders for the body in which the spirit lives.

Our intention is not to oppose the objective existence of the state by mere subjective whim, nor to claim the superiority of a "jurisdiction of the individual" over the possible outward existence of the state. On the contrary, what is to be shown is the limit at which the actual historical (and therefore always imperfect) state ceases to be a "true state," owing to the time-conditioned limitations of the existing state. The limit must be shown beyond which the state no longer has any "true" claim to obedience. The existing state, wherever it finds resistance within its boundaries, will attack this resistance with the means of power at its disposal. And those who rise against the existing state know that their behavior is dangerous for themselves. But power and danger never have any role in the decision about what is right and what is the truth. *It is humanity in its fullness of being, as present in the consciousness of a culture,* which determines the limit beyond which no state may retrogress without making it inevitable that those for whom the truth has clearly become the indispensable condition of a life worth living will turn away from the state. If a state which does not respect humanity, nor through humanity respect truth, if such an untrue state issues orders for its own purposes, then the very sacredness of the spirit prohibits man from delivering himself to the state as its instrument. Demonic powers never have any legitimate claim to dominion. If an inhuman, an untrue, state could really be shaken to its foundations by the refusal of obedience to it, and thus be brought to its downfall, this would be the very best thing that could happen. Jacob Burckhardt has said, "The blessing of a state consists in this: that the state is the shield of right."[9] If a state has ceased to be such a shield, not owing to temporary confusion but owing to inhumanity in principle, then it can produce no blessings but only curses which are not even limited to those who are its subjects. The fight against the state, the fight against a lying deformation in which the very idea of a state is dishonored, becomes a necessary task, a task in the first place for those whom the state would dominate, but also a task for the community of nations, particularly if the subjects of such a state are too weak to act on their own. Wherever humanity itself is attacked, no so-called "internal affairs" can justify the state's claim to enforce its goals without interference. For the state it is a command of justice to protect the personality of each individual—for instance, to withdraw the paternal power from parents who treat their own child in an inhuman way. Similarly, it is a command of justice for the *community of nations* to recognize the fostering of humanity as the very task which establishes the community and, therefore, to protect humanity if any given state is incapable of protecting it or is actually and explicitly injuring it. Then the community of nations has the duty of entering into the lists for the sake of protecting humanity.

Schelling taught us to understand the state as "the basis, the hypothesis, the transition point" of the development of humanity which leads beyond the state and beyond the individual. "If one considers that most men show but little affection for duty, then the fact that the state from outside demands our observance of the law appears very beneficial. Yet this does not suffice. Nobody belongs to the state, but everybody unconditionally belongs to the moral law."[10] "To set the state above all else means to show the servility of one's own attitude."[11] The opinion that the state is higher than man is not only of recent date; it already existed in the ancient world. The end of the ancient era was in sight when Christianity announced the non-finite value of the human soul and placed its home, its πολίτευμα, in the heavens.[12] The ancient tradition, thus interrupted, was resumed by the Renaissance. Machiavelli wrote his *Discorsi sopra la prima deca di Tito Livio* in order to reawaken the *antica virtù*. His glorification of the power of the state has become a temptation for many. The temptation was followed by the coercion exercised by the state, even to the point of shrewdly organizing the complicity in which a criminal government unites itself with its own nation.

In Pestalozzi's *Inquiries* of 1797 one section bears the title, "Rebellion Is Never Right." However, Pestalozzi sees the "causes" for rebellion only in the passive suffering of what is unjust, a suffering which one should bear in moral superiority. It is beyond the range of Pestalozzi's vision that those who govern could force the people into active participation in injustice, and that rebellion might spring from this coercion and perhaps ought to spring from it; rebellion which would in that case result not in "the liberation of wild instinct,"[13] but in the moral self-defense of an independent conscience. Historically, it was the military draft, the imposition on citizens of the duty of universal service, which first created the conditions for that kind of extension of state power. Yet even in the time of Pestalozzi, who saw that dangers are inseparably connected with the very essence of the state, these dangers were great enough to make the fight against them a moral necessity for him, just because he was filled with a patriotism which was humanly pure. He conducted this fight with strong words, words which nevertheless gave due importance to the inevitable tragic events connected with the government of the state. "Owing to its very essence, every form of government always sways between the selfish demands of our animal nature and the pure service of the public needs and the public will. Therefore, all governments are of value only insofar as they bring about the ascendancy of the pure will to minister to public needs over the animal claim to power, no matter in whose hands governments are."[14] "The state may make ever greater demands. The spirit of the age and the force of circumstances may compel the state to sever the ties of blood and the benevolent relationships of all men who are close to each other. The age may force the state to let the citizens feel the full severity of the state's power, so that the citizen may feel that he exists for the sake of the state and not for his own sake, and that his right is powerless when confronted by any demands made by those in power. The greater these demands of the state, the more the administration will undermine the very frame of mind which is essential to the inner nobility of the citizen. Therefore, the morality of a nation is always a consequence of the wisdom of the legislator, a wisdom which can be more or less profound and which would subject selfishness to benevolence and power to right."[15] Thus wrote Pestalozzi in his *Inquiries*. No less impressively did he say these things again in the ardent work of 1815, *To Innocence, to the Seriousness and to the Magnanimity of My Age and My Fatherland*, an essay challenging man to fight for the freedom of personal conscience and against the sinister demands of a "collective existence" of mankind.[16]

Five years later, in 1820, this essay was printed a second time. Soon after, there appeared in print a book which gave the strongest and most seductive systematic foundation for the subjection of the individual under the state, Hegel's *Foundations of the Philosophy of Right*. When the aged Schelling wrote the sentences quoted above [notes 10 and 11 of this chapter] he had long since read §258 in Hegel's book, a paragraph whose first section declared: "The state is the reality of the substantial *will*. It has this reality in any particular *self-awareness* raised to its own universality. Thus the state is what is reasonable in itself and for itself. This substantial unity is an absolute unmoving end in itself, in which freedom attains its highest right; likewise this end in itself has the highest right over the individual, whose *highest duty* it is to be a member of the state." In Hegel's view this unconditional surrender of the individual to the state has its basis in ontological truth. In §268 Hegel says: "A merely subjective certainty does not spring from *truth*, and is only an opinion. The political *frame of mind, patriotism* as such, being the certainty which has its stand in *truth*, and the will which has become *habit*, is only the result of the institutions existing in the state. Thus what is reasonable (*die Vernünftigkeit*) is *really* present in the institutions of the state, and it obtains its activation in actions which are in line with the state institutions." This means that the truth of the state must become the truth of the individual; for the individual on this earth the possibility of essential, substantial life exists only through the state.

To be sure, Hegel does not neglect to point out (§270) that the state "transcends into a higher sphere in which it has its true basis," namely into *religion* in which the state attains "for consciousness the highest verification and the highest obligation." "The state is divine will. It is the presence of the *spirit* which *unfolds itself* in a real manifestation and in the *organization of a world.*" According to Hegel the legitimate limits of the active power of the state are reached only where the supermundane demands its rights. Hegel himself has seen the seriousness of the demands religion makes upon the state, and he has called it, "the enormous transition of the inner into the outer." He has understood it as the very own work of world history in the making. Yet we need not be amazed when we find an echo of Hegel's glorification of the state in an essay on the doctrine of Fascism signed by Benito Mussolini in Volume 14 of the *Enciclopedia Italiana*.

The question arises: dare man let the state assign to him his "highest duty"? Hegel subjects the state to religion. But for the state this subjection is only a "postulate" (*Forderung*)! "As intuition, as feeling, as imaginative knowledge which occupies itself with God as the unlimited basis and as the cause from which everything depends, religion contains the postulate that everything be conceived in this relationship and that everything attain its own confirmation, its justification and validation in this relationship."[17] It is left to the state to decide whether and how it is to fulfill the postulate of religion. If the individual allows the state as such to determine his duties, then the individual exposes himself to the danger that his "trust" in the state, which Hegel demands (§268) will mislead him and that he will lose (to put it in terms of the Gospel of John, 5:44) the honor which belongs to God alone—and therewith the very possibility of being at one with himself. If the state which exists in fact desires to degrade the individual to a mere instrument, may the individual then appeal to that state which takes seriously the postulate that its very existence is permeated with the demands of religion, the demands of pure humanity? And if words are mere sound which dies away, may the appeal then break forth in actions? If these questions were answered affirmatively, then *the right to resist the state* would be recognized, the right which would become significant whenever the state disregarded its supermundane "basis." (The National Socialist state flagrantly disregarded this basis, in spite of the fact that in item 24 of the "unalterable" party program, the basis had been sanctioned explicitly: "The party as such represents the standpoint of a positive Christianity.") But it was very far from Hegel's intention to admit the right of resistance. In this respect Hegel did not go beyond the stand of Kant, who had said, in his doctrine of right, which appeared in the same year as Pestalozzi's *Inquiries* of 1797: "The *idea* of a state constitution which is simultaneously an absolute command given to every nation by a practical reason which judges according to concepts of right is *holy* and irresistible. And although the organization of a state as such has inherent flaws, yet no subaltern power in the state can oppose active resistance to the legislative sovereign of the state. But any inherent defects must gradually be corrected by reforms which the state performs on itself."[18]

During the time which has elapsed since the days of Kant and Hegel, painful events have deeply shaken the metaphysical optimism which would concede to the existing states the right over the life, property and powers of its inhabitants, a right which was supposed to be recognized under all circumstances. Kant and Hegel restrained the incumbents of state power with uncomfortable postulates. But these postulates have seldom been mentioned, even in political ideologies, since Nietzsche intoned his paeans to the will for power. Unmasked power finds its worshippers, and the religion which gives great powers their "basis" is only too often the religion of force. "The religion of force is surely a very seductive religion," says Edouard Claparède in the posthumous book whose bitterly true title is *Morals and Politics, or the Holiday of Probity*.[19] Since modern states have begun to demand that they be not judged according to the moral standards pertinent to the life of citizens, since they have declared that they must and dare stand above morality—declarations expressed in many statements by their responsible representatives—they have given the lie to that "trust" which, according to Hegel, should bind the intentions of the individual to the state. J. Huizinga, the great Dutch historian of culture, has spoken about the "moral, or rather the immoral autonomy of the state," and he has declared: "The pretension that the state could oblige its citizens to unconditional faithfulness and obedience, finds its limit on the one hand in conscience, but equally well, on the other hand, in the very egoism of human nature."[20] To be sure, the state cannot afford to renounce trust and faith altogether; such a renunciation would make it impossible for the state to exist. But of this Huizinga says: "The state is a being which, given the imperfection of human affairs, will behave with an apparent necessity under norms, norms which, however, are not those of a social morality which rests on trust, not to mention the norms of Christian faith. Nevertheless, the state may never entirely lose sight of the Christian and the social norm of morality, lest its own apostasy bring upon it the punishment of destruction."[21] But there is no longer any ideological mask which would permit the state the deception of claiming that moral, nay that religious, dignity which is the indispensable presupposition for the rejection on principle of every right to resistance.

Even in a man whose character has sunk very low, we still respect the fact that he is a man. It is still his task to ponder the demands which are addressed to him. As long as he knows himself as an I, it is his task to be himself, to strive for the idea of man. Should we not give a similar credit to the state? Does not the state retain its relationship to high demands, as Kant and Hegel have formulated them? This may be admitted. Croce has said concerning the state, that it is nothing else than "man in his practical activity."[22] However, a man who does not himself have a due regard for his honor is given little honor. And under certain conditions the honor paid to him will be paid in a way which shows up his insufficiency. Wherever a penal process endeavors to ascertain the just penalty for the accused, there, as Hegel has impressively shown, the accused "is *honored* as capable of reasoning."[23] The very penal process would try to make the accused aware of his dignity, and try it precisely by turning against his actual behavior. The honor paid to the accused does not protect him against the procedure of the community of law which is bringing him to justice; nay which, if necessary, would dispose of him. Similarly, the recognition of a right of resistance to the state cannot mean that respect be refused to the "idea of a state constitution as such." However, if that which poses as a realization of such a constitution resists the necessary demands which would spring from the constitution, then its claim to sacredness, its claim to be "a reality of the moral idea," is empty.[24]

In line with the spirit of Hegel, Adolfo Ravà declared that the state has a value in itself, a value as final purpose, not as mere means, a moral value ("un valore per sè, un valore di fine e non di mezzo, un valore etico e morale"), and that this value is based fundamentally on the state's historical mission; the realization of ethics is attained in history.[25] But what will become of the "reality of the moral idea" if the state endeavors to lower the tone of the moral life? if the state leads the education of children forcefully into paths of brutality, of inhumanity? This kind of state can be only the possessor of superior power in its relation to individual man. Man, however, is an autonomous subject of moral necessity. As such he has dignity, and this dignity demands of man's behavior that it reflect the unconditional. Man may not surrender this dignity to any power. The dignity determines his relation even to God, because it renders any divine service offered to a Power who would act by arbitrary whim impossible. All the more does human dignity call for defense wherever the state would use man as a mere instrument. Jurisconsults subservient to the power actually in control always want to confuse moral sentiments by means of artificial formulations. With regard to such artifice Kant's pronouncement is valid: "One need not have systematic knowledge and philosophy in order to be honest; nay, in order to be wise and virtuous."[26]

Schelling says with regard to the individual personality that it "transcends the state."[27] This formulation recalls a comment which Fichte had published as early as 1797: "Humanity sets itself apart from the nature of the citizen (that is, from the citizen's performance which he owes to the state) in order to rise in absolute freedom to morality. However, this occurs only insofar as the way of man leads him through the state,"[28] that is, insofar as man makes use of the state without being unconditionally subject to it. In Fichte's lectures of 1812 on the *Doctrine of Right* the significant phrase is repeated: "Every man's way leads through the state, yet man is not absorbed by the state."[29] The necessity of the state is acknowledged. In Fichte's lectures of 1805 he could be heard to say that the establishment of the state has its ground "in the divine idea."[30] But for Fichte the state lacks the totalitarian character which Hegel attributes to it in saying, "Since the state is objective spirit the individual himself has objectivity, truth and morality only insofar as he is a member of the state."[31] For Fichte the state is not an end in itself, but (as the *Addresses to the German Nation* explain) is "merely the means for the higher end of the formation of whatever is purely human in the nation."[32] Therefore, man may not sacrifice himself for the state but must sacrifice himself for the purely human end of the state. This, the superhistorical idea of freedom, is worth more than he, the individual, and measured against the demands of human dignity, the individual is ever so imperfect. He who loses his life in a just war dies for an end of the state for the fulfillment of which the state itself is only a necessary means. However, if a state sets up goals for itself which are inimical to the formation of the purely human, then that state loses its claim to recognition and allegiance. The state does not prove its right by its "legal form" but by its "last end," which is moral freedom.[33] The state manifests the fact that it serves this last end "by institutions for the formation of all toward freedom, toward man's ability to have as the first ground and origin of his actions his own will, a will to set for himself ends which go beyond the state." The state cannot manifest its last end "by any institutions of sheer training for mere skill, for mere agility, or for merely being tools of a foreign will. A despot and tyrant would turn man into his tool, but the state would form him" for freedom.[34] Thus Fichte in his Berlin lectures of 1812 on the doctrine of right. And in lectures given in 1813 Fichte speaks yet more distinctly about the freedom which must be granted to all men, as the end of every state constitution. "Everyone shall obey only God, according to his own clear insight into the will of God regarding him. And insofar as he should nevertheless obey another man, he shall do so only owing to his clear insight that, for him, the other man's voice is not the call of man but of God. Every power over the will of man other than the power of the conscience of each shall be invalid."[35]

The danger that man, and particularly the man of our time,

might be absorbed by the state is certainly not inconsiderable. In his *Zarathustra*, Nietzsche (although in the chapter "About the New Idol" he presents only a one-sided caricature of the state) names, as the "sign of the State," "confusion of tongues of the good and evil"; and (in the chapter "About Great Events") he says, "The state simply wants to be the most important animal on earth." One can hardly deny this. In comforting contrast to the modern tendency to sacrifice man to the state we find the challenge of Montaigne: "Every man must have sworn unto himself what the kings of Egypt solemnly let their judges swear: to obey no order against conscience, even if the order come from the kings themselves."[36]

4
CONCERNING HUMANITY AND INHUMAN "DUTIES"

On the 25th of January, 1851, King Maximilian II of Bavaria wrote to his old teacher and "honored friend," Schelling, that he was of a mind to make use of the money available beyond his private needs not, like his father, for the "strong promotion of art," but rather, in line with the needs of the time, for "a charitableness as comprehensive as possible" in order to "counteract therewith the very origin and the consequences of the real proletariat." He asked for Schelling's advice. And in a letter of the 15th of February, Schelling recommended the establishment of "asylums for children." Schelling says he is very much pleased with the king's intention to emerge in "his pure personality, from the abstract status of the chief of state." Schelling's letter praises the royal prerogative to forgive and to pardon and to adjust, from the hidden depths of humanity, whatever is unsatisfactory in a "state mechanism which is ruthless and is concerned only with what is general and with things in the round."[1] When we evaluate the praise which Schelling bestows upon monarchy, we must keep in mind the juridical conditions in the German lands of that time, and we must also remember the special relationship of trust which prevailed between the addressee and writer of these letters. Should we abstract from these conditions, then the privilege of the monarchy which Schelling praises would be no more than a proper "postulate"[2] whose worthy human fulfillment would be threatened by all the unpleasantnesses of a personal government. Schelling had in mind the conditions of his time when he praised the monarchic form of the state as a royal distinction which puts a personal duty upon the king who, as crown prince, had been under Schelling's guidance. (In public lectures Schelling presented similar views.) His term "state mechanism," however, points to the superhistorical problematicity of the state, to the insufficiency of everything that can be attained through legal order and through economic relationships. These relationships do call for concern. However, humanity thrives only where life has discovered that its foundation alone lies in these relations, and that one must look above the foundation for whatever ennobles humanity.[3] Therefore, in another letter addressed to the king,[4] Schelling declares very explicitly that the "directing of all thoughts exclusively upon the state" cannot but be disastrous for humanity. Humanity never finds its end in the state even though it has often sought it there. Such a search would lead men to accept and treat as an end what can be only a means. Men would not take the state for what it is in truth. Blinded by the splendor of the state's development of power, they would overrate the state. Instead, we should take note of the unconditionality with which our truly human desire resists every restriction which could limit our human possibilities. This human desire is to be superior to everything by means of which nature and society would tend to prescribe the ways in which we seek to give shape to our existence. More precisely speaking, human desire resists every restriction of which it has become aware; fetters it is not aware of it will bear, although not always with ease, without open resistance. In order to attain its ends, human desire needs history. In the historical process it obtains new possibilities. Yet though given, these possibilities are not necessarily recognized as such. They must always be explicitly discovered first, and those who discover them must make clear to their contemporaries the true significance of these possibilities, a significance which alone can amount to an obligation. Sometimes it takes harsh and painful striving to bring this about. Wherever true possibilities are discovered, they make demands upon man's humanity, and humanity cannot afford to let the state frustrate these needs. On the contrary, humanity must make every endeavor to teach the state that it has true dignity only in the measure in which, as a true state, it endeavors to assure for mankind the conditions of effective development. With regard to the state, Jonas Cohn says: "Power obtains its significance not from itself but from the whole of that life whose power it is, and from the ends which such a power then makes its own."[5]

The true dignity of the state must not be confused with its prestige. Prestige has its significance exclusively in the territory of politics—in relation to its own citizens or subjects, and above all in relation to other states. It is a relative value, it refers to changing circumstances, and it depends primarily on the shrewdness and the diplomatic skill of the government. In contrast, true dignity depends primarily on moral forces—on the seriousness with which the state endeavors to fulfill its essential task—the task of creating the prerequisites for a *human* formation of life. The state, as a state, cannot bestow dignity upon itself; it can only receive dignity by becoming a basis for a worthwhile human life. It is to furnish the ground in which human freedom and greatness can grow, and dignity falls to the lot of the state only if human freedom does not need to wrest from the state the conditions of its growth, and therefore does not find itself at odds with the state, but on the contrary finds the state willing to offer to human freedom those juridical and economic possibilities which further its growth. The state must not want to impose itself as an end in itself. The duty of the state to be a basis for humanity is valid with superhistorical unconditionality. The task is always a particular task, but always and everywhere the task requires of the state that it maintain itself at the height of the time—that it offer to humanity the best possible conditions at that particular time.

In its relations to the individual, the state stands as an independent power which claims him for its purposes. Yet the state has no existence by itself. Human beings are the medium in which and through which the state must exist—human beings subject to the challenge of humanity. Now it is possible for an individual man to sacrifice the absolute value of his human dignity for the sake of some relative advantage and thus to be unfaithful to his true task. Similarly, the state can let its true dignity sink down to the level of an empty postulate.[6] In such a case the state, like the individual, will treat the supertemporal ideas as if they were objects and make use of them, as far as possible, as means for its purposes. It will endeavor to dominate the realm of ideas and will try to restrain them within political limits. Thus the state may not permit freedom for scientific research. On principle, within its jurisdiction, such a state will leave the truths of the intellect undisturbed only insofar as they are not politically dangerous. And since the posture of such a state is false and inhuman, the state becomes suspicious, and so may see dangers even where there are none. Consequently it has secrets, and makes an effort to guard them even when such affairs have become quite transparent. It will forbid those officeholders who know the secrets to appear in court as witnesses—and will thus force the judges to make decisions against which they would cry out could they judge by their private insight. The state will impose its own purposes as the supreme law to guide the duty of its officials, who are not supposed to question the legitimacy of the state's purposes. The same thing goes for the sense of duty of soldiers, who can no longer be at home in the free sphere of independent conscience. The state will even try to keep the general catechism of morals in line with its own purposes. In order to enhance its own sway, the state will define new crimes, on the one hand, and on the other hand enforce actions which weigh heavily on the human conscience. For it is not the idea of what is true but the interests of the state's false way of life which determine such transformations in the values men are supposed to acknowledge. Even art will be made subject to the intentions of the state and will be shorn of some of its rights if these rights are not acceptable to those in power. In the whole realm of jurisdiction, the idea of what is just is given a place only insofar as it can be subjected to, and made part of, the plans of those who are in control of the state. In line with a decreasing tolerance for any development of life independent of the state, and with an increasing development of totalitarianism, there is a decrease in the possibilities for lawsuits whose decisions are not predetermined by the interests of the state. The supertemporal ideas themselves are managed. They are tools for the attainment of limited goals. They are no longer giving direction to the fight for free humanity. To be sure, the ideas still have power over human minds because it is impossible to live without the distinction between values, distinctions by means of which "reason has us."[a] The state is well aware of this power of ideas over minds, even over minds already exposed to unceasing deterioration. And the men in control of the state will make use of this power of ideas as a means towards their ends. The state must use threats whose effect is that weak minds will expect the powers that be to furnish authoritative interpretations of the very demands of conscience. The "existential" interest of the state claims dominion over the "merely" ideal values; the state determines the meaning and the limits of the values. An "idealism" which would attribute unconditionality to the values is mocked as unrealistic or, in case such idealism should seem to become spiritual power, is denounced as dangerous. (A theology confined by superstitious bias will go along timidly and will furnish an abettor's strange services, since such a theology, too, must fear the "truth that makes free" [John 8:32].)

In every age a public opinion which has lost its dignity has come to terms with imposed conditions under which alone the age tolerates faith in the true, the good, the beautiful. Martin Buber notes, quoting from chassidic literature: "The Israelites' exile in Egypt became in truth an exile in their having learned to bear it."[7] True, so far as historical reality is concerned, all that has been said about state totalitarianism refers without qualification only to extreme cases. Nevertheless all states until now have restricted freedom of conscience to some extent, necessarily perhaps. Even nowadays humanness is not yet much more than an abstraction in the theoretical domain and a postulate for the practical domain. It is still always possible for a state to foster its own time-conditioned interests by means of patent inhumanity without bringing upon itself any effective interference from other states. It is still always possible that an apostasy from the eternally valid—an apostasy thinly veiled in ideology, or not veiled at all—will strive for a time-conditioned splendor and gain the enthusiastic applause of the masses. This splendor is a deception because it has no basis in the ontological reality of this particular state—what it really is, the stunted kind of life it affords. And those who are not securely anchored in the truth are in fact being deceived. A state like this, deceptive and deceiving, will project an unlimited duration for its prestige: a long duration substitutes for eternity. Hence the proclamation of a "millennial rule."[b] And if the state we refer to had actually lasted for a thousand years, then for that length of time the life of its inhabitants would have been forcibly polluted with untruth and inhumanity.

Humanity can develop freely only on a foundation which has no built-in fetters to restrain the powers of body or mind. Truth can be experienced and known only in freedom. But wherever "freely acting beings"[8] live in mutual relationships—and only thus is a really human life possible—a collision of wills with different goals is inevitable. If the consequent strife is not to lead to the dissolution of the community, or even pose a constant threat to the community's life, an organization must exist having the power and authority to keep order among the juridical and economic relations prevailing in the territory of this society. This organization—the state—has for its end the development of the humanity of the community, of "the life of the spirit" (in Fichte's words, already quoted from his *Addresses to the German Nation*). All that is human—even what may be characterized as all-too-human—takes form in history, and is determined by the spirit, either actually or through the demand which relates what is human to the spirit, so that that which is human in ontological reality can be understood only from that relation. The state, too, must serve the spirit—and not only with police functions. The state exacts positive accomplishments from the inhabitants of its territory, and in a large measure their work will benefit only a time when those who have performed it will no longer be living. Thus the state assists in the education of its citizens (or subjects), helping them to understand their existence as historical. Within the wide horizon of the community which looks for an unlimited duration, the state makes demands which recall to the minds of all that they are not living for their own sake or the sake of their close relations alone.

This significance which the state has for the formation of what is human gives it its legitimate claim to dignity, a claim to which it holds fast. And the state substantiates the claim by carrying out its undertakings in the manner of a genuinely human institution.

Nevertheless, difficulties will arise in the state, pressures from within and from without which will often prevent it from doing what it would want to do and should do. Its measures can be taken, not freely but in dependence upon the political constellation. Hence the great task of the state cannot be perfectly accomplished; the state must be content with doing it as well as possible. All too often some misfortune forces the state into taking legal measures which bring those subject to the law into conflict with the demands of conscience. Pestalozzi, who recognized this, writes impressively: "Quite apart from external conditions, which may be better or worse, there are evils in the state as such, so intimately connected with its essence that one must consider them as very nearly perennial. The collective existence of our human kind implies in its very nature exigencies which are forever in conflict with the higher views of human nature and its essential destiny. Every state community has the seed of this contradiction within itself. In every instance of a collision of the collective existence of our kind with the existence of the individual, the state must put the former above the latter, and it must recognize this preference as a rule of its own behavior, as its law. Therefore the state must in every such case elevate what is unholy in our common nature above what is holy and divine in our individual inner essence. . . . No wisdom in legislation, no constitution, can fully eliminate the consequent inner weakening of a morality whose strength alone can fully satisfy human nature."[9]

Modern states are forced to draft men for military service. And under circumstances which tolerate no evasion, military service always implies the inhuman "duty" of being ready to kill other people. This is a clear example of the inhumanity which is inevitable in our states and hence in our human existence. As long as conscience preserves its voice, even when confronted with the inevitable and even when living with the inevitable, conscience cannot accept the inhumanity without resistance. Jean-Paul Sartre speaks of dirty hands—*les mains sales*—and dirty hands must be granted to those who would undertake the concrete tasks which our duty imposes on us in a dirty world. Yet conscience must relentlessly condemn dirty hands. The awareness of the sacredness of supertemporal values, of unshakeable truth, is obscured if one is seduced by the temptation to believe that it is morally permissible in time of war—indeed, that it is good—to use weapons which bring death to other men. It is *not* good; and even the greatest perils cannot *empower the state to decide between good and evil*.[10] Yet a man does not have the choice of remaining free of guilt—and therefore one who believes that God was made man must trust in the forgiveness of sin.

One must admit the necessity whereby man submits to the coercion of inhuman situations, accepts military service and, as the case may be, uses deadly weapons. Yet, unlike the moral necessity involved in the pure fulfillment of duty, this "necessity" does not provide the occasion of rising superior to what is intolerable in the situation's call to action. Rather, this "necessity" involves the submission to something wrong. It is a question of the "guilt of the age," and we are made to feel that it is not granted to us to remain free of compromise. Only a barbarian can carry out a "duty" which, in war, summons him to kill without suffering a psychic shock and overcoming some inner resistance.

A war conducted in the defense of our historical heritage can be called a "just war," and it is then still possible to speak of the "duty" of military service. Yet the fact remains, even here, that we shall not stay clear of guilty entanglements; whereas in the fulfillment of a duty which is unconditional in the true sense, the agent is free of the inadequacies of the situation in which he acts. The state which in fact exists under the conditions of history can represent a force of decisive importance to our freedom, and thus can make a very serious claim for survival. And if an enemy hinders the free operation of the state, its defense furnishes some slight justification for our action. Nevertheless such action remains negative, since it rests on the evidence that the dire situation does not allow for any humanly satisfactory solution. If it were not for this evidence, there would be no reason at all for calling any war "just."

Demonic[11] powers which cannot be subdued by the sheer force of a morally pure will alone exert their oppressive influence in a society, and then of course it is possible for one who becomes entangled with them to try to save his soul by a readiness for martyrdom.[12] But even then he runs the risk of appearing to be a deserter in his own eyes; because it would have been his "duty" to enter actively into the service of the better cause even if its moral validity was not unquestionable, or even into the service of the cause which, though not the better, must nevertheless be his own because it belongs to the framework which nurtured him, the order which has provided for him the possibility of being the person he is. Moreover, where demonic powers are active there simply cannot be any "good" cause. In Goethe one can read "Let an independent conscience be the sun of your moral day,"[c] and Kant and Fichte have defended the same thesis. But the demonic eclipses this sun, and only the half-light of ambiguity remains.

Duties which are free of any element of doubt can be experienced in the universally binding conscience of mankind. All supertemporal values shine as beacons guiding men towards spiritual community, and they are at the same time its conditions. To the ideal of universal community Kant has given the name "realm of ends." He says, "I understand by a realm the systematic union of different rational beings through common laws." And also: "Morality consists in relating every action to a legislation by which alone a realm of ends is possible." In line with his formula "act in such a way that the maxim of our action could, by means of your will, become a universal natural law," Kant demands that "all maxims issuing from one's own legislation shall harmonize in a possible realm of ends as if it were a realm of nature."[13]

It can readily be seen that all unconditional duties are in harmony, since they have their ground in a unifying law. When Kant demands that we relate "every action" to the universally binding law, he means this relation to be understood as the actual observance of the imperatives which are implied. Yet Kant's requirement does not take into account the "earthly remnant which it is embarrassing to bear," the residue which "remains for us." It leaves out of account the historical conditionality of all social forms within which our duties arise, and consequently, too, the "fragmentation"[14] of human life. And thus Kant's demand is a postulate which cannot be directed to the individual man as such because he is inevitably confined within limits of whose origin Goethe, after the words about the "earthly remnant," makes "the more perfect angels" say:

> When the strong power of spirit
> Has swept the elements into its own realm,
> Then no angel can separate
> The unified double nature
> The intimate unity of the two.^c

This powerful movement of the spirit which sweeps up the elements of human nature and holds them fast (that inferior mortal stuff which belongs to the foundation of what is human and only here has its justification) manifests itself throughout the history of mankind. It has conferred on social forms that inexorableness which constantly confronts the individual with options, none of which can be fully satisfied and none of which is unconditionally good. It draws into its vortex every individual, whatever the strength or weakness of his personal spiritual powers. The world in which we act and within which we have our duties is not merely *nature*, which is indifferent with regard to supertemporal values; still less is it merely an object,[15] from which we as subjects could maintain our detachment in timeless freedom. This world is at the same time *history* as well, and it is impossible for us to emerge from its bonds. (Even the great champion who introduces a new age by the sheer force of his personality—and is thus in conflict with his own times—can break only some of the particular fetters by which the time into which he was born is held. The new age he brings in remains historically conditioned.) The particular conditions of any given time nevertheless confront those living at that time with particular historically conditioned "duties."

Social formations which are more or less closed confront each other, each with its own history and therefore each with its own treasured heritage to be preserved. The historical heritage constitutes an obligation; the duties which arise from it separate religions, peoples and states, a separation which is productive of many enmities. These enmities force men into their fateful conflicts, quite apart from any personal guilt of individuals. The individuals have grown up in and grown into the particular cultural heritage of their community—nowadays, mainly of their state. Their obligation to this heritage is real, and therefore the institutions which would safeguard it make a claim on the person. However, warlike actions which involve destructive intrusion into a country whose people are fighting for its heritage ("the best defense is attack"!) cannot be related—at least, cannot be directly related—to that body of laws through which alone a realm of ends is possible. The act of war can be a "duty" only in the domain of a historically conditioned situation which demands such action, perhaps not without reason. However, one can and must say that this historical situation itself stands under the authority of the realm of ends, and that in this respect there is a direct relation even of this kind of action to the realm of ends— a relation which manifests itself, in that case, as a disquieting tension. However, while the unconditionally true duties are to be understood in terms of the dictum "you can because you ought to,"[16] wherever the historical conditionality of human communities asserts itself in its corruptness—and none of them is quite free of corruption—the fulfillment of purely human duty is impossible. "One age bears the burden of the other's guilt, but it seldom knows how to absolve it except by a new guilt." (Schleiermacher[17]) Moreover, in the area where demonic powers hold sway there is no action at all which could do justice to the ontological truth, at least insofar as the demonic rule is effective. For then there is an inherent contradiction between the men who are challenged to act and the situation in which they are supposed to act; the situation cannot be treated as what it in truth is.

To return to the general problem and to focus on it at this particularly important point—war—we can say that it is possible for one who is of a truly humane mentality to ward off the temptation to hate and to despise the enemy. Yet the force of events fraught with guilt inevitably overwhelms the individual's strength; he is swept into the mesh, and thus even a humane man becomes corrupted, however he may act.

Kant declared that every individual is directly subject to the moral command to relate "every action" to the legislation through which alone a realm of ends is possible. It is easy for us to understand today how such a statement could have been written in the Age of Enlightenment, when the human was identified with the "reasonable"—that is to say, with what in that age was considered to be the timeless! Owing to that identification, the Enlightenment could take history into account only in a very imperfect way; in particular, it was unable to see the historical conditionality of the whole of human existence. Seeing two hostile armies ranged against each other, the man of the Enlightenment, in consistency with his principles, could only have said that every act of war runs counter to morality. It is true, of course, that in the *Metaphysical Fundamentals of the Doctrine of Right* Kant has conceded to states a right to wage war, but only a limited right.[18] And above all, Kant did not acknowledge the legitimacy of *any* resistance on the part of a subject, even to the unjust orders of the ruler.[19] But if "duty" is so conceived, its observance would turn the subject into a tool of the government, devoid of dignity, and place the severest limitations on his ability to preserve his morality. Indeed one must admit that in many cases the unrestricted preservation of what morality demands is impossible in fact because it is precluded by historically conditioned circumstances. Wherever the limitations of the historical situation overpower the individual he is forced to be satisfied with historically conditioned "duties" which cannot be related directly and with unbroken coherence to the "realm of ends."

One must take into account the historical bonds of the state, which are incomparably more determining in its case than in that of the individual, if one seeks to answer the much-debated question whether any other morality than the morality of private persons is valid for the state (and therefore also for individuals insofar as they identify themselves with it as its members and representatives). The state is charged with the responsibility of safeguarding the conditions under which the humanity of the people can develop. The better the state fulfills this task, the more successfully can the individual maintain the freedom of his own sphere. To be sure, even there he cannot escape history, but neither is he fettered by it. On the contrary, it is possible for him to enjoy, and perhaps even to enrich, the heritage which he owes to history. For it is primarily from the individual that all those forces must come which make the relation of the state to superhistorical ends a concrete reality. Only in this relation does the state discover the task of preserving itself. Threatened by armed conquest, the state must defend itself. And for that very reason the state must be empowered to exact "duties" of its citizens which do not serve any "possible realm of ends" but for which the historical situation, with its moral shortcomings, is an extenuating circumstance. It is simply impossible to resolve the dilemma arising from this moral inadequacy in a manner which is morally unobjectionable. Even the best of states must adjust to the dangers to be expected from this limitation.

Fichte wrote a treatise on Machiavelli which contains some highly objectionable passages, although with regard to many points one must agree with him. It is not permissible, says Fichte, for a prince who has neglected military preparedness and thus brought disaster upon his people to "step forth and say: 'I have been committed to humane principles. I have believed in good faith and honesty.' A private individual may talk like that, and if he perishes as a consequence, well, then he perishes privately. But it is impossible for a prince to talk like that, for a prince does not perish in his own right, nor does he perish alone. Let him be committed to humane principles in his private affairs; if he errs, the damage is to himself. But let him not dare to risk the nation in this commitment, for it is not right that the nation should be drawn into the mire, and perhaps other nations along with it, and with them perhaps the most notable qualities which humanity has attained in a thousand years of striving. It is not right for this to happen merely so that it may be said of a prince that he had humane beliefs. In his private life the prince is subject to the universal laws of morality even as is the meanest of his countrymen. . . . But in his relation to other states there is neither a law nor any right apart from the right of the stronger; and this relation puts the divine rights of majesty, that is of fate and world-government, into the hands of the prince, under his responsibility, and elevates him above the commandments of individual morality into a higher moral order."[20]

Of course these last words fall like a dark shadow on the treatise, bringing it to a gloomy conclusion. A philosopher should never allow himself to use the phrase "the right of the stronger." Above all, what we hear echoed here in Fichte's presentation is the ancient conception of the dignity of the state, of which

Machiavelli also was the exponent—the idea that the state is a power standing above the individual in the moral sphere. If one ponders the foregoing passage of Fichte's with this concept in mind, then it would appear that the private individual who observes the universal commandments of morality in their full rigor without counting the possible cost to himself remains on a lower level of the moral order than one who serves his state with acts of war. But this conclusion is quite intolerable; on the contrary, it is precisely the "duty" to serve in war, no matter how solemn this obligation may be, which thrusts a man into an imperfect ethical order, forcing him to defile his moral life with the inequities of his century. (And, to look more closely, this is likewise true of one who by paying taxes supports the army of the state.)

Schelling says:[21] "The destiny of the world and of mankind is by nature tragic, and every tragic event which occurs in the world during the course of time is only a variation on the one great theme which renews itself continuously. The action which is the wellspring of all sorrow has not happened once and for all but is taking place always, eternally. One of our poets has spoken of 'what happened never and nowhere.' We would alter the phrase to read 'what always happens and will happen eternally'—it is that which 'alone never becomes obsolete.'" With the verses which Schelling rejects, Schiller is referring, in his poem "To the Friends,"[d] to the "eternal youth" of the life of the imagination, to the creations of art. Actually the incompatibility between Schiller's verse and Schelling's words is only according to the letter; there is no contradiction as to sense. But Schelling's thesis is concerned with graver matters: he is preoccupied with the superhistorical and problematic essence of man, who cannot escape from the necessity of acting in contradiction to what is eternally valid. Humanity finds its norms in the eternal verities, in the ideal of a "realm of ends." Nevertheless man cannot reject his historically conditioned "duties" even when (like military service in wartime) they call for inhuman actions; for such duties find a relative justification in the acknowledgment that under existing conditions a situation which is humanly intolerable cannot be redressed by means which are wholly humane. To be sure, judged by absolute standards, these "duties" remain unjust. But for that reason, when the conditions of the time have made them inescapable, they are a call of distress; man should not have such "duties." (Speaking of his drama *Maria Magdalene*, Hebbel says,[22] "we catch a glimmer of consequences which only in future centuries, perhaps, will be accepted in the catechism of life"). Owing to the "reason which has us," we men, in our relation to what is valid unconditionally, are always caught up in a tension calling for ever renewed resistance against what we recognize as defective in the human sense. The ontological truth of these historically conditioned defects is their appeal to the possibilities offered by the age for the improvement of the historically conditioned foundation of human life. Even one who has renounced the "world," who refuses from the authorities of the world any commands which would bring him into conflicts of conscience, is free of the reproach that he has forsaken the duty which the historical situation put upon him only if his superhistorical stand as such does in fact also fulfill a serious task of the time. Fichte has made it strikingly clear[23] that the meaning of duty as it bears on us personally is made manifest only in the world of sense. The sensible sphere incessantly gives moral content to the formal thought of duty. If cowardice should induce a man to take religious vows, if he were to enter the monastery in order to avoid the stress of the "world's" undertakings, he would remain still subject to the world even within the cloister—the world whose moral inadequacies he would fancy himself to have left behind.

All those conditions of an age which fall short of true humanity *must* be fought. To turn away from the demands which arise from the needs of the historically conditioned situation would mean to abandon the field to the overwhelming forces of evil; it would mean the uncharitable abandonment to these powers of the fate of other men's souls, insofar as that fate somehow depends on the deserter. The heroes of the old myths are liberators, men who brought higher possibilities of life into being; yet, judged by modern standards, they cannot all be said to have behaved in a notably humane way. Often they had to wield a club in order to broaden the area within which the humane could survive. The age of the heroes is past. But what has not vanished is the grievous necessity of using inhuman means in order to come to grips with the perils of a still worse and more enduring inhumanity. Only by way of arbitrary abstraction is it possible to attribute to individual man an existence which is self-sufficient; in reality he is a member of the community, and this life is historically conditioned. His personal conditions have roots reaching back into time immemorial. The power of other wills of the most diverse origin has helped to determine his specific character, and not all of them have been at a high level of humanity by any means. In their history, social groups—following their protagonists with an imitation which often approaches involuntary caricature—have unceasingly deepened the cleavage between subject and object, only to spend themselves in a restless endeavor to bridge this gap and fill in the crevices (though often with little success). The plowed field does not have an exclusively objective existence; a deliberate will has made the field into what it is, and this will recognizes itself in the field. Cottage and palace have an objective existence, yet in such a way that the human spirit has poured itself into them in characteristic manners. The printed book of Kant's *Foundations of the Metaphysics of Morals* is an object, but not only an object; it is not a dead letter but rather the vehicle of great and profound thoughts, capable of bringing into being in the mind of the reader thoughts which are his own. The possibility that such an "object" can be bought has a long history of mankind as its prerequisite. But Hitler's *Mein Kampf* likewise can and could be bought, and the historical conditions under which it was brought into existence supported the will which the book embodies, the will to delude and to enslave. In its own way the *state*, too, has objective existence, and in wartime and for the enemy soldier it has almost nothing but objective existence. Yet for the man for whom the state means home it is above all the will of that destiny which embraces him and which at this present moment has entrusted him with the task of throwing himself with all the forces at his command into the fight for its aims.

Moral obligations present themselves not over against an objective world but in an historically constituted sphere whose process of formation is often disturbed (by misfortunes and by enemies, but by its own bad will too). Hence it is afflicted with many ambiguities. If a war breaks out, both sides endeavor to present it as necessary and just. Those who fight on each side, believing in the justice of their cause, will take their stand, and as men do their bloody duty in the opposing armies they act against each other and in their action can affirm the "realm of ends" only as the goal of a now impotent longing. Can they be men of good will all the same? Though Kant's formulation of the question remains, of course, within the limits of the eighteenth century, within those limits it is well pondered. That will is "unconditionally good . . . whose maxim can never contradict itself if turned into a universal law."[24] The conditionality of the relations of human life does *not* permit us an "unconditionally good will," not any one of us. For the example of the soldier in war shows something quite universal. The unconditionally good will is an ideal; it points out only the direction in which we must seek moral self-affirmation.

5

INHUMAN TRUTHS AND HUMAN UNTRUTHS

Will one who seeks direction for his life in the ideal of an absolutely good will tell the truth in all cases? Must he tell it? Dare he? Kant quite peremptorily says yes. "To lie means to cast aside one's human dignity and, as it were, to annihilate it. To communicate by means of words which deliberately express the opposite of what the speaker is thinking involves a goal strictly contrary to the natural efficiency of one's power to communicate one's thoughts. Therefore it means to renounce one's personality, and the liar presents himself as nothing but the deceptive appearance of a man, not as a true man."[1] Thus says the *Metaphysical Principles of the Doctrine of Virtue*. Another treatise published in the same year (1797), *Concerning an Ostensible Right to Lie from Human Charity*,[a] declares that it is a duty to answer truthfully the question of "a caller bent on murder" who asks whether the victim he seeks is at home—if one cannot evade answering.[2] "It is a sacred command of reason, unlimited by any considerations of convenience, which bids us unconditionally to be truthful (honest) in all our declarations." Fichte spoke no less forcefully. His *System of the Doctrine of Morals (System der Sittenlehre)*, only a year after the quoted words of Kant, repeats the example given by Kant with only a slight variation. Fichte says we must refuse to answer the question of a pursuer who comes with "naked sword" inquiring about someone's whereabouts. In the extreme case, the one to whom the question has been addressed must let himself be cut down. "After you are dead it is no longer your affair to protect the life of the fugitive; and at the same time, as dead, you are safe from the danger of telling a lie."[3] As late as the *Doctrine of Morals (Sittenlehre)* of 1812, published posthumously, Fichte writes: "To tell the truth in spite of every danger develops in man an immediate feeling and consciousness of his higher self, which is beyond all earthly consequences."[4]

The bishop in Grillparzer's play *Woe to Him Who Lies* stands in the beginning for a similarly rigorous morality, but at the end the admission escapes him that in the "mottled confusion of the world," the strict truth becomes indistinct; as long as we live on earth we are in "the land of deception," incapable of bearing the truth in its purity, though we are nevertheless aware of it.

This insight of Grillparzer's bishop that the eyes of men are in danger of being blinded by the rays of pure truth finds an impressive confirmation in a drama of Ibsen's, *The Wild Duck*. Gregers Werle is a fanatic for the truth. As a youth, he had sought everywhere the realization of the "ideal demand" which he "carries in his heart." Even as an older man, he still makes this demand of everyone he would esteem as a "genuine, a true man." Hence he is determined that his friend Hjalmer Ekdal shall "open his eyes . . . see the situation as it is." Gregers Werle remains faithful to himself: after the catastrophic denouement he comforts himself with an illusion. He thinks himself justified in replying to the realistically minded Relling that Hedwig did not die in vain. "Have you seen," he asks Relling, "how the grief liberated what is sublime in him (Hjalmar)?"

Here is another example (unfortunately not from a work of fiction) of the insight gained by Grillparzer's bishop. A Protestant pastor learned from a physician that the latter's wife, an orthodox Christian, was suffering from cancer. Her husband had kept the dreadful diagnosis from her. However, she was full of foreboding and feared to learn the truth. She took counsel with the pastor, and he summoned her to contemplate with him what her spiritual condition would be, supposing that her illness really should be cancer. The effect on the woman was horrid; her husband having forbidden further pastoral visitations, she died "a lonely death in indescribable pain."

To be sure, there are people from whom it would be unjust to conceal a medical prognosis which gave no hope. Such people find, in precisely such an outlook, the occasion for the richest unfolding of their human depths, a development which likewise exerts a beneficent influence on their environment. But even

Gregers Werle had learned to direct the "ideal demand" only to men who were "genuine and true." Admittedly it is possible to endure the certain imminence of a long-drawn-out, painful death; indeed, perhaps to accept this certainty in pious submission and with an intensified inward experience of one's superiority over the world. However, this possibility depends not upon a man's intellectual acceptance of any orthodox doctrine as true, but merely on his mature formation as a man.

> The infinite gods give everything
> whole to their favorites;
> all infinite pleasures,
> all infinite pains, whole.[b]

What is essential is that the influence arising from his human depths should be so efficacious as to permit him to look forward to the tragic fate which awaits him. And only such depth in another man will equip him to be the bearer of the melancholy truth—to judge whether this fate can be spoken of in words before it has announced itself unmistakably. Only genuine humanness makes it possible to understand man. It is inhuman to substitute for an individual understanding some "ideal demand"; it is inhuman to place burdens on people without having an adequate measure of the personal strength they have to bear them. Wherever a person breaks down spiritually under the weight of "ideal demands" it is because these demands, contrary to their truly human meaning, have been interpreted as abstract imperatives universally applicable in the sphere of experience. The real goal for each individual is the attainment of the height of his own potentialities. (The ideals only indicate the direction in which that height must be sought.[5]) To assume without convincing reasons that a given man's capacities equip him to reach a height of personal development far above the average, and having made this assumption to impose on him a "truth" of annihilating weight, is moralistic inhumanity. It is precisely this kind of inhumanity which would be involved in those cases in which the murderer is shown the way to his victim, or the one asked for the way offers up his own life instead of answering.

The word moralistic here refers to the behavior of one who

holds that morality is an end in itself which can furnish the very meaning of life. An ostensibly religious interpretation would identify this kind of end with the will of God. But as poet-philosopher Max Brod says in a beautiful phrase, "The lover assents to the will of God."[6] And the lover is always the whole man, never the one whose regard is focused wholly on a moral will. The moralist does not understand that although morality is indisputably necessary for a spiritual life—that is to say, for a life worth living—nevertheless the demands made from case to case become clear only within the all-embracing, ever-changing contexts of life. (Even the recognition of one's own duty often becomes excessively difficult, because often outward circumstances beyond one's immediate control affect the context. And above all, the moral evaluation of the decisions made by another in a problematic situation becomes impossible. Thomas Hill Green has rightly pointed out that the evaluation of such a decision would presuppose the—never attainable—complete knowledge of its place in the total history of a life, in the total context of a character.[7] It is impossible to formulate a universal dictate of morality having a definite content and at the same time being supported by the certainty that there can never be any case in which it would be immoral to consider the dictate as binding.)

In answer to the question, what is a "will which is simply good," Kant said that it is a will which "is not evil." Hence it is a will "whose maxim can never contradict itself if turned into a universal law."[8] By maxims one must understand sentences with a definite content. Kant says a maxim is "the rule of the agent which he himself, for subjective reasons, makes a principle for himself."[9] But the very definiteness of content, and therefore the limitations, of a maxim should make it impossible for the will "which cannot be evil" to make the maxim binding. Maxims would reduce the will to such a state of passivity that under unfortunate circumstances it might observe as morally binding what is really inhuman—as is illustrated by Kant's own decision of the issue with regard to answering the murderer seeking his victim.

Kant speaks of the duty to tell the truth as of a principle allowing for no exceptions. But the only principle valid without exception is to behave in a genuinely human way. The will can be simply good only if it preserves the freedom to make a new decision in an unprecedented situation. (And no situation can be truly evaluated from an exclusively moral point of view.) A man in quest of the good in the sphere of action cannot obtain his certainty regarding it from rules inflexibly laid down by his own subjective decision, even though with the best of intentions. Man does not live as a moral monad which could, "for subjective reasons," venture to force its actions into unchangeable patterns. The domain of morality is the world of coexistence; the man of good will seeks to find his place in social structures which are moved by the most manifold interests, all the while adhering unerringly to the ideal of humanity which is the real goal of those structures. (This means that at times he quietly puts up with the given order and at others offers resistance to its shortcomings.) Fichte says (and here he speaks without moralistic narrowness): "In the proper sense, there is no duty of the single individual, but only a duty of the whole community. . . . Therefore, it is the task of every individual . . . to develop in harmony with what is universally valid in others, and to help them to develop in harmony with what is universally valid in himself."[10] Fichte calls this universal validity "the image of the concept which creates the world," "the image of God." His doctrine is that "the creation of the world from God is in no way finished." In the true world, the world of the spirit, God continues to develop his own image with ever increasing clarity. He reveals himself in "visions of the spirit" (*geistigen Gesichten*) which have the effect of removing from man all arbitrary self-will. "At this point, however, the immediate divine action terminates, and henceforth God makes use of the freedom and independence of man in order to transmit to the whole of mankind the effect of the action which irrupted at this one point." Mankind's task is to shape the life of its spirit into a "likeness," into a "perfect impression of that first vision manifest in the single point"; insofar as mankind is in the deepest sense human, it is the image of God.[11] A great painter, Cuno Amiet, wrote some striking sentences about the formation of a work of art. "All parts are subject to the whole. Together with the other parts, each has only the one goal: the formation of the whole. The whole, then, is a faithful image of its creator."[12] Thus, though the painting may represent a landscape or a bunch of flowers, it is yet "a faithful image" of the painter! In the very same sense, the world for which we are responsible is destined in its unceasing movements to become a faithful image of God.

For the moral sensibilities an untruth told deliberately must seem reprehensible if it is considered in isolation, apart from its context. But such isolated utterances are mere abstractions; real life is not composed of elements which exist by themselves. And a sentence uttered in the encounters which life brings about does not have its true meaning and value in its relation to (objective) truth. Rather, it is the degree of appropriateness and significance with which sentences fit into the context in which they belong that furnishes them with their meaning and value. In his work, *Types of Ethical Theory*, James Martineau[13] writes: "We speak, not in order to be truthful, but in order to tell some experience, or to elicit it from another, or to stir some sympathetic or antipathetic emotion, or to influence the will of our companion. In all cases, the incentive is supplied out of the familiar list—be it Wonder in quest of information, or Passion in an explosion of anger, or Affection in the tender of sympathy. Moreover, the impulse, whatever it be, does not spend itself on speech as an end, but merely wields it as an instrument for reaching its real object, viz. a certain effect upon another's mind. . . . our own states of mind are just what we long to transfuse into the mind of our fellow." It is the humanity or the inhumanity of the *purpose* of our talk which determines the meaning and value of what we say.

A score of years after Martineau, Hermann Cohen argued in a similar way, and what he adds is apposite. "Truthfulness does not have the formalistic sense of directing me to say yes or no thoughtlessly and without examination, to speak by rote without conscience, without inquiring who it is who asks me. Truthfulness rests on knowledge. Therefore, it demands a critical examination of all circumstances of each particular case."[14] The manifold nature of human affairs is not favorable to moral maxims.

This is the place to mention Benedetto Croce. He would restrict the use of the term "lie" (*menzogna*) to the utterances of ill-will, and he would be far from assuming that a lie was at the bottom of every untruthful statement. Croce believes in the real existence of the moral sense (*senso morale*), and he maintains that the moral judgment is confused only in the minds of the abstracting rationalists (*raziocinatori astratti*). The liar introduces disorder into life with his untruth; but there are likewise malicious truth-tellers (*dicitori maligni del vero*) who bring disorder into life with their "truths." "With the little word 'truth' one can, under certain circumstances, kill a man." Croce furnishes a philosophical justification for this stand, in which the unsophisticated moral judgment is sanctioned, by taking into consideration the fact that, properly speaking, truth is quite incapable of being communicated. "Truth is not a commodity which can change hands. It is the thought itself in the immediacy of the thinking act. How could that be 'communicated'?" We can influence other people, or try to influence them, in a certain way by what we say; but what is going to happen in their minds is no longer within our control.¹⁵ We do have a moral responsibility for our words, but it cannot be measured by the objective truth of our statements. The question is whether we advance the life of others, changing it, elevating it.

Could Kant have been persuaded by such reflections? As if he had anticipated this question and wanted to answer it in advance, Kant declared: "Man as a moral being (*homo noumenon*) may not make use of himself as a physical being (*homo phaenomenon*) as a mere means (a talking machine) not regulated by the inner purpose of the communication of thoughts; rather, the condition which requires that his actions conform to his declaration as a moral being is binding on him."¹⁶ This is to say that the "inner purpose of the communication of thoughts" binds man to his obligation as a moral being. This inner purpose imposes on our relation to other men a limitation which must be observed unconditionally: "Truthfulness is a duty which must be considered the basis of all the duties which rest on contracts. The law of which this is the basis loses its stability and becomes quite useless if one admits even the smallest exception to it." It is for this reason that Kant speaks of an "unconditional principle of truthfulness" and calls it "a principle acknowledged *a priori*, and therefore apodictical."¹⁷ But it is at this very point that we must recall—in line with Croce's *Philosophy of the Spirit*ᶜ—that anything a man may say at any time is always situated in a conditioned context. The very situations a man would try to influence are conditional, and so also are the men whom he would influence. And in particular the intelligence (*Verstand*) is likewise conditioned, the intelligence without whose help consciousness could never become aware of any maxim or principle, and through which all expression receives its form. True, whereas our existence is conditioned, we are nevertheless unceasingly related to the unconditional and under obligation to it. But unconditionality urges us to transcend the domain of the single, separate functions of our psychic life and to reach a unity which embraces the single functions, the unity to which every single function is bound and in which alone it can find its true meaning. The unconditional determines the measure in which every person can bring his own humanness to a fulfillment which corresponds to the height of that person's potentialities. The unconditional also determines the measure in which objective truth must be communicated if justice is to be done in a particular situation. Kant and Fichte alike have failed to rise above a certain confusion: they mistake for an unconditional obligation that truth which is subject to the conditions of life, confounding it with the unconditionally true with whose requirements the conditionally true may, under particular circumstances, be in embarrassing contrast.

That truth which binds us unconditionally is final; the truths of the intelligence are not. In scientific research, for instance, the truths of the intelligence never lead to a result which is absolutely certain. And when it comes to the various affairs of social life, then the truths of the intelligence prove to be so very ambiguous that even a lie can be concealed in them. It requires only a little clever attention to one's language to make our words, which do in fact say something true, strike the hearer in such a way that he must understand them in a sense other than their "true" sense—that is, he will understand the words the way the speaker wants him to understand them. Of course, by his words the speaker has told nothing but the truth; yet he has lied to the hearer. Let us admit that even such sharp-witted and treacherous practices imply a proper sense of the worth of truth as an idea (though of course it is a regard which remains quite abstract!). In particular they can be recommended, it seems, when it is necessary to put someone off who is rather too forward in asking inopportune questions. In rare cases, indeed, taking such a course may be the only way of meeting an unpleasant situation as it deserves to be met. But if we make a habit of behaving in this way with the notion that we do so with no prejudice to the truth, then our conduct is worse than a deliberate lie, for it seduces us into believing that we are better than we are: we persuade ourselves that we never lie at the very time that we are actually lying very methodically.

It remains to be said that untruths and outright lies can be expressed not only in words but in gestures which have the meaning of words. Even the concealing of objects and of persons is equivalent to the untrue statement that the object (say, in a customs inspection) and the person is not there (think of the numbers of fugitives during the Second World War whose lives were saved by protectors who risked their own!). We shall have to equate the first of these examples with a lie, the expression of an evil will; the second, however (Kant and Fichte notwithstanding), we must see as an action of high moral value, an heroic action.

If evil were confined to the inward intentions of the will and had no power to render the situations in which human life takes its course ambiguous or even to poison them, and if moreover human frailty did not call for our forebearance, then one could not understand how there could be untruths which were genuinely humane. The paradox of the genuinely humane untruth has its origin in an area which transcends conceptually formulated, rationalized norms. When the intelligence tries to clarify the opposition between good and evil for moral experience, its very forms misapprehend this contrast owing to a conceptual rigor which is incongruous with the real relationships of life. To be sure, our moral experience cannot dispense with the services of the intelligence; however, its operations cannot attune themselves to the sensitiveness which is the mark of the genuinely humane.

Everyone experiences his own life, of which he is at the center with respect to the surrounding world, a center which is his in trust. At the beginning of life, to be sure, man is a very dependent being, powerless and lacking in orientation; but quite early he becomes aware of the threats to his existence and seeks security against them. The well-defined consciousness of himself as a responsible being develops from such beginnings. The value contrasts of true and false, good and evil, beautiful and ugly, just and unjust, evoke in him a capacity for holding security in low esteem as compared to the courageous determination to fight against the false, the evil, the ugly, the unjust. But he also discovers the possibility of evading the fight, or of undertaking it only with a view to his own safety. These are the temptations which induce him to come to terms with what is reprehensible, unworthy of man. The dependency of childhood *can* become a thing of the past, and that reason which "has man" would remind him that that dependency *should* belong to the past. But the decision remains each individual's own affair. It is not a decision reached on a purely rational level, for there are quite different sets of values and quite different points of view from which one can interpret the fight a man must undertake out of the awareness of the value contrasts of good and evil, just and unjust.

If the security of his existence seems to be the only meaning which a man's struggle involves (that is, if the true goal is not his independence, his freedom), then the uncertainty of the issue may easily dishearten him, and then the physical weakness of his earliest years readily turns into moral weakness, into guilt. This is a type of life attitude which only too often manifests itself in innumerable variations. Other types can be distinguished. In their case the struggle against the evils of life is undertaken with earnestness: there is a real willingness to comply with the demands which the contrasts of values make. But again there arises the task of reaching a decision, though it may present itself with less clarity. Now the intellect generalizes the experiences into which the fight has led a man; the intellect formulates commandments and maxims. Above all, it produces negative formulations: "Thou shalt not kill, lie, commit adultery, steal." And in so doing, it is performing a necessary task. Yet *all* the intellect's accomplishments remain somehow unfinished: so, too, in this area. For what really matters is this, that the formulation of the commandments should not hide their true meaning—humanity.

Commandments are stopgaps. There is no unconditional truth

in them, there cannot be. Nevertheless the need for security makes itself felt here too: *moral consciousness seeks a shelter* in the imperatives which speak so forcefully. An intellect grown robust gives firmness to the formal expression of the imperative, and now the will espouses the commandments, endowing them with its unswerving loyalty. The will intends well; but in its espousal of the commandments, in its faith commitment to the formulas in whose strict observance it seeks security, the goodness of the will is restricted and less pure.

The only decision which can give morality its true meaning amounts to the liberation of the human in its purity. And the human transcends every limiting commandment: "The sabbath was made for man, not man for the sabbath" (Mark 2:27). No law, however formulated, is capable of fixing the content of a life worth living, at least not in a way that is fully trustworthy. Sets of general instructions are nevertheless necessary for education. (Of course, for quite some time the demands made of the pupil must be kept free of the extraordinary.) And all administration of justice fulfills a function which is socially pedagogical. But humanity in its wholeness is subject to no law. "The son of man is lord even of the sabbath" (Mark 2:28).

Needless to say it is humanity in its wholeness, perfected humanity, which needs no laws and which, if it ignores a law, does it for the sake of humaneness itself. The laws themselves—if they are good laws—have their origin in the humane. But owing to their rational form, which gives them the semblance of finality, they are narrowed in their implications and are hence never ultimately valid. Life is always challenged to make its own decisions. Laws would induce these decisions to follow paths which, although they satisfy social needs as they are recognized in the general consensus of the age, can nevertheless become restrictive, even frustrating, in the event of extraordinary calls to action. In such cases, our decision should substantiate the very meaning of our existence without any antecedent law but with the free necessity of what is purely human.

No matter what we attain, it is always imperfect. Often there is a culpable hiatus between what we accomplish and what we should accomplish. Often, too, the culpable act of another is a call for help to those whose experience is more profound; it is a call for help because suffering wants a remedy. To be truly human means to be always ready to help; to seek to help the guilty as well as the innocent victim of misfortune. Even the mere moral will (*die moralische Gesinnung*) as such shows itself as benevolent, for it is rooted in humanness. Yet, as the doctrines of Kant and Fichte demonstrate, mere morality would offer no protection against inhuman harshness.

Humanness is the source not only of morality but of every movement in which the human spirit tends to realize itself, and of every form in which the spirit manifests itself. By humanness we mean the unity of everything which enters into the making of personality. The creatively unifying bond is love.[18] The moralist has not good intentions towards anybody, not even towards himself.[d] He maintains the unity of his various potentialities under the pressure of moral consciousness alone, and thus he prevents them from interpenetrating. (If, for instance, he should be endowed with an artistic gift, he would regard it with suspicion.) The inner unity which love affords for the personal life is only love seen from one aspect, that in which it benefits oneself; the other, truer aspect is the unifying force which love manifests in its effect upon other men—indeed in its contemplation of all that is. Rabindranath Tagore says, "He who lives his own life in truth is living the life of the whole world."[19] Of course, what is meant here is not love as a natural impulse but a love which is, "though free of nature, yet not without nature" (a significant distinction made by Franz Baader[20]). Impulse is blind, but a love not fettered by nature is productive of the certitude which belongs to the acts of the intellectual, moral and aesthetic domains. As the manifestations of the distinct single movements of the human spirit yield the immediate certainty of freedom, so likewise does the love which integrates these movements and thus constitutes our humanness—whenever and wherever that love becomes effective. Love liberates man and comprehends him. It understands human weakness and human guilt. Confined to the limits of rational norms, one could not possibly do justice to the weakness of a child, still less to human guilt. Both the weakness and the guilt are a call to understanding love.

The very nature of the child makes him lovable, makes his weakness touching. To help a child is a joy whose experience calls for no great depths of humanity. When a guilty man needs help, needs the comfort which revives, it is a different matter. Yet it may happen that a man released from a penitentiary, almost breaking down under the weight of his deserved misery and hence very much in need of encouragement, meets an upright man well established in active life; and the latter, in order to encourage the ex-convict, tells him (untruthfully) that he himself once shared the convict's fate, but that by keeping his courage up he has succeeded in rising above his mistakes and their bitter consequences. Will anyone call these words of comfort a lie? The comforter's claim is a fiction, it is untrue; but it is undeniable that it may be the most impressive help that can be offered to the unfortunate man in this situation. In no other way could the comforter present himself as so unreservedly a neighbor to the ex-convict. He "pours oil into his wounds," and with his untrue words yet treats the ex-convict as what he is in truth—a human being. One must assume, of course, that such Samaritan-like words of comfort could occur only to one who had for long reflected on the mental condition of an ex-convict weighed down by his guilt and shame and hence could sympathize intimately with the lot of the man now before him. In this respect it might be said that there is a deep fundamental truth in his words: he knows from his own mental experience the weight which the other man must bear.

Yet all this does not alter the fact that the objective content of his words is untrue. Is this a case where the end sanctifies the means? One may perhaps answer yes, keeping in mind that in this case the end is nothing but the unconditional value of humanity and that the means have no significance apart from the fact that they are means for this end.

The disturbing fact remains that every deliberate untruth sets the one who makes use of it at odds with himself. Kant is of the opinion that "a man who does not himself believe what he tells another man has even less value than he would have as a thing." For a thing can be put to effective use, but a lie can not.[21] The latter argumentation may not apply to our example, but it is quite true that any deliberate untrue statement interferes with the speaker's being at one with himself. Yet even this interference is not susceptible of unconditional generalization, because there are two questions which we must distinguish here. One is, "Do I remain at one with myself by acting in line with the goal of humanity?" This question must be affirmed. The other question is, "Do I remain at one with myself when I am using an untrue statement as the means towards an unconditionally valuable end?" In answering this second question one must grant that in it I am using as a means (like a hammer or a tong) something which (in distinction from a mere tool) in itself has a relation to the idea of the true; that I am setting aside this relation, and that it is precisely this setting aside which results in its usefulness as a means! The conflict (stressed by Kant) between what is said and what at the same time is thought concerns only one's own consciousness. (It is different in the case of a common lie, wherein the conflict reaches further and in some ways defiles the relation to other men.) In our case the conflict does not bear on the human relation between the speaker and the listener; it is altogether the affair of the one who makes the untrue statement. For him the meeting with the ex-convict returning to civil life has become the occasion to say words which unhesitatingly put at stake the speaker's self, for the sake of offering the help needed by the former convict. The fact that the objective sense of his words is untrue concerns only the speaker. But the interests of his own self are not under consideration at this moment. As the son of man is lord even over the Sabbath, so one who acts under the highest necessity, the necessity of the purely human, is lord over the objective truth. The love powerfully at work in him lets him find the words appropriate to the case. Man does not exist for the Sabbath, but the Sabbath for man. Even objective truth is not an end in itself. It, too, exists for man—for the humanity of man.

6

THE CLAIM THAT
THE DEPTHS OF TRUTH MAKE ON MAN

In a discussion of pictorial art,[1] it has been said with regard to the cathedrals that by means of them "even in this world, another, greater world began to exist for one who knew how to enter through devotion the gateway which pictures provided." (The writer chose the past tense because his argument was concerned with the *modern* man who "believes very little.") Pictures speak to the aesthetic sensibility (and only through it to the whole man). What a picture shows *objectively* is not decisive for the aesthetic response, any more than the "truth" revealed by the work of art is the truth of the intelligence which is concerned with seizing objective relationships. For instance, the intelligence may record that on a given altarpiece the enthroned Madonna with the Child Jesus may be seen, and on each side, to the right and the left, two saints. This does not mean that this grouping of personages exists or ever has existed in heaven or on earth. Nor does it mean that what the intelligence records contains anything essential to what is artistic in the work of art. The aesthetic value of the picture is nothing objective. What genuine aesthetic experience makes us aware of is the fact that reality is not confined to the objective realm, and for that very reason pictures can serve as "gates" into the "other, greater" world which nevertheless extends into the order here below. But as the text we have quoted justly observes, pictures must be approached "devoutly" if they are to lead us into that other world. And only the *whole* man can be devout—not his aesthetic sensibility alone, which (having only the intelligence for its support) could enjoy only the feast afforded the eyes (a feast not, of course, to be despised).

But for modern man, the work we are quoting would tell us,

the cathedrals are no longer what they were of old. Shaken by the experience of two world wars, modern man is calling everything into question, he is no longer attuned to faith. But what, in this context, does faith mean? Does it mean to accept the truth of certain objective relationships although they belong to a higher order which transcends the world of sense?

In his work *Hither and Thither* Max Brod writes: "An old Jewess who had fled to Palestine from Romania said to me yesterday: 'All my life I have believed in God. When the Germans came and killed our husbands—and the women and old men—then I still believed in God. When they killed our old pious rabbi, having tortured him first, I still believed. But since I have seen how they take suckling babies and smash their heads against tree trunks so that their brains splatter out, I have stopped believing that there is a God.'"[2]

It is easy to believe as long as things here below merely point beyond themselves; when it is a question of what is known below giving access to the realm above—which is what occurs in the experience of the beautiful. But when events take place for whose possibility there is no room in the imagery of belief, then faith is shaken. Thus indeed did the eighth-century missionary who felled the sacred oak of Donar shake the faith in the old gods. For he went unpunished for this sacrilege—surely something which, in the imagery of the faith in which Donar lived, the gods (and surely Donar himself) would never have permitted.

In the history of peoples and of individuals alike, events which have a jarring impact on religious imagery are of great significance. The hold which imagery has on belief is loosened, and either faith becomes purer or it loses its vitality, dries up, and vanishes.

The Old Testament still contains vestiges of the primeval cult of nature (e.g. II Kings 18:4, Jer. 2:27). The beings worshipped in such a cult are powers; but for Israel they have become the righteous God: by his very power he shows that he is just. His commandments carved on the two tablets are not the utterances of arbitrary rule; they are revelations of the truth which is of necessity, they have humanity as their object. If Israel faithfully fulfills the commandments, Yahweh will support Israel against its enemies. But if Israel does what displeases Yahweh, then he is provoked to anger and brings great calamities upon his people (Judges 2). He does not ask for the performance of liturgies; he exclaims, through his prophet Isaiah:

"What to me is the multitude of your sacrifices? . . . I have had enough of burnt offerings of rams and the fat of fed beasts; I do not delight in the blood of bulls, or of lambs, or of he-goats. . . .

"When you spread forth your hands, I will hide my eyes from you; even though you make many prayers, I will not listen; your hands are full of blood. Wash yourselves; make yourselves clean; remove the evil of your doings from before my eyes; cease to do evil, learn to do good; seek justice, correct oppression; defend the fatherless, plead for the widow." (Is. 1:11, 15–17)

No doubt those words sounded very scandalous when they were voiced in the eighth century before Christ; scandalous in the ears of those for whom propitiating their God by prayer and sacrifice was a serious business. But Isaiah had the certainty of God which calls for the surrender of the whole man, the kind of relationship which cannot be kept within the limits of specific observances. For the only words and actions capable of pleasing God are those whose goal is to bring man into harmony with himself. Only then can they be religious. A worship lacking in such harmony is a lie. Isaiah foresees the downfall of a people steeped in untruthfulness and injustice; he proclaims that only a remnant of them will return to Yahweh (37:31f.)

Two centuries later, under the stress of the Babylonian Exile, a new certainty of God takes form in Deutero-Isaiah. The prophetic word of old has been confirmed. Yahweh reminds his people of it: ". . . your teachers have been guilty of prevarication regarding my Truth. Therefore I profaned the princes of the sanctuary, I delivered Jacob to utter destruction and Israel to reviling." (43:27–28) Now Israel laments: "My way is hid from the Lord, and my right is disregarded by my God" (40:27). And so it is fitting to understand this God in a more profound way, and in the depths of one's own being to overcome the effects of the shock which painful misfortunes bring upon the faith. God sends sufferings to his beloved. To prove one's humanity even in suffering, indeed precisely in suffering, means to live for the greater glory of God. The people Israel is God's servant (41:8). This is why the most intense suffering must be their lot. Israel's calling is to glorify God by bearing the cruellest blows of fate in a manner superior to the world, thus revealing the true God to all nations: "Behold my servant, whom I uphold, my chosen, in whom my soul delights. I have put my Spirit upon him, he will bring forth justice to the nations. . . . I, Yahweh, have called you in righteousness, I have taken you by the hand and kept you; I have given you as a covenant to the people, a light to the nations" (42:1,6). Israel, bearing up under its destiny, is to be a radiant revelation of human fidelity, and the fate of the nation requires every individual Israelite to do his own part in glorifying the truth of God: "every one who is called by my name, whom I created for my glory, whom I formed and made" (43:7). The high calling makes the utmost demand—the unconditional willingness to accept the mortifications which God imposes: the servant of God takes upon himself the guilt of those who torment him. "Yahweh has laid on him the iniquity of us all. He was oppressed, and he was afflicted, yet he opened not his mouth" (53:6,7). Yet through him, through his sufferings, Yahweh's cause was to be victorious; for all the nations such sufferings must become the proclamation of the true God. Their ideas of justice must undergo correction: "For my thoughts are not your thoughts, neither are your ways my ways, says Yahweh. For as the heavens are higher than the earth, so are my ways higher than your ways and my thoughts than your thoughts" (55:8,9). God's paradoxical revelation supersedes the divine imagery of old. (Cf. 53:1–3.) That imagery is transcended by the greater, deeper truth with its heavier demands. Therefore Yahweh says: "For as the rain and the snow come down from heaven, and return not thither but water the earth, making it bring forth and sprout, giving seed to the sower and bread to the eater, so shall my word be that goes forth from my mouth; it shall not return to me empty, but it shall accomplish that which I purpose, and prosper in the thing for which I sent it" (55:10,11). A few centuries later, what Deutero-Isaiah had spoken in prophecy, the acknowledgment of the bonds whereby man is held within the sphere of God's love was poured forth in the poetic form of the book of Job.

The Claim That the Depths of Truth Make on Man

For long centuries Christian theology saw in the "servant of God" only the Christ who had been prophesied; only lately has the insight gained acceptance that the phrase designates the people of Israel. In recent times the lot of Israel's people has been called a "Job-like fate." It can only be called that. How significant the trust in life, life understood as a blessing and a calling, has been in this history of the Jewish people is well known. Margarete Susman says: "The ability to wait under conditions which have become intolerable is the blessing which the people receive from life itself. . . . The people live in waiting; by waiting they hold life in trust; the nation sins only when it cannot wait, when it loses its trust in life. Only today can we fully evaluate the burden which has been laid upon this people by the need to wait. There is hardly any living Jewish individual in whose heart the psalmist's outcry has not risen at one time or another: 'Happy shall he be who takes your little ones and dashes them against the rock!' And yet the great wave of Jewish life advances. It can advance only as long as this waiting is not an empty waiting, as long as it is trust: trust in life, Messianic hope."[3]

It is the "servant of God" for whom the traumatic experiences clarify the imagery of faith; it is he who can withstand the shocks and nevertheless persevere in his course towards personal wholeness. The content which fills his life, ever growing in depth, becomes ontological truth.

Alfred de Vigny wrote a poem, "The Mount of Olives," whose topic is the night in Gethsemane. The last verse, with its phrase about the "silence éternel de la Divinité," sounds chillingly anti-Christian. The silence of God made Max Brod's old Rumanian Jewess lose her faith. The fearful nature of this silence is something with which Margarete Susman has become familiar: "The people cry out to their God and no longer find him. . . . Can we discover a sense, no matter how hidden, in which this total withdrawal of God is a part of their destiny?" She has learned the answer: "Once again it is the lot of Job which is the key to a meaning, to the ancient, eternal meaning of this withdrawal of God. God loves his people as he loves his servant. He wants what love wants: he wants the whole.[4] . . . Can any Jewish individual interpret as mere contingency the fact that he was born in this hour as a Jew and made subject to the Jewish destiny? Is not God making use of Satan today in order to make the Jew understand what He wants of him? ... It is the almost unutterable mystery that the dark fate with which God has today ringed his people about is the very encircling of His love."[5] In a later part of her book she refers to the assault upon Job which Satan launches, against God's wishes yet with his consent. The biblical conflict becomes a key to the agonizing enigma of the present time. Our view becomes clear: the poetic symbol has *universal* validity. "To experience a presence behind him [Satan], who will not be allowed to remain the victor ... the presence of the One who sends him, and who even in the darkest hell of temptation never lets go of the soul—this means to live from the very depths of truth."[6]

Truth in its depths, hidden from one who has abandoned himself to baseness, demands the *whole* man. It claims him as one who stands superior to the events in the objective world and above the concerns by which this world is agitated. It claims him as one who is called to resist even the greatest, the most awesome power. It makes demands on him insofar as he is not merely an individual but a responsible partner, a recipient, sharing that which makes life worth living: the human calling. Through his personal calling he is united with all men, and all are related to it. According to Yahweh's promise of old, Abraham is to become a blessing for "all the generations on earth" (Gen. 12:3; cf. 22:18).

Within the context of the external world a liar will try to triumph over objective truths by subtle deceit, sometimes with considerable success. But there is no possibility of triumphing over the depths of truth. One who surrenders himself to those depths in the search for personal certitude will learn by experience, if he is able to persevere even in the face of appalling events, that in these events too the higher will of God seeks, and can obtain, realization. The truth makes us free. One who believes in its unfathomable depths also believes in its immeasurable freedom. Evil, too, receives from God every freedom which is not wholly beyond its capacity. But this freedom is never unconditional; it is confined within structures immersed in the mystery of the non-finite, a mystery impenetrable to the intelligence, the mystery of all conditional existence. And in this way even the freedom which evil has remains in the service of the eternal.

For those who, in extreme distress of soul, experience the liberating power of God's truth the imagery of faith, whether or not they are aware of it, has been transformed: what was content has become a means, a tool. As such, the imagery of faith may be indispensable; yet the depths of truth are beyond any image we can form. Nevertheless it is these depths which we are experiencing. A superficial mind does not want to know the depths of truth; and yet truth in its depths holds firmly within its encompassing grasp all the decisions which man can make. Our freedom has no power over the ground from which it derives; our freedom is responsibility, it is responsible to ontological necessity. Reason is active in us, ordering our freedom with its law which forces us to distinguish between what is of value and what is a negation of value; yet it forces us in such a way as to leave to us the outcome of our distinguishing and deciding. And the law of reason permits what is a negation of value to make use of enticements of every kind to make us unfaithful to the truth and induce us to surrender consciously our personal wholeness.

The thoughtless individual fails to recognize the seriousness, the *true* significance, of the decisions which life unceasingly forces us to make. An individual existence dominated by the trends of the "world" lets itself be determined by the temptation to have little regard for the definite but unwelcome demands made by the law of reason. It evades at will what is good and just. It cultivates the beautiful only insofar as it is pleasing or flattering. But where a man makes his decisions in accordance with the demands of reason his action is based on the experience that there is a union of mankind under God (*menschlicher Verbundenheit*). This union is immediately manifest only within a limited community, but in principle it is universal in its implications and never tolerates any limitation of the humane. A ruthless disregard of one's own mere self-interest is necessary for every kind of experience of the depths of truth. It is moreover necessary if we want to resist the ignoble desire to recognize the demands of humanity only when they can be made to depend on the interests of a social group. The Jewish people is not walled off as a people from the rest of mankind for the very reason that in ancient times it burst the bonds of national religion, and ever since then it has known, as the very content of its own existence, the universal truth, which is universally binding. To quote Margarete Susman once more: "From without and from within, the challenge of his responsibility confronts him [the Jew] more rigorously than all other men. From without, the world would make the whole people responsible for the deeds of a single Jew. And what the world would force on the people from without is urged on the individual from within by that personal certainty that every single Jew is responsible for a fate which he did not seek, did not choose, but which has chosen him: which is laid upon him as a particular task, as his personal responsibility—the very meaning of his being man. This responsibility alone is basic to the essence of the Jewish people; the boundaries of this people, which has neither form nor boundary, are precisely coextensive with its responsibility."[7] But such vicariously borne responsibility is a challenge to imitation. All peoples are challenged to acknowledge, as the very content of their existence, the universally binding truth. Thus far, however, the God announced by the Christian message has only too often become "the German god."[8] And again and again the attempts to give effective reality to a league of nations have been swallowed up by untruth.

Formulations designed to have dogmatic finality or to render communicable the insights found in the depths of truth, are symbols. The imagery which they evoke addresses itself immediately only to the senses, and through the senses to the intelligence, whose orientation is objective. Thus it can happen that the impression they make remains a sense impression and stops short at the level of the intelligence. So it may come about that (in Goethe's phrase) "for the sake of the pure concept of the Cross and Christ/ One will forget precisely Him and His Cross."[a]

Schelling calls the reason which has us "a knowledge of God which is itself in God."[9] It is in God as Nature also is in God. God himself transcends the distinction between values.

Now it is true that Nietzsche also wanted to be above the distinction between values, and not only "beyond good and evil." In the first section of the book which bears that title, he presents us with the question: "Granted, we want truth; *why not untruth instead?*" Nietzsche would call one who takes the "popular" notion of contrasting values seriously a believer in metaphysical superstition; that notion is only a "foreground assessment," "a preliminary perspective."[10] The philosophers still to come, the reader is told, will be "no dogmatists. It will be an affront to their pride, even to their taste, that *their* truth should also be a truth for everybody—as was precisely the secret wish and implied meaning (*Hintersinn*) of all dogmatic endeavors. 'My judgment is *my* judgment: it is not likely that another is entitled to the same judgment' —this is what such a philosopher of the future will probably say."[11] For Nietzsche, not truth but life—"Dionysos"—is the highest reality. According to his doctrine the will for truth has emerged as a product of life itself: at a certain stage of our biological development the will for truth has become useful as a tool for enhanced self-assertion. Logical forms are fictions.[12] There are far-reaching consequences of the devaluation of even the ultimate ground on which a universally valid framework for man's self-formation could rest. To make the range of these consequences clear to oneself calls for a courage which loves life in spite of its cruel savagery—even because of it; in spite of and because of its being an adventure full of terrors. Nietzsche's art of persuasion makes an appeal to a biologically caused trait of character in the strong and noble man (in contrast to the flawed personality). One who would live in the spirit of Nietzsche must be hard, he must lack compassion. (Compassion would seduce him into deviation from the rigorous course he has chosen; in compassion lurk the greatest dangers for precisely the most superior breed of men).[13]

Thus the endeavor to advance beyond the contrast of values has a biological orientation, and the proposition that Dionysos is beyond the value contrast has a *biological* meaning. But the meaning of the statement that *God* is beyond them is the expression of our faith in *ontological* truth. God transcends the contrast because he is truth itself, goodness itself. (God's divinity does not become a reality merely because there is a contrast between God and the Devil. This contrast is nothing but an intellectual construct, although it is, of course, important at least as a transitional phase for our human consciousness, which does move towards truth by way of contrasts.) Ontological truth is without contrasts.

In the *Tibetan Book of the Dead*, the *Bardo Thödol*, we read that one who dies, or is at the point of death, has an experience of the "rays of the unshadowed light of pure reality," that at that moment his consciousness is "shaped into nothing and is in reality empty." Yet this emptiness is "not to be regarded as the emptiness of the void"; rather, it is "radiant, exciting and blessed, true consciousness, the all-benevolent Buddha." The "condition of complete enlightenment" (which permits the dying man to experience absolute truth in his God) elevates the mind above reason and reason's formal contrasts and their relationship to the world of appearances. The *Bardo Thödol* connects this insight with Buddhistic images regarding the fate of the soul.[14] But the insight retains its meaning apart from the Buddhistic imagery. Carl Gustav Jung, whose psychological commentary is added to the German edition, expresses profound admiration of the book's "magnificent world of ideas and of its problems, its profound humanity and still more profound insight into the secrets of the soul."[15] In European philosophy, Spinoza came close to this mystical insight when he saw that the ultimate depths of truth are veiled for us by the contrast between good and evil. "Cognitio mali cognitio est inadequata"; our very knowledge of evil is a defect of knowledge itself. The human mind contains the idea of evil only because it is denied the cloudless purity of knowledge: "If the human mind had none but adequate ideas, it would not form any notion of evil."[16] In our consciousness the ideas of the true, the good, the just, the beautiful occur only by way of contrast with the experience of the false, the evil, the unjust, the ugly. And it is precisely the distinction of the valuable from that which is a negation of value (life continuously gives us occasion to make these distinctions) which lifts us above the merely relative and relates us to the eternal, to the divine.

It is quite proper to say that it is in becoming aware of the reason which has us that our becoming human consists. As we experience the necessity of seeing what is of value in contrast to what is a negation of value and of espousing the former, we are lifted into an order superior to mere existence, and we discover what has been put in our charge—namely, the possibility that our own existence can become meaningful. *For us* those distinctions between values are of unconditional validity (though in the absolute they lose their meaning), and through them we contingent beings transcend the merely conditional. In the immediacy of our being we become related to the unconditional. By means of the reason which possesses us, truth itself takes us into its care, directing us towards our real selves. In this reason we are enabled to acknowledge the love of God for mankind. Through this reason we share in the truth of God. By means of a series of decisions which determine the course of our conscious life, reason enables us to advance by ever renewed efforts towards the attainment of the height which gives meaning to our existence.

7
ABOUT THE GOAL OF MANKIND

The imagery in which faith represents itself is not the same in the various religions, and as it differs it is able in very different measures to give support to deep experience. The "visions" of which prophets—true prophets—have spoken elucidate the faith, strengthen and enhance it. New truths which become manifest in visions lead to a understanding of life and of faith which is more profound and more comprehensive. New symbols are added to the traditional store of imagery, and insofar as the old symbols of the faith are not displaced, they attain a fuller and deeper content in terms of the new. What is impressed upon the prophets themselves in their great hours, they fix in written words, and wherever their proclamation is accepted, they furnish the basis for a fuller and purer relationship to the truth.

Every experience of the truth, even the most trivial, gives an immediate certainty of our superiority over a vexation which may be brought upon us by a theoretical or practical task. When the teacher asks, 'How much are 5 and 3?' and the first-grader, from lucid conviction, gives the correct answer, the child shows that he can master the manifoldness which demands synthetic unity.[a] In problematic situations, of course, the elements of the manifold are not easily unified, and as long as the synthetic unity which comprehends the elements has not been found with full certainty, the human intellect is unsure of itself. Hermann Lotze concluded his *Metaphysics* with the oriental saying: "God knows it better."

That truth which metaphysics, every metaphysics, must seek is not a truth valid merely for theoretical consciousness. Even when metaphysics "would present itself as a strict discipline"[1] (and metaphysics does not always elect to do this), it cannot do so in the same sense as mathematics or zoology. But theology and

About the Goal of Mankind

jurisprudence and medicine, too, want to be respected as strict disciplines; and in the "solution of the general question of the *Prolegomena*: How is Metaphysics possible as a discipline?" Kant himself says that the need for such a discipline is "something more than our mere craving for knowledge." If therefore truth in general is experienced as synthetic unity of manifoldness, then in the case of metaphysics, this manifoldness will have to comprehend more than the elements of theoretical consciousness.

Thoroughly at home in the history of philosophy, Hegel and Schelling were able to base their own doctrines on the historical heritage as what could be taken for granted. They did this well before Nietzsche, and after Nietzsche none has been able to do it in the same measure as Benedetto Croce. Nietzsche, only superficially at home in the history of philosophy, was unable to do it. He challenged the noble man to set a goal for existence from his sheer subjectivity. In the first main section of his work *Human, All-Too Human*, he says: "Mankind as a whole has *no* goals."[2] In the Zarathustra-Book the section "A Thousand Goals and One" concludes: "As yet mankind has no goal. But tell me, my brethren, if the goal for mankind is still lacking, is there not as yet a lack of—mankind itself?" Later in the book comes the section, "About Old and New Tablets." There, Zarathustra says: "When I came among men, I found them sitting on an old conceit: Everyone felt he had long known what is good and evil for man. . . . One who wanted to sleep well would talk, before going to sleep, about 'Good' and 'Evil.' I disturbed their slumbers when I taught 'what good and evil are *no one* yet knows—except he who creates! But the creative one is the one who creates a goal for man and who gives to the earth its meaning and its future. This man first *creates* the fact that anything *is* good or evil.'" And in the last speech of the same section there follows the emphatic challenge to himself: "Oh thou, my will! Thou turner of all care, thou, *my* necessity! Protect me from all small victories! . . . Save for the last, oh my will, thy last greatness, that thou mayst be inexorable in thy victory!" Before the background of a mankind as yet without goals there unfolds in sovereign subjectivity the desire for power in the creative will.

To be sure, only a noble will is to determine the millennia of the future by its own setting of values. Nietzsche saw the danger that the aimless multitude might submit to an unworthy man. "A great power-lord might come, a shrewd fiend, who would impose his favor and disfavor, constraining and compressing the whole past: till it would become a bridge for himself and an omen and a herald and a cock's early crow."[3] In fact the awareness of values develops in and through its own history, and only where, among the masses, this awareness loses its orientation and comes to doubt itself is it possible for profane (*ungeistige*) power-lords to gain demonic power. But Nietzsche is mistaken when he expects that the goal—or rather, the goals—of mankind can be set by the creative will of noble men, of the "new nobility." ("What is needed in order that there shall be nobility is many nobles and many kinds of nobles! Or, as I once said, in a parable: Divinity consists precisely in this, that there are gods, but that there is no God!"[4]) His descent from Schopenhauer made it almost impossible for Nietzsche to understand Hegel, who, far surpassing him, could have taught him that the life of the spirit has its necessary goal in the conformity with itself, a goal superior to all that is subjective and arbitrary. "The aim of the spirit is to attain the concept of itself."[5]

Implicitly and explicitly Hegel's philosophy of world history gives what is very much more essential than a construction of the factual sequel of historical movements. It characterizes the "gradual steps" by which the spirit moves towards its goals. In its first phase, comparable to the period of childhood, it is submerged in what is natural. It enters into its second phase when it attains the consciousness of its freedom. "The third phase is the elevation from this as yet particular freedom into the pure universality of freedom (man as man is free)."[6] This is the content of the Christian message. "The spirit is at one with its concept."[7]

This goal sets an immense and infinite task for mankind, and much more is needed than the mere efforts of the intelligence when the spirit, which finds its realization in history, is working to attain its own concept. The domains in which the different value contrasts hold sway over human development must all jointly furnish the stage for the activity of the spirit. In all these domains inner and outer resistances must be overcome (outer resistances in the fight against natural urges, inner resistances when we take a stand against the demonic powers of self-alienation). And beyond what is thus to be accomplished in the interest of the particular cultural domains there remains the greatest, the highest task of unifying them—in the very synthesis for the sake of whose conceptual determination metaphysics must labor. This determination is realized where the "at-oneness of the spirit with its concept" comes about.

8

ABOUT HUMANITY: ITS ONTOLOGICAL GROUND, THE DANGERS TO IT, AND ITS HEIGHT

Augustine identified truth with God.[1] For him the word *veritas* has this highest meaning of an all-comprehensive essentiality; as everything that is has its being only from the fullness of God, so according to Augustine's philosophy every truth is true only in God, from God and through God.[2] Thus the value contrasts of true and false, the gauge of logical thinking, is related to an ontological ground which makes the contrast unconditional. For the finite consciousness it is unconditionally valid—and is valid in such a way that consciousness has no need to make an effort in order to acknowledge the contrast, nor indeed could it make such an effort. (To be sure, the effort is necessary in case consciousness should endeavor to refuse acknowledgment to the contrast—sophistically, and not without self-contradiction.)[3] Even when we err, our intellectual experience remains aware of the meaning of the word "truth," and our very error asks to be taken for the truth as long as we are confined in it. Even error springs from reference to the truth as a goal, and the tacit affirmation of the goal alone can give it a logical meaning. No matter how much uncertainty is embodied in our judgments, the distinction between true and false is constitutive for the theoretical I. In that distinction the I has always found itself. If the I falls into error, the distinction nevertheless prevails—and likewise when an erroneous judgment is corrected. All intellectual life rests on the distinction—and not alone intellectual life: it is effective in all forms of the life of the spirit (because this life is never without an intellectual ingredient).[4] To abandon the distinction between true and false would mean to abandon the very being of our spirit; but, owing to the unconditionality of the distinction, to acknowledge it means also to acknowledge its ontological ground. For the distinction between these values does not furnish its own ground. At times we humans may fancy that our intelligence is infallible, but we are so uncertain of it that, in fact, we must make the distinction anew in every moment of our thinking activity. Yet, we do not make it arbitrarily, but rather in line with the necessity of reason from which the intelligence derives the validity of its formal laws[a] and, along with these laws, the (often unjustified) claim that the accomplishments of the intelligence are always valid. Insofar as this claim involves the necessity of the distinction between true and false it has its legitimacy from reason and is therefore unshakeable. Through reason the claim of the intelligence unites all "finite rational beings," and it finds its confirmation in experience by uniting all men. (The thought of primitive man moves in forms different from ours. It is caught up in magic presuppositions, and hence is very far from our intellectual patterns. But even for primitive thought the distinction between true and false is indispensable. It is unconditionally valid wherever judgments are being made.)

When we meet with judgments, as we hear them or read them, or formulate them ourselves, the interest we show for them is not usually attributable to the fact that they take a stand for the true and against the false (and that even as untruths they pretend to take this stand). For we take this fact as a matter of course. Our vital interest is concerned with the particular truth content of the objective statement. But this content can always be doubted in some measure; remember the Meditations of Descartes.[5] The human intelligence receives only a faint reflection of what, free of all contrast, is the ontological truth. A reflection is fragmentary and comes in refracted rays. Its interpretation requires the help of mental images, whose bearing is always influenced by the current trends in cultural life. The mental images among primitives are different from those in civilized regions, but even in the latter they are subject to a usually slow but steady change. (Aristotle's concept of cause was different from the concept of the eighteenth century, and that in its turn differs from the concept of today. And one must always ask anew the question of the extent to which thinking in terms of causality is legitimate, and what types of causal concepts must be distinguished and acknowledged.) Our judgments seek truth, but what they can grasp is uncertain.

However, our judgments do not occur in isolation. Other judgments in the contexts of which they must be understood give them some security.[6] The individual links of an objective structure of judgments, e.g., in the natural science of an age, support each other—but, of course, within the framework of that conditionality beyond which no objective judgment can go.[7] Thus, the desire for an objectively fixed truth leads to the boundless, and even given infinite time, the truth of the intelligence could not get any closer to the unconditional truth. True, every activity concerned with knowledge designates a path of liberation for the life of the intellect. Nevertheless, if this activity reflects upon itself it becomes aware of its own frailty[b] and of the fact that all the objective and apparently fixed certitudes are conditioned by the steady movement of intellectual history, and within that history, by principles which are not clear and are surely not unconditionally true.[8]

Kant tried to understand these forms of objective knowledge as "conditions of the possibility of experience" and to verify them in a timeless, systematic manner. These forms constitute the *I* as the self-aware subject of objective knowledge. However, the knowing subject is purely spiritual only in abstraction. In reality it always has a basis of a natural kind, and it does not in the least stand in rigid opposition to that basis as if it were a spiritual reality different in essence from the natural. (Such a difference might be supposed if one were to interpret Plato's comparison of the body with a prison of the soul literally.) Our own body is not given to us merely as an object;[9] it participates in our subjectivity. But since objectivity is still of its essence, the very questionable character of everything objective plays its part in our knowledge. "One understands only on the basis of what one is."[10] In a deliberately anthropomorphic phrase, Schelling has said of nature that it is that in God which "He Himself is not."[11] If we reduce Schelling's phrase to the original relationship from which he has borrowed it and thus refer it to the nature of individual man, it then signifies that that in us which we ourselves are not—namely, the unfree, particular "self-will of the creature"[12]—seeks to influence our decisions and does influence them. With us it is not as it is in God—the basis of our existence is not entirely subject to the life of the spirit. We men know this basis as what ought to be "merely a carrier and, as it were, a receptacle of the highest principle of light."[13] And yet we know it as that which continuously threatens our certainty of self and our freedom, and only too often overwhelms them. And the basis not only threatens our knowledge: in every man it manifests itself as his peculiar urges, and, through these urges, as particular dangers to his humanity.

Similar to the effects of the *individual* basis of natural being, and in fact deriving from the natural basis of individuals, there are also the effects of the economic and juridical basis of *social* existence,[14] effects which influence "that which one is"—*ce qu'on est*. Both economics and law are necessary conditions of human existence, but both also involve temptations and fetters for our humanity. Therefore both must be made the object of responsible concern.

In its passive thraldom, an animal existence which is nothing but animal existence is not aware of how constrained it is. Mere chance bestows upon such an existence circumstances of life which offer the possibility of satisfying urges, the animal will enjoy existence. Humanity gladly helps further such enjoyment. (It is painful to see an animal suffer.) Humanity also wishes every joy to the child who as yet bears no responsibility—the unconcerned joy of existence. But this joy is no longer possible as soon as the movements of the human spirit reach into a realm where opposing interests are at odds with each other. As the growing child moves into this realm, the awareness of his responsibility is awakened in him. And responsibility demands a meaning for existence, a meaning which can be neither secured nor enhanced by enjoyment, a meaning which even suffering can not call into question. As long as man gives himself up to the natural and the social drive of the basis of his existence, the meaning of life remains closed to him. He would sink to the level of the animal if his responsibility did not continue to distinguish him from that level. Franz von Baader has said, "Unfortunately, man can stand only above or below the animal."[15] The meaning of the existence of a little child is experienced by those who are in charge of his education; through education the child ought to mature so that he himself can experience the responsibility which he must take in person.

Wherever men become deeply aware of belonging together, the meaning of human existence is fulfilled. All peoples belong together, and in the long run this has become so deep and universal as to bring about their actual unity. The readiness for this feeling is prepared within the narrower framework of every particular community of culture. Every community has strong and weak members, highly or less highly endowed. Yet the desire for true culture is manifest in the endeavor to relate the life of all to a unity which embraces all in such a way that the accomplishments of the strong and gifted will benefit even the weakest and most wretched—though through manifold mediations. (The abolition of serfdom in Prussia was brought about very decisively by the influence which one of the strongest and most gifted men, Kant, had upon a student of law, the later minister, Theodor von Schön.) A high culture in a nation presupposes that the difference in natural talents shall be recognized, and that no arrangement of life and no regulation of schooling shall try to reduce everyone to the lowest common denominator, nor shall artificial privilege create gulfs which could swallow up the superhistorical task of human community.

In spite of all the differences with which nature equips the conditions of a personal form of life, nature is impersonal; and so it remains, even where social influences have turned the life of natural urges towards the goals of civilization. We have not acquired our urges by personal choice, and wherever our urges determine our life it takes its course in line with the impersonal "self-will of the creature"—in line with the trend of that in us which we ourselves are not. The more decisively the individual defends himself against the vexations which arise from the basis of his existence, hindering the development of the humanity for which he is responsible, the better he secures the possibility of a meaningful formation of his own life. (He also secures the formation of his environment, a formation which is inseparable from the formation of his self. For wherever we take a hand in the development of the environment we also shape something in our selves. And whatever we do for our own inner formation becomes significant for the active stand we take within our environment.)

The very fact that responsibility is his makes manifest the specific unreliability of man—this reverse, this wrong, side of the freedom which, to be sure, man ought to realize but whose realization is never assured. (Unconditional freedom would not have any "reverse" and could not be made answerable, not even answerable to itself.) Our human existence confronts us with tasks: but it is uncertain how well or how poorly we shall do them. The more that reverse of our freedom asserts itself, the more our freedom lacks substance and becomes illusionary: it ceases to be true freedom. Then we merely imagine that we decide; in fact our action will be determined by our natural urges (whether innate or conditioned by social circumstances). Man's responsibility directs him to seek the center of his decisions in the depths of himself. Yet our nature has great power (immediately, and also mediated through social circumstances). Ours is a nature from whose hold we must first liberate what is personal in our being, in order that our nature shall become what it ought to be, the mere foundation of our being.

In a famous phrase,[16] Pascal demanded that man should be aware of his baseness as well as his greatness. Man should not grow despondent and faint-hearted, but neither should he misjudge the possibilities of greatness which are given to him. In particular, he ought to avoid mistaking a mere display of power for human greatness. To be sure, power always affords some freedom; but such freedom can spend itself in the realm of illusion. In order that it should be true freedom, the responsible will which subjects power to the service of humanity is needed. If man strives for power as a goal, the power will alienate him from his true self, and his consciousness of freedom becomes a fateful self-deception—fateful for others also if the power tyrannizes them. We ascend true heights only by doing our true tasks. Life, in its height, finds its superiority over its basis. But this basis is subject to constant, cumulative growth deriving from the facts of our individual past. As the future becomes past, our liberty becomes irrevocably restricted by the fresh data on whose ground we must now make our further decisions. Thus even the height of life which we may have attained confronts us ever again with new obligations. Interminably our very accomplishments prove to have been dependent on the shortcomings of the time at which they were attained and demand to be surpassed. When conscience resists the tendencies deriving from its foundation in nature, it measures the performances produced under the conditions of time against what is demanded supertemporally. Thus one sees clearly the distance which separates what man is, what he has done and what he is doing, from what he ought to be, what he ought to have done, and what he should do. Man always lags behind the concept of his humanity which would oblige him to be at one with himself.[17]

The concept "humanity" sums up that which gives to all human "reality," to all human "existence," its tension, its orientation towards the supertemporal ideas of the true, the good, the just, and the beautiful. Fichte saw[18] that to eliminate the tension would involve turning man into God. But the greatest undertaking that is within man's reach is to direct his own life towards the height of humanity attainable in his time[19]: and yet "humanity" involves transcending time, it involves the supertemporal. Moreover, one must not forget that the heights of humanity at a given time cannot be determined unambiguously; currents of very different kinds are operative in the movements of culture—currents which may be opposed to each other and currents which have no immediate relation to each other. Each current, after its own fashion, permits us to represent the humanity of the time. If it is said of a man that he is at the height of the humanity of his time, this does not mean that he is no longer limited to his particular interests in culture. These interests determine his sphere, and within this sphere he has the capacity to realize his humanity in a conservative direction as well as in an attitude of active faith bent upon a desired change. "Greatnesses which have opposite meanings do not cancel each other out."[20]

The illimitable meaning of the word "humanity" excludes its

application to concrete human beings; none can represent the meaning exhaustively. And on that account mythology alone can point across the chasm between real man (who is always historically conditioned in many ways) and the "concept" (the Idea) of man. Such mythology is most necessary and wholesome. In the very true sense it brings about wholeness.[c] It may seem to voice objective truth, but this can seem so only to a mind which does not understand what it means to be a self, and which is bound by the objective formulations of its religious symbols. Yet even for such a mind, mythology points the way to the eternal goal of perfect humanity. But where the objective symbols are recognized as symbols, where the sensuous imagery has ceased to hamper the free movement of the spirit, there the symbols are experienced as parables which embody ontological truth. Their symbolic expression points beyond the possibilities accessible to objective consciousness, it points to that truth which is unconditionally true. Human consciousness must acknowledge that truth, though it be unable to comprehend it in the forms of finite consciousness: for such comprehension would mean to limit the truth, even to deny its unconditionality—although not denying it deliberately.

The forms of cognitive consciousness permit comprehension of the finite as such. These forms prove fruitful in technology, because technical thinking considers the parts which make up its constructions only as finite, and uses them as finite. A complicated machine which has its use in the present will become obsolete after a time. The principles of its construction, however, retain their validity: at every future time, the machine could be built again, and the operation it performs today objectively it would perform again. The forms of social life (the constitutions of states, the laws, the educational systems, the economic institutions, forms of transportation, etc.) become obsolete in a very much more comprehensive and deeper sense; they do not stand on a timeless ground but are time-conditioned manifestations of supertemporal life-forces. If, after centuries, one should want to make use of these social forms again, they would by no means be able to serve the purposes they serve today. They would bring about quite unsupportable conditions. Finite objects have no inner relationship to the time that happens to be; men, however, live in their own time, and every social practice belongs to its time. To be sure, in abstraction, men, too, may be considered as if they were finite things; for instance, the size of their body and their weight can be determined quantitatively. But, for their humanity, everything objective which can be distinguished in man is only a basis, a vehicle, a presupposition. The specifically human which develops, making use of this basis, is beyond the reach of the categories of finite things.

[Since humanity is not an object] the word humanity has no objective sense. We can know what it means only from our immediate experience, and this experience points beyond itself—it points to the greatest breadth, comprehensiveness and depth. Many examples of history, even of the most recent history not yet recorded by historians, could furnish illustrations for such experience. But to illustrate is one thing, to use the predicate of humanity without qualification is another. Unqualifiedly, the purely human can be predicated only of single actions detached from their context by abstraction. Were we to bestow the predicate upon the whole life of a man, then many qualifications would appear as a matter of course—though they might be deemed of little importance. They would appear for this reason only, that a perfect realization of the purely human would require perfect conditions of existence. Imperfections of the frame which holds and narrows a life will always enforce decisions which set man at odds with himself. Under given circumstances, such decisions may be the best possible, but they cannot be perfect. With every postage stamp which we buy from the state we support the state's goals. And in spite of the very best will of those who are responsible for the necessary tasks of the state, the goals of the state cannot be attained without some inhumanity. With every service we furnish to the state (and rightly must furnish) we give our assent to the state—we partake of its unavoidable guilt.

The humanity of man is always only relative. The meaning of the word humanity makes us aware of the measure of this relativity, and in that measure it sets the goals for every historical epoch—though without concrete specificity. *What* is to be done in order that man may be furnished the conditions of the best possible at-one-ness with himself—to determine this *what* is left to the perseverance and to the insight of man (to the correct evaluation of the real situation). Yet it is left to man's judgment only where deep love fills the imagination and lifts it beyond the time-conditioned level. With good reason Raymond Savioz (taking his cue from Gabriel Marcel) has spoken of "the light which gushes forth from the mystery."[21]

Humanity and love cannot be separated. Likewise, inhumanity and uncharitableness go together. "Love" signifies a communion which has its ground in man's inwardness. Even nature has its own inwardness (for this very reason our body is not given to us as a mere object). But for humanity nature is merely a basis. Of natural love, the remark of Baader[22] is true, that "notwithstanding all the charm and all the delight found in the innocence of natural love, it still carries infirmity within itself, nay death." Love is human only when, by faithfulness, it has overcome the contingent, the altogether too transitory, which belongs to the merely natural. And genuine faithfulness results from the fact that the inwardness on which human community rests is experienced in responsible existence. In the measure in which the love which creates a community is human, the demands of the day as given by the particular situation furnish the goal for the union between the members of the community. The fact that the community is bent upon this goal manifests itself in the undesirable form of imperatives only in borderline cases. Normally it is love which determines the direction towards the goals, and love is the spontaneity of the drive of life. Fichte once asked, "What is it that gives to each individual the exclusive character of his particular life?" And he answers: "It is the love of this particular and individual life. Reveal to me what you truly love, what you seek with your fullest desire, and what you strive for when you hope to find the true enjoyment of yourself—and you have already interpreted your life for me. What you love, you live."[23]

Now to be sure, the members of a community (no matter whether a religious denomination or a political party or a student fraternity) belong to the community with very different intensity. Consequently they are not all in the same measure aware of the character of the community, which can be more or less pure, humanly speaking, and which as such forms the personal life.

The mightier and purer the love which lives in an individual and the more unambiguously it is committed to what is truly human, the better the individual will understand the human meaning of the community, and the more decisively he will find in that meaning the reason for his own belonging to the community. What his faithfulness has in view is the community's human meaning. Empirically, to be sure, faithfulness seems to be demonstrated best by one who would adhere to his community through thick and thin, through right and wrong. But true faithfulness has its principle in conscience, in the responsibility for what is human, and in order to preserve the integrity of the human it may be that an empirical tie must be loosened or even cut. Nietzsche began his academic studies at Bonn, where he joined the "Franconia" fraternity. After two semesters he returned the ribbon.[d] In the accompanying letter there are the sentences: "I must notify the assembly of the Franconia that I hereby declare my resignation. I do not cease to hold the idea of fraternity as such in high esteem. But I will frankly confess that I take little pleasure in its present form. . . . May the Franconia soon outgrow a stage of its development in which it now is. May it always have nothing but members of worthy intentions and of good manners."[24]

The inward aspect of nature becomes valuable when its energy —though it belongs to that in man which is "not he himself"— serves humanity and in humanity serves truth. Where this subordination is lacking, nature may show itself in instincts which are indifferent to values or outright wrong. Then the love by means of which the inward aspect of nature affects social forms keeps these forms on a level which is humanly low. The more his bad instincts tie an individual to a social organization (which on that account need not be bad itself) the more unscrupulously he will be "faithful" to the organization, even if it moves in devious paths, for he takes pleasure in that which is all too human in the organization. Then his faithfulness, instead of being subordinate to conscience, will rule conscience in a large measure. Such faithfulness will also display a moral unction and will thus try to justify the evil way in which it represents the common cause. To be sure, there may also be genuinely humane motives, for instance motives of selflessness (man is never a devil in all respects); nevertheless, evil instincts determine the goals for which the moral forces work. In every state there is probably a considerable number of such "patriots" to whom the state is dear precisely because of the tragic necessity of inhuman procedures. Such patriots find it unforgivable if an individual wants to keep his conscience clean wherever the state gives an evil suggestion or an outright order. Moreover, if the officeholders of their state are humanly worthless fellows, then they have their most reliable supporters of their rule in such patriots. . . . Genuine patriotism acts as *responsibility for the humanity of the fatherland.* A distinguished theologian has said that love is "worth exactly as much as its object."[25] The same thing can be said of faithfulness. But just as every synthetic unity of elements of judgment, owing to its categoric form, depends on the idea of the true, and so far partakes of the true, even if that which it claims is false, thus also in love and faithfulness that which is formally essential for all humanity shows that the individual's relation to the community is subordinate to humanity even if the content of the relationship is inhuman. Only that faithfulness has value whose empirical substantiation springs from genuine humanity.

Dire inevitability can *force* man to inhuman actions. Owing to the frailty of our existence there are times when nothing can prevent an overpowering gloom being cast upon what is truly human.[26] Yet even warfare is under obligation to humanity: it ought not permit full vent to evil instincts. One who is under obligation to an inhuman "duty" can find in the light of his conscience the painful but unerring awareness that the fulfillment of that "duty" is guilt belonging to the time into which his ill fate has thrust him and by which he, too, is soiled. However, his conscience will also make clear to him where the limit is beyond which he must reject impositions which are presented to him as "duties." He may help carry the guilt of his time—he is a member of the present human race and its imperfect social orders —but he will not contribute to a relapse into the barbarism of an earlier age. (When two men do the same thing, it is not the same. [German proverb.] This is true also with regard to brutalities found among primitives as compared to those committed by a man whom a rich cultural heritage obliges to a higher level of humanity.) If a man ordered to do something inhuman submits to the order as inevitable, consenting likewise to the deceit involved in describing his action as "doing one's duty," he is guilty of the denial of truth and a fatal weakening of his humanity. Precisely when the man lacks the courage to admit to himself that wrong is wrong, it is fatal to the ability to feel true human love. On the other hand, one who is of a humane mind need not be crushed by the awareness that he is living in a world weighed down with guilt, living in it as one who has been drawn into its guilt not only through his own will but without it. To acknowledge the guilt of the present time (in which the individual's personal guilt is comprehended) means to attain to clarity with regard to the shortcomings of the present time (and the shortcomings in particular of the little piece of the present which we ourselves are)—it is a clarity which constitutes an obligation, light in the obscurity of life. In François Mauriac's novel *Woman of the Pharisees*, the wise priest hearing the confession of a lady (the identical woman of the Pharisees) makes her feel ashamed of the excessive importance she is attaching to her own sins, "as if she did not know that God uses even our sins for his own purposes." Properly understood, the awareness of guilt becomes a light on the path to humanity.

The so-called great religions have the distinction of evaluating the natural as that which has been conquered and is to be conquered. The adherent of such a religion is aware that the meaning of life is not to be sought in the objective world. Its enigmatic nature remains without decisive influence on the meaning of human existence, and it is this meaning which is of central significance.[27] One who tries to ascertain the meaning of existence objectively will not find it. It is a meaning which must be experienced, and it can be experienced only by one who does not let his natural drives take possession of him but, as one who loves, holds himself "available"[28] for appeals to his freedom. Through these appeals the order which is superior to mere natural existence, from its ontological depths, reveals, from time to time, that which is authentically human.

The deities of nature have their whims. The gods of the Greeks were not good. In the great religions, the content of the myth is purely human. "Seeking its proper path, my heart accepts what is divine only insofar as it is human."[29]

To be sure, the great religions do not, at every point in their history, stand in such definite opposition to the nature religions. Religious communities have to maintain themselves within the conditions of the changing circumstances of the times, and hence they are not free to renounce their desire for power completely. Through this desire for power, the natural basis of humanity threatens to exalt itself over what is human. And wherever it succeeds there is fresh confirmation of the words which Rabindranath Tagore, in one of his dramas, puts into the mouth of the king. Receiving the report that his brother is plotting against his life because the goddess, the Great Mother Kâli, demands his blood, the king says, "When the gods are at stake man loses his humanity."[30] But even Ramakrishna, for whom the religious life was nothing but all-embracing love, humanity in its purity, was a priest of the Great Mother Kâli. It is not the gods who are at fault, but the guilt of men when the gods demand what is inhuman.

9

CONFIRMATIONS

Every experience of truth enters into consciousness as the unity of a manifold. In a scholarly book every sentence endeavors to comprehend a multiplicity of elements of judgment. Every chapter seeks to unite a manifold of individual insights, in a more far-reaching cognition. And the entire book presents itself as the unity in which the different chapters are joined together in order to offer the kind of knowledge which the title of the book promises: one comprehensive truth would present itself.

Most situations in which we find ourselves require some action on our part. By moral action we must understand an action in line with what the situation truly is.[1] In order to accomplish this a multiplicity of individual actions of different kinds must be performed. Schiller sings the praises of the faith which, in 1325, Frederick the Handsome of Austria kept with Louis the Bavarian, to whom he had given his knightly word that if he were unable to persuade his brother Leopold to accept Louis's terms, he would return into captivity. This keeping faith on Frederick's part called for quite a number of individual actions—from resistance to temptations (made more inviting by the Pope) down to care for the baggage.[a] These actions were unified by Frederick's conviction that the word he had given determined his situation unambiguously. The situation being what it was in truth for him, he could not deal with it other than by returning into captivity. The realization of his experience of truth was the purpose which meaningfully joined, in a comprehensive unity, the very different individual actions which were needed. But a criminal purpose, too, gives coherence to the preparatory actions. In that case, however, the situation is not at all dealt with as what it is in truth. The means are related to their end only by intelligence, which always serves only a conditional truth and is neutral towards the meaning of human existence, neutral with regard to good and evil. And the evil end has a merely subjective ground, as for instance in a desire for revenge. Its realization, therefore, cannot help the agent to be ultimately at one with himself. For the existence of a man is not contained within itself, but has its roots within the comprehensive social contexts which—be they what they are[2]—demand a morally pure behavior. The kind of action which, in subjectivistic manner, would disregard the ontological truth brings the agent into inescapable conflict with the social context as well as with the depth of his own being. (It is one of the tasks of criminal procedure to make the criminal clearly aware of that conflict.) The intelligence is impersonal: it is incapable of furnishing the ground for the unity of personality.

Endeavors toward justice are similar to moral actions; they, too, would unify a multiplicity of different expedients under one guiding point of view. However, there is this distinction, that these measures can be enforced; and furthermore, that their justice is substantiated only if they are freely recognized as just. In civilized states, court procedure is public as far as possible: the judgments are addressed to the entire community under the law, and they anticipate the community's agreement. But especially important is the agreement of those who are immediately concerned, and of them the judgments often expect the serious subjugation of selfish desires. At all events, the realization of what is just occurs only in a synthesis of the enforced and the free. It occurs when the enforced is freely made a matter of one's own will.[3]

In the current of life it is possible to set goals whose content is determined by sheerly subjective arbitrariness. Within the domain of the economic and juridical basis of what is human, such goals can even meet with success. (The police do not apprehend every criminal. And even if he is brought before the judge, then, owing to an all-too-clever defense, the criminal may not receive "that which is due him," that is, the personally befitting punishment, not to speak of the reform meant for him.) In a similar way, the value of a work of art can be restricted to what is subjective, for instance, to the fact that the work shows taste, and this value may be sufficient to bring its creator popularity and economic gain.

One cannot argue about taste (or, what amounts to the same thing, one cannot argue endlessly), simply because taste is merely subjective. However, since the meaning of art implies what is irreplaceable for the humanity of man, art does not merely satisfy the demands of subjective taste, nor is it merely a manifestation of the specific life of an individual, but as irreplaceable it is the revelation of ontological truth. To be sure, this essential meaning of art manifests itself only under the particular conditions of the history of the time: therefore, it takes into account the prevailing taste. (Of course, in order to blaze a trail for a new time and for the new beauty of that time, it may deliberately go against the taste of the present.) But that which, in the life of mankind, gives necessity to art is the superhistorical truth which speaks through art.

The harmonious fusion of a multiplicity of sense elements is indispensable for all art; it can be found even in the most superficial work of the artist whose performance, quite lacking in real substance, is a cultivation of what he vainly calls his own taste. But the pleasure taken in what has no substance becomes a danger to our humanity, to our personal wholeness. The harmonious synthesis of the multiplicity is experienced in the deeper sense where great art ennobles what is time-conditioned, raising it to the level at which the voice of the eternal is heard, joyful or reproachful.

Of the fullness of this eternal reality man is a sharer in this, that starting from the individual basis of his existence, it is possible for a personal center of self-awareness to come into being and develop. From this center, through the working together of the autonomous functions of the human spirit, man looks out on life and becomes aware of the meaning of his own existence. High art speaks not only to the aesthetic sensibilities but to the undivided humanity of man. And on that very account it speaks to everyone who would plumb its depths in a personal way; only to him is it fully accessible.[4] The more a man who encounters art is himself a unified personality, the more the truth of the masterpiece will touch him—and the deeper the level at which his meeting with art will reveal to him the substance of life which gives direction to the forces of his own existence, the substance in which these forces find their liberating unity.

To make the reality of this substance of life the matter of living experience is the endeavor of the great religions. The verbal expressions of these religions are very different, and even within one and the same denomination one phrase contradicts another; but in religion words have an inevitable inadequacy. The liturgy, however, is of assistance here; it gives a practical interpretation of the meaning of the words and affords an experience of the unutterable. The depth of human existence can attain a form of awareness whether a man remains within the existing order of sacred tradition or is struck by the certainty of a new mission. ("You have heard that it was said to the men of old. . . . But I say to you . . .) (Matt. 5:21ff.) In such certitude the depths of our being claim authority over all our personal potentialities. This activation of the depths means personal wholeness, the overcoming of our spiritual fragmentation and inward uncertainties. Of course even now the intelligence in its impersonal operations can fall prey to doubt in situations which are not rationally clear, to dilemmas from which it sees no avenue of escape. Nevertheless, like all other autonomous functions, it remains even then unalterably in the service of our humanity. Wherever the depths of being in its purity break through into our conscious life, doubts and errors and their often very undesirable consequences are accepted as part of our human enterprise. Even demonic aberrations lose their power in the light of insights granted by Grace, and the path of highest necessity becomes luminously clear. The autonomous functions do supply what they are meant to supply for our humanity, for the necessity of what is human is experienced in these functions. And insofar as man's body serves as a foundation for his humanness, the necessity of the human finds its own experience even in the body, thus securing the unity of the person.

Wherever humanness is realized it bears the stamp of personality; each man's potentialities are exclusively his, and the more strongly humanness in its purity is manifested in him the more conventions decrease in importance; and, at the same time, that element in his personality which is not interchangeable with others becomes better defined. In all those areas where the social order makes its claims the powers of the person keep faith with the superhistorical ideas. This is a faith which needs no orientation spelled out in explicit commands; for our humanity the ideas do not merely mean what they are named, which may seem to point in separate directions (e.g., the good, the beautiful); they involve a reference to the human in which they are unified and which does remain one and the same in the very distinction of the separate directions in which it develops. This identity cannot be grasped like an objective image, but it can be experienced—experienced as love which proves itself in actions where actions are called for. Rabindranath Tagore says: "Love is the ultimate meaning of everything around us. It is not a mere sentiment; it is truth."[5] The person who loves becomes aware of that which, in the sphere of superindividual life, is the ontological truth of his own life.

One must have a right understanding of the word love. A devotion which simply diffused itself would not be viable.[6] Devotion always presupposes a self which boldly takes its stand. On Pestalozzi's tomb there are the words "Everything for others, nothing for oneself." It would be foolish to try to take these words literally; their real meaning is that self-fulfillment was not a final end for Pestalozzi, he kept it within the narrowest possible limits. From the beginning of his career he endeavored to acquaint himself with the urgent problems of his time. In these troubled situations he saw human need where his contemporaries did not see it and did not want to see it; acknowledging the need would have the consequence of demanding self-limitation instead of self-fulfillment from the "higher classes"—the "Haves." Pestalozzi kept his eyes open to the need of the time, and this was a very essential part of the service which, as he knew, truth demanded of him. (He often wrote the word truth reverently.) To fight strongly and with dedication against a known distress was in Pestalozzi's eyes a service of God. In the suffering poor he saw the suffering God. He often praised the splendor, the "Godlike" quality, of human nature, but he saw how the distress which weighed upon the poor prevented that glory from revealing itself in its full radiance.

Yet it is not only by the poverty of those who must remain without hope in a life of misery that God's splendor is dimmed— the pre-eminent but not the exclusive preoccupation of Pestalozzi; everywhere and always there are clouds of distress. To put it in Christian terms, that need makes its appeal to the willingness to make sacrifices, to that will which loves God in men. "Yet even a little pagan saying does no harm."[b] Rabindranath Tagore would say: "The higher nature in man always seeks something which transcends itself and yet is its deepest truth; which claims all its sacrifice, yet makes this sacrifice its own recompense. This is man's *dharma*, man's religion, and man's self is the vessel which is to carry this sacrifice to the altar."[7] To be sure, the thought that our humanness finds its fulfillment only in self-sacrifice is one which does not readily enter the Western mind. Yet it could not remain unspoken: a glance at the Christian cross was bound to evoke it. We have the verses of Angelus Silesius:

> The rain does not fall for itself, the sun
>   does not shine for its own sake,
> For others thou too art created, not for thyself.[c]

Even the proof of the existence of God which Descartes produces in his Third Meditation speaks of the longing which draws man beyond himself to the immensity which ever increases, the goodness which endlessly becomes more perfect.

However, a far stronger influence on the Western mind is exercised by the idea that for man, the "crown of creation," the self-realization of himself as an individual is the unquestionable ultimate goal. The most greatly admired are those individuals who, having themselves a passion for life, are able to communicate this passion to others, stimulating in them the courage to be themselves—selves fully contained within the bounds of nature. Almost without exception, in the lives which are representative of Western history and have given it its character, we can observe very little of what Tagore, in the passage quoted, has called *dharma*; but an abundance of the *entelechy* which explains the stages of individual development as the manifestation of a principle of self-fulfillment determining the individual's proper form. In its origin the concept of an entelechy was meant to explain natural organisms unaware of their teleological development, but in Western culture it has become a guide for the interpretation of the moral domain as well. On September 1, 1829, in a conversation about God and immortality, Goethe said to Eckermann:

"I do not doubt the continuation of our existence because nature cannot dispense with the entelechy." We are not in the least denying that it is permissible to apply the concept of entelechy to the life of the person: for the life of the person, even including the life of the human spirit, belongs to the life of nature and hence shows the characteristics which determine all life. Our question is whether that concept extends to the question of the person's ultimate goal. For naturalism, materialism, psychologism, biologism, insight into the truth of the idea of sacrifice is precluded. Insofar as those "isms" have anything whatever to say about a goal of personal existence, it is a goal which must be sought in the self-realization of the individual as such. "Become the one you are!" The old dictum has this impressive echo in Nietzsche.[d] The injunction has been understood as a summons to austere inflexibility, and in Europe it has for long been heeded by people who knew nothing of Pindar. Such Europeans have appointed as Lord of Hosts (asked to bless their weapons of war) the God who made manifest on Golgotha his relation to men and their actions. Simply because they have "given their lives," those who have fallen in battle have had their deaths solemnized as Christian deaths following in the line of Jesus (even with a daring allusion to John 15:13).

But as we have said, war cannot be waged without a guilt in which all participants share.[8] The death of a soldier means that the man has fallen victim to an evil fate. But the Crucified manifests in his dying his transcendence of a fate full of the utmost horror, proving to the last his total adherence to the will of God in the fulfillment of his personal mission.[9] Tagore says (just before the passage we have quoted): "The bearers of revelation were always those who led a life of self-sacrifice." And a little further on: "Love has its end in itself. In all other instances we ask 'why?' and search for a reason. But when one says 'I love,' then 'why' has no place." "Why" asks for a reason: but for the immediate self which says "I" there are no reasons. Reasons are addressed to the self as subject—the subject of the experience of truth; all argumentation presupposes that there is a self which can evaluate reasons, consequently the self as such cannot be based on reasons.

But how far does the province of this immediate self extend? We all know the phenomenon of people who, in certain matters, are inaccessible to reason. We cannot discuss these matters with them; they have so fully identified themselves with them, so passionately, with so much love—love which is worth "exactly as much as its object"[10]—that they are unable to separate them from the immediate reality of the self. (And this goes on as long as their passion endures.) The "patriotic" nationalist says, "Right or wrong, it is *my* country which is at stake." He identifies his love with his deepest, most inward self. Nevertheless he may have to admit that the situation he will not talk about may be "unjust," and by that admission he acknowledges the existence of a free self which transcends the self which is bound by history and likewise his historically determined love. He recognizes the unifying self which makes the distinctions between values, distinctions in which "reason has us"—between true and false, good and evil. This free self directs even him; yet he uses his freedom to disregard its verdict. His empirical self is so possessed by his passions as to be powerless to resist them.

Though a man awakens to an awareness of his own self, yet in the course of his personal development, no matter what or who is the object of his love, every purely natural impulse of love is bound up with all the elements in opposition in historical life. Never is it simply love; it is always also rejection, and very often hatred. (The nationalist's love for his country is hatred directed against the "enemies" of the fatherland whom he invents if he cannot discover them.) Often the natural urge is ambivalent: love and hatred are directed to one and the same person, one and the same institution. Social relationships make their unceasing demands, and often they enforce participation in the ambivalence which motivates them. They require us, and try to coerce us, to love on the one hand, to hate on the other. Occasions for hatred are easily found in known injustices, and particularly in injustices suffered personally; but in injustices personally done as well. (It has been said of an important man in an important position that this was part of his greatness: he would bear no grudge against those to whom he had done an injustice.)

But men have become aware long since that hatred is a sign

of unfreedom, of inner weakness. God does not hate: what is hateful does not exist for him.[11] The Gospel of Luke (even more impressively than the parallel passage in Matthew which speaks of the evil and the good, the just and the unjust) says that the Most High is kind to the ungrateful and the wicked; men show themselves to be sons of God if they love their enemies (Luke 6:35; cf. Matt. 5:45). But man *must* hate; what is hateful does exist for him. This is a consequence of the poverty of the human being, who becomes aware of truth only by way of the opposition of true and false and is incapable of apprehending truth unconditionally. It is impossible for man to free himself from this way of knowing in order to know in the manner of a pure spirit. The worth which his life can attain is bound up with his making use of the possibilities which are given to him. For man, awareness of the true comes about through contrast with the false; good is known through contrast with evil. No exception to this is made even with respect to the earthly life of the Son of God, in the image of it presented by the New Testament. A mitigation of the need to hate is possible (and for the noble and humane man is a matter of course) only because, according to a teaching which goes back to the Old Testament prophets (Rom. 12:9, Amos 5:15, Micah 3:2), hatred is not necessarily directed towards persons. Evil must be hated; but men are to be loved even if they are evil, even if they are our enemies. This is the utmost achievement possible within the limits of our finitude: to love the doers of evil in spite of all; to hate only evil itself, hate what is base and inhuman. This hatred is a human obligation; but man's hatred must be above egoistic motives.

In the love of our enemies the divine diffuses its radiance with a power which is equalled nowhere else in the world which unfolds before our consciousness. "Love your enemies"—it is a wondrous phrase. Because the word enemy has a meaning only within this world of contrasts, *love* directed towards the enemy is the denial of faith in this world. To "believe" in the *world* means to entrust oneself to it, to seek life's meaning in the fulfillments which the world can provide. But faith and trust directed outwards, and hence towards what can be determined *objectively*, is always exposed to legitimate doubt. True faith is a certitude that there is inward depth in one's own being.[12] This certitude cannot be attained by a single, particular function of the life of the human spirit but issues from a harmony of man's spiritual forces under the sign of truth, of the humane. (The "faith" of a man who is torn by inner conflicts is always imperfect, and if it poses as religious faith it will only with difficulty escape the danger of tyrannizing the intelligence, ignoring the latter's legitimate exercise. The difficulties involved in the relation between faith and knowledge spring from a misunderstanding of the true meaning of faith, which leaves the investigation of objective reality to the intelligence quite unreservedly.) Wherever the powers of the human person are gatherd into unity, the intelligence is presented with *its* true task; it is impossible, then, for it to be used for inhuman activities.

The man who is whole is capable of love—love which, as Louis Meylan says, makes the intelligence clairvoyant.[13] The richer and more comprehensive the love, the more perfect is the integration of the person. Unlimited love—which is an Idea—transcends all the contrarieties of life. One who hates nothing but what is inhuman does not fall prey to these oppositions or lose any element of himself to them; always and everywhere he is free of them. Of course, even one who feels no hatred against any man stands within the conditions of the world owing to what is objective in his own existence. He remains exposed to the attacks of inimical forces: they are at liberty to assail him, but he is not their enemy. The love living in him is the revelation of the divine in man; it is the truest[14] humanity.

According to the words we have quoted from Luke, God does not know his enemies as such, but He loves them, the ungrateful and the wicked alike. This statement would be seriously misinterpreted if it were to be understood as a contribution to the characterization of an otherworldly reality, and on that account called a "revelation." What the statement reveals is the divine depth of our human existence. It does not undertake to make us a gift of transcendent knowledge; its intention is to awaken in our hearts an echo of recognition of the statement as a call deriving from the deepest source and the necessary goals of our own being. Thus understood, what the Gospel of Luke is saying here is that the idea of humanity, in its deepest synthesis constituted by true integration and personal wholeness, points in the direction of that life in which man has ceased to belong to himself, ceased to seek the fulfillment of his being in his own individuality. For his individuality is bound up with the world, and what can be attained in the world is never free of confusion, never fully open to truth. At the end of Romain Rolland's *Play about Death and Love*, we read: "Wherefore, wherefore was life given to us?—In order to overcome it." Only a life lived entirely for the "glory of God," a life that has become wholly sacrificial, raises man beyond any doubt as to the meaning of human existence, for such a life fills him with unlimited truth. To believe in this meaning of life means to have religion.

The objection suggests itself that there are religions which contain no awareness of any such desire to overcome the world. The answer is that during the course of mankind's historical existence many foreign elements have infiltrated the very roots of the religious experience, and this admixture persists in occurring, so that it is possible for what is purely human in true religion to be buried under superstitious elements. Nevertheless, despite all the murkiness and obfuscation, *true* religion must be understood as nothing but a rectification.[15] Even those ritual exercises which would only serve to satisfy the desire for a tolerable relationship with the powers which rule one's own existence have, implicit in the longing they express, the sense of a desire to be in harmony with the being which transcends phenomenal reality—the desire for *truth*.

10
RELIGION AND CULTURE

The insights of the intelligence are the result of the work of man. The way to unconditional truth is barred to them. However, the functioning of the intelligence is the prerequisite for all conditional truth. For the intelligence the reference to unconditionality has a merely ideational significance. The relation which the personal functions of the human spirit have to the unconditional is the ontological source of all their depth and fullness. From it is derived the truth-content which permits these functions to transcend the contingency of the merely subjective, reaching into the domain of unconditional validity. In this way art, morality, justice are anchored in the superhistorical structure of truth, and only by a narrowing of the horizon of reality can the thesis be maintained that the full meaning of truth is consummated in the fact that truth can be the predicate of a statement, which is either true or false. The meaning of Augustine's dictum that God is truth becomes clear: if a man's experiencing of a situation in which he stands (whatever it may be) is fully adequate to the reality of the situation in its depths, then in the experience he knows God. Thus our cultural interests acquire a definite relation to our religious life, though a relation fraught with problems, and the alleged incompatibility of *autonomy* and *theonomy*, so much discussed in literature, loses its appearance of validity. For now it is evident that it is only when a man has not developed to the height of his personal potentialities, when his personal autonomy has not proved itself within the context of reality, that his willing and acting are not identical with the will for truth—the will to conform to God's will (which unceasingly reveals itself in the world, though it is often difficult to interpret).

Kant saw a grave danger for "the true and only religion" in whatever is "according to statute."[1] The "will of God" with respect to statutes can be only this: that in our free decisions they are to be taken for what they are in truth—that is, means for the symbolic representation of the supersensuous which have been handed down to us from specific times. Thus understood as a means, a statute cannot have the ground of its validity in itself. (The danger is that a statute raised to unconditional validity will be productive of uncharity, since it will represent many a limitation which was historically justified as having a severity it does not have in the realm of truth.) If, with Kant, we purge the concept of autonomy of all libertinistic connotations, then we can readily understand that to acknowledge the true significance of statutes is precisely the course which the autonomous personality should take. The formula that I should take everything that concerns me as what it is in truth has a relative significance inasmuch as it must be interpreted with reference to the particular nature of the historical situation (of the organizations of community life, and within them of the individual person).[2] And just as our personal relation to statutes is subject to historical conditions, so also is the attitude we should adopt with respect to the whole theological enterprise. Of course the insights of theology, like the insights of other disciplines concerned with the humanities, are not merely the product of impersonal reflection. But they share with all forms of theoretical knowledge the fact that they are produced by men. For it is within time-conditioned limitations that they bring forth the ontological content which it is their task to offer. The idea of autonomy is capable of realization only in the context of historical relativity.

Where statutory prescriptions are such as to fill a religious community with the superstitious fear[3] that opaque dogmas and commands which seem unreasonable and even inhuman have been revealed in order to test the obedience of faith, the concept of God has been falsified and the concept of autonomy along with it. For now autonomous man is seen as a rebel against God, and God is seen as a dictator. Of course, a man enmeshed in superstitious anxieties will reject the thought of rebellion, believing that it is his religious duty to submit. But a man who yields to a dictator does so at the expense of his humanity. His readiness to obey, whatever the circumstances, a commanding coming from without involves a disregard for the rights of his conscience, which would summon him to act autonomously. If the dictator is the God in whom he believes, then an unworthy concept of God will hide from him the depths of the freedom intimated by calling men the children of God. He is not at one with himself: his repudiation of an autonomous, a truly free, will cuts him off from the possibility of leading his life as an integrated personality. Inevitably his inner life is full of discord. His personal relation to truth is unclear. In principle a clarification can come only if, in the worship of God himself, truth is worshipped—the ontological truth towards which all the life functions of the human spirit are directed.

Yet each of these functions has its own autonomy and hence its own history. The words art, morality, science seem to indicate entirely separate areas. Nevertheless humanity is at work in all of them in an insistent movement of self-formation. Here, however, is the recurrent question in cultural life, which indicates the disintegration by which it is threatened: Is what takes form in the history of art only art or is it the product of man whole and undivided in his humanity? Does art help man to prove himself as human in every new endeavor? Does the cultivation of science serve only the expansion of knowledge (which then can be exploited at will), or does it serve man, who needs the resources of all autonomous orders if his age is to attain the height of its development and he is to attain to genuine humanity in his age?[4] Art, science, morality, economics, law: whenever one of these dominates the formation of human life the humane is thereby fragmented. This dominance hides from view the inner limits set for each particular function of the human spirit by its integration in the comprehensive unity of the human. When they remain mutually exclusive of each other they are mere fragments of the human. Unmistakably they belong to it, but they cannot present it in its fullness any more than the fragments of a vase can represent the vase itself.

The life of truth which makes man human has set his end in the unity of his whole being. The realization of this unity is a non-finite task,[a] and man is increasingly aware that it is beyond his powers. Nevertheless his humanness forbids him to abandon the undertaking, compels him to *believe* in it.

One can disavow one's faith, but only by inhumanity. This need not mean turning inhumane with regard to one's fellow men, but it always means a fateful insufficiency which will limit the experience of essential truth. "One who does not hear the voice of poetry is a barbarian, whoever he may be."[b] The *depth* of being can never be expressed in prose. Every one of the functions of the human spirit is an irreplaceable way to truth. However, just as the once shattered vase retains the cracks after all the fragments have been found and cemented together, and so has lost its unbroken wholeness, so humanity can be cracked even if none of the functions of the spirit is lacking. For the orientation of their activity towards the truly human depends on their being raised and maintained in a higher unity. This orientation is not a matter of course. It is true that we have our faith in unity as a high value and faith in filling our life with meaning. But faith may become confused in difficult situations or situations obscured by passion. Then we become only dimly aware of what the hour calls for, and the powers of temptation find us an easy prey.

Religion claims to provide the true interpretation of the unity which is demanded of man. Religion speaks of the peace of God, which the letter to the Philippians describes as surpassing reason (4:7). What this last phrase may mean in its context does not concern us here. (Perhaps it is a parallel to the warning against philosophy voiced in the letter to the Colossians, 2:8.) But it is true that the "reason which has us" provides no security against our "liberty" to be tormented, as inwardly alienated men, by the question of our life's meaning—to be tormented ever anew and with ever decreasing hope. Reason forces us to distinguish between what is of value and what is a negation of value; but in so doing it merely confronts us with unceasingly changing, unceasingly multiplying tasks. Reason leaves it up to us to seek positive solutions, and it is precisely the most meaningful solutions which are threatened by the "resistance of an indifferent world." Reason cannot *give* us peace, nor will it: peace is the freedom of one who transcends the world.

But are not the troubles of life the fate of men in general? Even the man of religious faith remains exposed to them! Religious or not, the man beset by difficulties will endeavor, while his courage lasts, to equalize the tensions, to resolve the contradictions. On earth and under the conditions of the hour, he will try to break the force of historical events if it threatens his humanity with offense or bondage, or if these evils are an accomplished fact. He will try to measure exigencies, claims, and desiderata against supertemporal standards. What men can accomplish is historically conditioned; even what has the semblance of perfection retains it only for an epoch which passes away, slowly or quickly. Nevertheless if it is born from the faith in supertemporal values and gives that faith expression it is no longer a product which could have resulted from the mere interaction of historical factors. What is genuinely human in our history is the consequence of the incorporation of freedom within historical conditions. In the first of his *Monologues* Schleiermacher spoke of this freedom within necessity and necessity within freedom: "My act is free, but not the effects I exercise in the world. The latter are subject to eternal laws. Freedom is pitted against freedom, and whatever the outcome, it is marked by limitation and by the community."[5] Freedom has its effects in history; it cannot lead out of history, within which alone it finds its sphere of operation. The possibilities which history offers are always time-conditioned, and whatever is done in pursuit of those possibilities remains subject to the conditions of time. But wherever the supertemporal values give direction to men's actions, freedom and humanity become effective.

In this view, it would seem to be not religion but culture which provides the framework within which the possibilities of human development can find their goal and within which they *must* try to find unification in their inescapable contact.[6] For the historian of culture it is an accepted fact that he can form a comprehensive image of a people or nation with regard to a definite period only if he gives to the religious life the same consideration that he gives to science, morality, art, economics, technology and the administration of justice. Of course, when the historian of culture treats religion, his concern is not with the possibilities of religion as a supertemporal and supermundane phenomenon but with the time-conditioned manifestations in which it is objectified and with the objectively ascertainable relations, whether friendly or hostile, in which religion finds itself with regard to other historical forces of the time. Yet one may not rashly conclude that religion is nothing more than one sector within the cultural process.

Culture seeks unity, but its realization must issue out of discords, oppositions, conflicts. In culture man seeks to draw into unity all of his possibilities which are worthy of realization; yet culture always leads him into fresh temptations. Nevertheless, cannot culture reproach religion for rendering the undivided humanity of man an impossibility? Religion cannot but leave man in the world, and yet it sets before him an otherworldly goal. Through this dualism it alienates man from himself and hence seems to diminish his humanity. One may remember the biblical story of Abraham, who has become a very exemplary character in the eyes of the faithful owing to his willingness to execute an inhuman command of his God. Of course one might remark in passing, with regard to the story, that at the time to which it belongs its precise intent was to disentangle that mythological situation in a human way: God wants no human sacrifice.[7] The later consequence of the story—the acknowledgment of a duty of obedience which leaves humane considerations out of account—sprang from a misunderstanding, and for many still does, through what can only be called the persistence of a dead weight of aberration.

Whether it is culture or religion which determines the meaning of life through its quest of unity and humanity, in either case man falls short of the ideal of perfect humanity which is held before him. And this fact will disturb a man who is concerned with developing his potentialities to their fullest height. There is, of course, this difference between culture and religion, that in a man who is aware of the peace of God, restless anxiety does not penetrate into the ultimate citadel of self; in calm resignation he can accept his restlessness as what it is in truth, the tribute exacted by the conditions of his human existence.

The tensions of his situation lead a man into manifold activities, and the "reason which has him" induces him to take a stand with regard to them. It makes him aware of the norms deriving from his spiritual functions and, as one and the same reason, urges him not to acquiesce in the mere multiplicity of his functions, though it does not determine any specific form of the desired synthesis. In the movement of opposing forces which constitutes the life of history the desirable synthesis becomes again and again the content of disputes in which the religious and the secular interpretations of man's goal confront each other. In spite of all these confrontations, which are often impassioned, religious and secular interpretations are interrelated because their common goal is to shed light into an epoch which is always problematic. The precise nature of a just solution in a given case, where the situation is tense, will be a matter of various opinions, all influenced by the various factors bearing on the individuals concerned—their breadth of vision, freedom from ulterior motives, opportunities for action, and so on. Thus one individual will find meaningful something which will not satisfy another. If then, as so often happens, motives of collective selfishness obscure public opinion with regard to the course which should be taken if the action is to be meaningful, and so deflect the public consensus from its orientation towards the supertemporal ideas, then the opposition between parties can become venomous and implacable. The ensuing struggle, which runs counter to the spiritual element in history, can bring victory to one party, conferring on it the power to control the situation. But in such a case it is not to be expected that this party will do justice to the situation. The consequence is not that history is given its meaning but that it is rendered meaningless. That even such meaninglessness retains its relation to meaning scarcely needs to be re-emphasized, nor need we stress the fact that what is true of social groups is likewise true of the history of individual persons.

In the final analysis everyone believes in some way in the meaningfulness of human life. Admittedly the sense in which "there is" such a meaning is not the same as the sense in which there is a Milky Way or butter on one's bread, and hence the "freely hovering" intelligence can be seduced into denying the meaning of life. But even sceptics and agnostics have grounded their intellectual life on this faith in the reason which holds them; it is a faith which brings their actions into a kind of unity and makes them wish that the actions of other men may not be too harshly discordant with theirs, but on the contrary compatible. At work within the changes of history, the faith in the meaning of life confers on works of art the religious or secular character which accords with their epoch. (Owing to the small measure of independence which weak artists and craftsmen are able to develop, they tend to move along safe paths which have been blazed by stronger men.) This is likewise true with regard to the spheres of economics, jurisprudence, morality and science.

The faith in the meaning of life is itself caught up in the movement of history, and hence it is never quite free of ambiguity. In the human mind this faith has the role of supporting the diverse powers of the spiritual life, ordering their interrelation, and drawing them into a harmonious synthesis. Nevertheless in social institutions, and even more in the lives of individuals, this or that function of the human spirit can for a time take control, and the faith in the meaning of life can manifest itself now as a faith in culture, now as a faith in religion.

Faith is confronted by doubt. Doubt has a role of pre-eminent importance in the face of everything which is insufficiently established and which calls for the improvement of precarious conditions, provided that our desire for truth is strong. Every advance in the movement of culture receives its strongest impetus from doubt.

The steps of progress presuppose not only the level beyond which they would rise but also the standards of value in the light of which they can be pronounced progressive. This would seem to imply that those standards are not subject to the doubts which stimulate cultural advance. We must take into consideration, however, the fact that in primitive times even the norms of truth assume a primitive form and have their effects in a crude way. The greater the degree of clarity developed by our cultural consciousness, the more clearly the true meaning of the norm emerges; and at the same time the necessity for methodological rigor with regard to the norm becomes more evident. Hence doubt retains its legitimacy even in relation to that which is not to be doubted, insofar as the doubt is directed towards the historical conditionality wherein the latter enters into consciousness. The boundary of the domain of doubt is drawn by the superhistorical necessity with which the life of the spirit relates itself to truth. Philosophy tries to determine these relations, but its formulations belong to their century and are capable of improvement. There are no meaningful words, however, in terms of which we could doubt the self-certainty with which the human spirit affirms truth. Doubt is meaningful only in the service of truth; the inevitability of doubt characterizes the finite consciousness, which must strive towards truth along paths which are by no means always free of obscurity. In the non-finite consciousness of God (the *intellectus archetypus* of the *Critique of Pure Reason*,[8] insofar as there is any meaning in the notion of an archetypal intellect), doubt has no role. To doubt and to question is necessary for us human beings because in every sphere of the intellect's operations its relation to particular truths is enmeshed with uncertainties; hence, even though unconditional truth is its ultimate concern, its relation with the truth is clouded by these uncertainties.

Either immediately or because of an inextricable entanglement with it, the intellectual operations whereby we can encounter truth are directed upon an objective world of which we can have only a conditionally valid knowledge. Even what is unconditionally certain comes into consciousness only within the context of the conditional world; hence it is conditional and unconditional simultaneously. The conditionality refers to the form in which it becomes accessible; unconditionality, to the content it would express. The certainty with which we experience the truth as the power which determines the very being of our spirit may be impaired by the resistance it encounters from our nature and from the yielding of our enfeebled will; but that certainty cannot be touched by honest doubt. What is unconditionally certain is the validity of the distinction between values, between true and false, good and evil, beautiful and ugly, just and unjust; and likewise unconditional is the value of humanness, which finds its realization in the recognition of those distinctions. In this certitude all men are united, and all receive the blessing of the demands which flow from certitude. But men are free, and what stands they will take with regard to the truth of their own being is for them to decide. If they are committed to the defense of human values, then the unity which binds them in the innermost depths of their being manifests itself as the love which will acknowledge every limitation (say, the limitations of marriage as the community of two human beings) only as a limitation to be overcome, never one to be seen as final. (A true marriage can enrich everyone who enters the home of the marriage partners.)

What is true only in contrast to what is false belongs within the framework of a consciousness limited by the conditions of finiteness. It is not the same truth which is revealed in works of art and which, in moral conscience, demands of us that we take every situation for what it is in truth. Value contrasts which rule the domain of intelligence can at best hint at what is unconditionally true, beyond the reach of intelligence, and yet must be acknowledged of necessity.

All human experience of the absolute is linked with the accomplishments of the intelligence, and therefore to what is subject to doubt. And, particularly for the intellectualistic cast of mind, this interlinking turns into a temptation—the temptation to find in the unconditional only what is conditional and can be called into question. Connected with this temptation is the discovery that the weakness of the human will is a universal human characteristic and thus seems to provide confirmation for the justification of relativism. The faith in culture, provided that it seeks self-definition in philosophy, may issue in a critical metaphysics full of questions without answers or in outright skepticism. For such a faith it suffices to acknowledge the necessity of the *quest* of truth; and it must be admitted that even for religious men truth remains an open question for consideration. But religious faith is a commitment. In an environment which has put its faith in the development of culture, religious faith may easily come to be regarded as subjection to superstition. The testimonies of religion which are either misinterpreted or handed down by tradition in an erroneous interpretation will lend support to the hostility to religion. But although often they have a very weak title to it, every religious creed demands that it be taken as a profession of belief in the truth. (Though it is not, of course, a truth which can be judged purely by the intelligence.) And truth calls for intellectual freedom.

The example of the afore-mentioned story with regard to Abraham's "obedience" teaches how a religious message handed down without change may become unbelievable for one seeking a religious experience, owing to historical change. (The once significant truth that human sacrifice is irreligious may have become something taken for granted.) Having become unbelievable, such a story is doubted with good reason and must be rejected.

The truth of faith cannot be fixed at all in objective prose. Gabriel Marcel says: "To think, to formulate, to judge—in the last analysis it is always to betray."[9] Hence the danger of misinterpretation is inherent in the proclamations of religion, and in face of a misinterpreting tradition, the danger of acceptance here and rejection there. The danger increases wherever ancient records of the faith find overruling veneration. A notable theological work has this to say about the Bible: "There is no difficulty as long as one accepts the validity of Scripture as what it is in fact—namely, a collection of human testimonies about God. But the moment one sees more in the Bible, sees it as 'the Word of God' or '*Holy Writ*'—then it becomes a different matter."[10] Whenever the institutions charged with the care of religious life accept the ancient records of the faith *without adverting to the historically conditioned form of the expression* and the form is supposed to have a religious effect on the congregation, absurd interpretations are quite likely to arise. But every absurd interpretation is a challenge to our cultural consciousness, and this consciousness will defend itself against this "truth" which is alleged to be an article of faith. In this way the Enlightenment disposed of the obedience of Abraham, insofar as it had been taken as the essential message of the biblical passage, as an offense to morality.[11] The convincing attack upon the ostensible authority of a mythological story and its interpretation will give to a really free religious life the sense of having been liberated from something painful and confirmed in its confidence in the rights of a living immediacy. In that immediacy man attains the certainty of the depth in which he finds peace in spite of all the unrest of the world. How could peace have come from so heart-rending an act as the butchering of one's own son!

Wherever immediate experience places a higher value on

humanness than on the venerable age of a doctrine to which a community of organized religion passionately clings—a tradition, that is, whose content immediate experience can no longer find venerable—there our cultural consciousness gains, along with religious freedom and depth, a new strength and clarity with regard to itself. Cultural growth comes from the questions presented to us by everything that has been handed down in human history, just because what has been handed down does not give unconditional satisfaction. Questions which lead to actions, for good or evil, come forth endlessly. In the current of history, what is truly of value for culture springs from the desire for a deepening of the human content of existing circumstances—the desire for more goodness, more beauty, more justice, more knowledge. (What was experienced in former times as the realization of supreme Beauty, and may well continue to speak to men now living, nevertheless may fail to address itself to that innermost center of self which they find in their hopes and troubles, their new longings and desires, and therefore it is no longer experienced as intensely as in the past.) In the spirit of a culture there is always the abiding will to transcend the present situation by means of human effort.

But a religion certain of the content of its doctrine declares itself competent to pronounce upon the transcendent origin of all the true values which have appeared in the course of human history. This claim can lead religion into a strained relationship with powerful cultural trends. Religion sees in what man has wrought not merely the human as such but the revelation of an other world. Religion views evil as man's sinful disdain for such revelation (and may even see its origin in a mythological background). In what makes human life essentially human religion reveres the blessing presence of God, from whose fullness comes all that gives genuine value to life. "When there was talk about the misery of the land" in the orphanage at Stans, and the children, feeling compassion, were happy, Pestalozzi said to them, "Is not God good, God who created sympathy in the human heart?"[12]

Such an interpretation of life is intolerable to an irreligious cultural mentality. Nietzsche demanded that all men's achievements should be credited to them alone. As early as the first volume of his book *Human, All-Too-Human,* he writes, under the heading "Forbidden Openhandedness," "There is not enough love and goodness in the world to permit some of it to be given away to imaginary beings."[13] And as late as his sketches for the *Will to Power* he speaks of the "royal liberality" with which man "bestowed gifts on things, only to his own impoverishment, only to be more aware of his own misery. This has been man's greatest selflessness until now, that he admired and worshipped, and knew how to hide from his own eyes the fact that he himself was the creator of what he now admired." But now Nietzsche wants to "reclaim all the beauty and the sublimity which we have conferred on real and imagined things, reclaim them as the property and the product of man, as man's most beautiful apology."[14] Between the works referred to, Nietzsche produced the *Zarathustra.* There we read, in the same sense: "Men bestowed all their good and evil upon themselves. Truly they did not take it, they did not discover it, it did not descend to them like a voice from heaven. It was man himself who first attributed values to things as a means of his own self-preservation—he first created the meaning of things, a human meaning! That is why he called himself 'Man,' which means 'the Evaluator.' "[15]

But are not values degraded when they are reduced to acts of evaluation which are subjective and therefore historically conditioned—above all when these acts have the biological goal of the self-preservation of men? In the distinction of what is of value from what is worthless we must acknowledge the necessity which man has not created but wherein he attains the consciousness of his being man. It is within this necessity that he has awakened to the boundlessness of his horizons—the necessity which, as "reason which has him," is antecedent to his existence and leaves to his "evaluation" and "creation" nothing greater, yet nothing less, than a design which is oriented towards the height of his time.

Nevertheless "subjectivist" would be very inaccurate as applied to Nietzsche; in any case, his inconsistencies make a concise and unambiguous characterization impossible. The passage quoted from *Zarathustra* elevates value-creating love above "the sly self devoid of kindness, which seeks its own gain in the gain of the many." In *Beyond Good and Evil*[16] this contrast is elucidated by the distinction between the noble morality and the slave morality. Of course the evaluations whereby Nietzsche explains this distinction are themselves very subjective. While every error is indeed subjective but has the abstract acknowledgment of super-subjective truth as its presupposition, so also all evaluations presuppose a norm, and the question of whence the claim of the norm to validity is derived cannot be dismissed.

Nietzsche did not evade the question but asked it repeatedly with the greatest possible generalization. In the *Dawn of Day* he asked, "How did reason come into the world?" And he gives the answer (not a very fair one, to be sure): "As is fair, in an unreasonable way, by an accident. One will have to guess what accident, like a riddle."[17] In the section about the "mad man"[18] in *The Gay Science*, the deep seriousness of the question seems to assume the form of a symbol—immense, shattering. The answer with which the work, in its first edition, then concludes is: Eternal return, Zarathustra. And it is repeated in the concluding portion added to the later edition. But in what respect can the annunciation of Zarathustra claim to be an answer?

The section about the "mad man" showed most impressively that with the loss of faith in God, man has lost every possibility of orientation towards anything fixed. There is no world reason. The verses of Nietzsche's Prince Free-as-a-Bird express our plight, saying that the world is but a play, though imperiously mixing being and seeming; an eternally foolish game into which we ourselves are drawn.[19]

However, for one who, pervaded by the conviction that there is "no longer any reason in what happens," is able to muster the strength to accept the doctrine of eternal return, it becomes of the "greatest import," transforming him and permitting him "always to rise higher."[20] And in this vision the question of how reason came into the world, or from what source the claim of human evaluations to validity arises, is lost to sight. It is immeasurably surpassed by the doctrine of the eternal return: "The rolling world-wheel grazes goal after goal. . . ."

A variant version of the odd question as to the origin of reason

Religion and Culture

is to be found in the second section of *Beyond Good and Evil*: "How could anything spring from its own opposite? For instance, truth from error? or the will for truth from the will to deceive?"[21] Here, in line with what was said in *The Gay Science*, the answer is that faith in the contrast of values cannot be retained at all. Nietzsche denies (without, of course, being able to remain consistent) that reason stands in contrast with the universal world-unreason, that they are different in essence. For him reason is a form of life like all other biological formations. From the viewpoint of biology, the problem loses its seriousness, for that view ignores the fact that the concepts "error" and "deception" are meaningful only in relation to the idea of truth. Truth is the presupposition even of error and deception. After all, for biologism, "truth" would cease to be what it is, and it would be faint praise for anyone to be called "a genius of truth"[22] if reason had come into the world as a biological mutation "in an unreasonable manner." But we have said enough about all this.

Pestalozzi's words about God who has created sympathy in the human heart were said to children and are to be understood accordingly. It was Pestalozzi's intention to let the children of Stans^c feel that man is not merely man—not merely the pitiful being at the mercy of the overwhelming blind rage of forces which would senselessly destroy. God's goodness is active in man. In innumerable passages Pestalozzi has spoken of the divine in human nature. For him the relation of man to man was determined essentially by the presence of God in man. All the relations of communal life, and therewith also of all personal life, thus gain an immeasurable, an absolute meaning—a meaning which unites all men in their profoundest depths and which therefore seeks its empirical realization in the practical consequences of this unity, in inalterable love. The Gospels speak of it, but the life of a Francis of Assisi as well, or of Pestalozzi himself; and in a time still closer to us, the life of a Ramakrishna.

The cultural world also holds human personalities in high regard. The great names, though only they, are shining lights. Yet it is not as if there were no regard for the little people, those who are inconsequential so far as culture is concerned. The greatly gifted man is well aware that his work should be a contribution to the culture of the sphere in which he works, and perhaps to that of his nation and even of mankind as a whole, and he wishes this to be so. If he is so fortunate as to learn that he has enriched many ordinary lives, filled them with greater content or supplied them with greater and more enduring powers of resistance, it will be for him a happy confirmation of the value of his own life. Men who are lacking in social conscience may show considerable success in some area of human endeavor—they may, for example, be important representatives of a science or an art —but they are not perfect representatives of a culture. Culture calls for an individual's own particular development, on the basis of his personal possibilities, in such a way that he is a new coin minted from the humanity which constitutes his bond with other men. Hence culture demands of his personal development a positive relation to all the supertemporal ideas of humanness in its purity. The values for which a man obedient to the exacting demands of culture lives are universally valid, and it is the responsibility of one who is capable of great achievements to play his part in the improvement and enhancement of that which produces unity among men. Not every man who is the vehicle of culture can be popular: often he will be understood only by a small circle of fellow specialists; all the same he knows that his works have their ultimate value in effects which spread in the widest circles.

The achievements whose lasting value makes a name great in history always belong to some one sector of cultural life. So Copernicus belongs to astronomy, Mozart to music. The significance of a universal personality like Goethe must be judged in various spheres of culture—poetry, natural science, etc.—in accordance with their respective standards. All representative figures are fixed in historical relativity, and the truth as to their cultural significance would have to be grasped within the historical context as a frame of reference and on the basis of a broadly humanistic knowledge.[d] (Such humanistic knowledge is never quite adequate in its realization, since it is conditioned by the position in history of the one who is making the judgment.)

With regard to the religious position of man it is quite otherwise. Here value judgments have only a questionable place. They may be found in explicit and emphatic form, but in that case they have been formulated, as it were, only by way of misunderstanding. This happens particularly in the twilight of religiously obscure contexts. Thus [if God is conceived as a stranger] man's relation to God cannot seem other than wholly imperfect as soon as he himself or his fellow-man judges him with respect to true values. Then he is only the man who fell short of the infinite summons, the sinner who can hold no brief for himself:

> Ah, what agony of trembling,
> When the Judge, mankind assembling,
> Probeth all beyond dissembling!

If man imagines himself face to face with the God who will judge him in terms of those concepts of value which are the norm of his actions and exert their powerful effects in his conscience, if he imagines himself thus called to account before God, then this God becomes a *Rex tremendae majestatis*—a king of dread majesty. Man, on his side, crushed by the sense of his unworthiness, is brought to despair:

> What shall wretched I be crying?[e]

However, religious experience cannot be confined within a value system so rigorously conceived.[23] A Chassidic story tells about a discussion, at the close of the Sabbath, among devout and sincere eighteenth-century Jews concerned with the account to be given of a man's soul. "Moved by the fear of God and by the sense of humility, it seemed to them that they had greatly sinned, and they agreed that there was no longer any hope for them; their sole comfort was the thought that they had been the disciples of the great Zaddik Rabbi Nachum; he would lift them up and save them." And they started out at once towards Chernobil, the city in which their master lived. But this latter, on the same evening, was giving an account of his own soul, and it seemed to him "in his great fear and humility that his sins were so many that there was no longer any hope for him except this: that those Chassidim who had attached themselves to him in their zeal for the service of God might yet confer some benefit on him. He stepped out his front door and stood looking towards the place where his pupils lived, and after a while he saw them approaching. In this moment"—so the narrator, a grandson of that rabbi, concluded the tale—"two arcs joined together into a circle."²⁴

Transcending all human evaluations, religious experience is a certainty of the blessedness which derives from the divine ground in which the relations of men with one another have their origin. This experience draws a man out of even the deepest abyss of misery and affords him "perfect joy."ᶠ Even in the midst of the most grievous feeling of guilt, the soul remains open to the joy which has its source in the security found in the love of God, though this joy is not now unshadowed. Tradition records the following words of the founder of Chassidism, the Baal-shem-tow (1700–1760): "The sinner who knows that he is a sinner, and therefore holds himself in low esteem—God is with him, for 'God dwells with them in the midst of their impurity.' "²⁵ In the last chapter of the Gospel of John, Peter is reminded of his three betrayals by the Risen One's thrice-repeated question, "Do you love me?" Peter is grieved, but out of the certitude in the depths of his being, those innermost depths into which sin cannot reach, he remonstrates with the words "Lord, you know everything; you know that I love you." In Hinduism likewise, all Yoga-Ways have their meaning and their goal in the certainty of an existential depth in the face of which all sinful beings become as naught, a depth which constitutes the experience of blessedness.²⁶ And in Japanese Buddhism it is the trusting confidence in Amida Buddha which assures even the sinner of the blissful communion with him. We cannot avoid falling into sin; however, as a wise priest of another day (Koa Shonin, 1269–1330) says: "You need not think so little of yourself as to despair, but you must fear sin."²⁷ One who thinks that sin is a trifling matter lulls himself into false confidence; when a sinner has true confidence the awareness of his own sinfulness is very much alive.²⁸

A man can refuse to believe in the original ground of his being, and this defect of faith may prevent his own conduct from manifesting the ground. But even man's sin cannot defile that ground; over the ground of his being man has no power. No matter the extent to which guilt has defiled the individual, the original ground of his being nevertheless urges him to transcend the relativities of the world in which he is ensnared in secular standards. Religious truth does not declare that secular standards are invalid; our world has need of cultured lives. But the ultimate, the absolutely "binding," responsibility of the human person remains beyond the ken of cultural consciousness. When it is the meaning of our lives that is in question, religion removes from secular standards their ultimately decisive significance. The ultimate meaning of man can belong only to his relationship to the absolute, the relation which he has to God. The phrase "absolute relation" as an expression of the contrast with the relationships consisting in our ties with the world contains an element of risk; yet the contradiction it involves is of real import with regard to human existence. (Thus the gifted stylist Schelling has attributed to the organism a "divine relationship"[29] as opposed to its "relative aspect, the aspect of his being which is determined by other things.") Guilt is one ingredient of the unavoidable destiny of man. We were born into a somewhat impure world, and it is our solemn moral obligation to strive against its defilement. Nevertheless only moralistic fanaticism (which, of course, can afflict those who consider themselves sincerely religious) seeks to grasp the ultimate truth about man's relation to God on the basis of the awareness of his sinfulness. The relation is, on the contrary, precisely the certainty of that original ground of our being into which sin cannot reach. The Gospel of John and his epistles have a real bearing here—John, the disciple "whom Jesus loved" (John 19:26), who was "lying close to the breast of Jesus" (John 13:23). These expressions are symbolic formulation of John's certainty that to know Jesus one must go beyond what was then being said about him. (The reader of John's Gospel should know that any connotation of a friendship, indeed a bosom friendship, between John and Jesus is excluded by John's recognition of the fact that the figure of Jesus is definitively removed from the conditions of the merely human. For John, Jesus is the one who, even during his days on earth, is "he who is in heaven" (John 3:13). True faith rests on the experience of being held in the grasp of God's love in spite of everything.[30] As with regard to Buddha, so in the Gospel of John, the phrase is "Come and see."[31]

Wherever dogmatic restraints would keep religious experience in bondage, hedging about with anxieties the very thought of asking why a lasting claim should be made upon us by the denomination which was charged with the historical task of our education, it becomes impossible to experience the "truth that makes us free" of which John's Gospel speaks. It is not our view that to avoid becoming the prisoner of the "accident of birth"[g] a religious man should make the various faiths and creeds the matter of his personal experience and then make his own decision. Ramakrishna, who has done this, reached the conclusion that God can be discovered from many starting points. Such discovery is accompanied and even determined by certain imagery, but in no case is the imagery a likeness of God.

For a primitive believer the divine is only the supramundane. Of course even primitive faith knows the divine only by personal experience; but primitive faith takes it for granted that the experience is to be interpreted exclusively in terms of transcendence. Man will be all the more inclined to take this transcendence for granted the more impressed he is by the idea of power, of being simply at the mercy of such power. What gives substance to this attitude is his experience of the powers of nature, which, though they benefit and foster life, are at the same time the sources of danger and destruction. The powers of nature seem to point to transcendent goals which should concern man. But Kant justly observed in the *Critique of Judgment* that the teleological conception of nature taken only in itself can furnish nothing but the basis of a demonology, never of a theology.[32] And a few years later he says, similarly: "With regard to moral-mindedness, it all depends on the highest concept to which one subordinates one's duties. If the worship of God is primary, and if, therefore, one subordinates virtue to that worship, then that object is an *idol*."[33] There was no longer free access for Kant to Augustine's thesis that God is truth, and he had not yet found any new way of approach to it; but in many a passage he is very close to it.

It is not merely the notion of power which determines the interpretation of a religious experience in terms of transcendency. The proposition that the certainty of God has its origin in one's own experience, and is therefore immanent, requires a complement which secures the rights of transcendence[i]. Quite apart from any secular or religious bias, man's experience compels him to anchor his humanity in a reality which is greater and deeper than what is merely human, merely immanent; he is aware of a transcendental dignity, a dignity which seems to refer to a transcendent reality. A restriction to immanence would forbid us to go beyond the position of Nietzsche, who sees in human achievements the glory of human creativity but views both the achievements and the creativity as contained within the biological process and conditioned by it. (Hence the fact that the human which Nietzsche elevates beyond the bounds of humanity frequently deviates into the inhuman.) The unconditional reality to which all the qualities in man that constitute his humanness refer disrupts all our attempts to be satisfied with an explanation in terms of mere immanence. Paul Tillich formulates the problem in this way: "Man has an immediate awareness of the unconditional as something which is antecedent to the separation of subject and object and to all the interactions between them, in the theoretical as well as the practical sphere. . . . The unconditional is not mediated by observation or by inference. It is present whenever we advert to it, and it has the character of unconditional certainty." The explanatory sentence follows: "It is man himself, not man's knowledge nor his feeling, which is aware of the unconditional." And soon after this comes the important statement: "That which is antecedent to subject and object cannot become an object in relation to which man acts as a subject, in thought and action. God is not an object for us as subjects. He is what is always antecedent to this distinction. And yet we talk about God quite unavoidably, since everything which becomes real for us enters into the subject-object relationship. This fact, which is productive of much intellectual tension, has led to the notion of the 'existence of God,' a concept which is nearly blasphemous and dangerously mythological; it has also led to the impossible attempt to prove the existence of this object. To such a notion and to such attempts atheism is the necessary religious and theological answer, as has been fully recognized in the experience of the intensely spiritual in all ages. The 'atheistic' manner of speech of the mystics is surprising. It leads beyond God to the unconditional, which negates every attempt to fix the divine as a definite object. But in non-mystical religion as well we find the same sense of the inappropriateness of all the 'names' for God. True religion cannot be conceived without an atheistic element."[34]

Interpreting a sculpture on the temple of the "Great Mother" in Dakshineswar, Ramakrishna has expressed this "atheistic" truth in a very memorable comment: "Mankind must die before the godhead can reveal itself. But this godhead, too, must die before the Most High can be revealed. On the corpse of the dead godhead, the blessed mother dances her celestial dance."[35] And cautioning against "an identification of God with that which is already past because every revelation we can know has already occurred," Fritz Marti declares: "It might well be said with precision that for God, being-no-longer is the condition of His being as the most totally free."[36, h]

If the transcendence of the divine is asserted exclusively, religion declines into a slavish cultivation of superstitious practices and becomes pretty much what Sigmund Freud imagined it to be. It ceases to keep men aware of the unconditional obligating depth of the relation between man and man. (It is a matter of common observation that strict orthodoxy and inhumanity often go together. Dogma suffers a diminution of its superobjective truth wherever it is assumed that doctrines are records of objective relationships in a transcendent reality.) Among the great religions that of Israel is the closest approach to a profession of faith in God as wholly transcendent. Yet in precisely that religion men became aware very early of the danger of falsification through superstition, and the danger was always faced with moral earnestness. It was overcome in principle by the prophets, who recognized that it is in man's heart that the will of God becomes manifest for anyone who seeks it.[37]

Whatever the interpretation put on religious experience, where the experience is genuine it becomes transparently clear that in the last analysis the relation of man to man has a dimension beyond the human, that it is grounded in a depth of reality which is no longer at man's disposal but at whose disposal, on the contrary, he is. It lays its obligation upon him and is the source of everything which makes him "human," everything which in truth makes life worth living. As—the thought so beautifully expressed by Paracelsus[38]—God himself is present to the physician in the suffering patient, so it is true for everyone that in some way all his relations to other men have a meaning which transcends the merely human: again and again the religious man experiences the presence of God. The "eternal silence of the divinity"[j] does not oppress him, for he sees with his own eyes, hears with his own ears the voice of the God who speaks to him, recalling him to what is purely human in his duty. Often, too, it is the voice of the suffering God. Let the reader not misunderstand this: the imperatives which are sounded in each particular situation can also be heard by the man whose mind is concentrated on moral culture, and he too can obey them. The decisive factor here is that the religious man would see the image of God in the individual person, whereas faith in culture is faith in universally binding supertemporal values which have exerted their effects in their respective historical spheres.

In the sphere of social work both the practitioner of morality without a connection with religion and the religious man find the task which awaits them. The man of moral orientation who takes an alcoholic in charge sees with compassion the latter's shattered relationship to his wife and children, to his community and to the state. He tries to understand him within the context of the mutual relationship between him and the community, a relationship essential to his physical and his "human" existence. It is evident, from the standpoint of morality, that every man must live his life as a sharer in the responsibilities of communal structures founded on values, and in the maintenance and if necessary the repair of these structures the moral will find its constantly renewed task. The actual work done by the religious social worker need show no "objective" differences from that done by the one whose approach is moral and cultural. The difference is in the way they see the undertaking. The disturbed relationships between the drinker and his family and the whole social structure is not what counts for the religious social worker. He will not underestimate the importance of these factors and will refer to them when he is making his evaluations, but they are not what he has ultimately in view. If the man who has lost his bearings can only attain to the true experience of the depth of his existence, order in those objective areas will return of itself. What concerns the religious helper is the imperiled man himself, not the relations in which he stands or should stand with others—in brief, the man's absolute relationship, his salvation. To use Christian terms (and along with it the terms of almost all other religions), one can say that the absolute relationship is the relationship to God—the calling whereby man is distinguished from all other creatures of the earth, the calling which manifests itself in his very existence as the divine ground which supports him in love yet disquiets him with admonition. The great non-Christian religions are familiar with this calling, too. Ramakrishna is said to have recognized the "Great Mother" whose priest he was "even in the most depraved of human beings, in the street walkers." According to the testimony of his pupil, Vivekananda, Ramakrishna would "cast himself down at their feet, which became wet with his tears: 'Oh, Mother, Thou art this! In this form Thou art here in the street. In another form Thou art the universe. I greet Thee, O Mother, I greet Thee. . . .'"[39]

By his own experience the religious man has the immediate certainty that he is charged with a mission. He will acknowledge to himself that in many ways he has fallen short of this mission; yet it continues to claim him unconditionally, thus assuring him of the citizenship in the kingdom of God which is given to him and which he has retained despite all. In the cultural context every action, every event, is seen in relation to others. These relations have meaning, and the claims expressed in them derive their legitimacy from the fact that they are human claims. But for religious experience the relations, and with them the whole of human history, enter into a field of vision which has been opened up by the certainty of a personal calling which distinguishes human life. According to Plato's report,[40] Socrates lived in the awareness of a divine mission to which he could not become unfaithful even if the infidelity could avert the impending sentence of death. In the New Testament, Mark's Gospel reports that Jesus, as he emerged from the Jordan after the baptism, saw the heavens opened and received the announcement of his election. Thereafter in a series of passages, particularly in John's

Religion and Culture

Gospel, Jesus speaks of his mission, and when his career draws to a close he himself sends his disciples into the world as he himself has been sent into it (John 17:18). Rabindranath Tagore, in expressing his gratitude to his hosts in a house near Lucerne in July, 1926, said: "I have a mission." It was no whim which had brought him from the Far East to the Western world. The conscience of every man is rooted in the unconditional, he has a mission. The newborn child, by the mere fact of its entrance into life, makes those into whose care he has come feel that he "concerns them unconditionally." The baby comes into the world with a mission of which he is unaware. The task incumbent first on his educators and later on himself is that of assuring his growth in the consciousness of his mission.

The acknowledgment of the mission, which is to be confirmed by the man's life, and of his absolute relationship confers a religious character on personality. Marriage and family life (as distinguished from the community, the state, professional organizations, etc.) have this particular quality: within their sphere the individual has a title to something he cannot lose—namely, the claim to be loved for his own sake. For his own sake, and yet not as a self-contained end but as a manifestation of the presence of God which is the source of joy and at the same time of obligation. This does not always mean joy in any earthly sense; rather it is joy as coming from the hand of God. Everything which comes from God enhances life and therefore banishes the dismal note—audible, for instance, in Ibsen's *Architect Solness* —sounded in the "ugly, unpleasant word" *duty*, "so cold, so sharp and so stinging." Wherever duties have their foundation in true love they have some element of joy in them. Yet there is an element of severity as well, for it is not the readiness to fulfill all the wishes of one of its members indiscriminately which proves one's love for the family. What matters here is expressed in the words of a theologian whom we have already quoted, commenting on the first epistle of John: "Perfect love consists in letting the other have his share in man's communion with God."[41] In an early work on the philosophy of history the same author had written: "With regard to no gift of God—and great men are such a gift—is it a matter of course that the desire directed upon such gifts shall penetrate the gift and, behind and above it, grasp God."[42] As great men are for history, so are all the members of a family "gifts of God" for each other. And if they are so recognized and so treated, it is the sign of a religious home.[43] In a very literal sense, marriage and the family are "by nature" religious structures; therefore, considered empirically, marriages and families are in conformity with the concepts of them[44] only if they involve a community life informed by the *holy* Spirit. (This is by no means to say that mutual understanding and communication are always reached with ease.) In a nation whose faith in the religious meaning of the community of marriage and the family is vanishing, the ontological foundation of humanness becomes obscured. For in that case the human, deprived of certitude with regard to its ultimate foundation in the real, is threatened by decay: the eternal origin of human life is no longer treated as what it is in truth.

At the beginning, all culture is determined by religious motives. It comes into being within the transcendent relationships and interpretations of experience, whether concerned with the events of everyday or the forces of destiny. Culture is humanized to the extent that the idea of the true makes its influence felt, an influence which is at the same time a criticism of experience and a probing of its breadth and depth. Culture secularizes those possibilities which are opened up for us by that divine reason within whose grasp we have our being. But whatever is accomplished towards the realization of these possibilities is always nourished from a variety of sources, and this multiplicity renders our orientation towards the idea of the true more difficult, even where no passions enter in to direct the course of our actions. The task of resolving the oppositions and antagonisms which break out is always new.

We can speak of the depths of life only in symbols which are not susceptible of objective confirmation. But if the critical mind is not engaged by an endeavor concerned with what is of value in the history of the human spirit, it is inclined to concentrate its activities in the objective domain. If it does so, it becomes an accessory to the leveling of culture. For in that case the critical mind has little comprehension of the language of symbols, and the misapprehensions which ensue are only too readily supported by libertinistic tendencies deriving from our instinctual drives. Libertinism is a freedom without substance, without ontological truth; yet without this truth libertinism would itself be impossible. The goals set by eternal reason—the true, the good, the beautiful, the just—are precisely the source of men's freedom to make their own decisions with regard to those ends. In a world devoid of such antecedent, necessary norms, nothing could occur but chance events without orientation to any finality; there could be no "decision."[45] Paul Tillich's comment with regard to this is justified: "A secular culture is by its very essence as impossible as atheism; for both presuppose an element of unconditionality and both express something which concerns us unconditionally."[46]

Nevertheless it is inevitable that culture, in its development, should often be oblivious to its religious origins. At all events, these origins are never present in the consciousness of mankind except in the form of historically conditioned images against whose inadequacy the critical function of cultural life must constantly wage its war. It is a warfare full of danger and the risk of tragedy, for the very humanity of culture is imperilled when the spirit of criticism exalts itself over the structures within which it has its legitimate sphere of operation. Then, not knowing what it is doing, it will blunder into a spiritual estate which it cannot but misunderstand, and as a consequence all cultural functions are threatened by the dire possibility not only of losing their meaning but of becoming subservient to trends inimical to the human spirit. For then the cultural functions are in bondage to the cult of their mere forms without substance (something which occurs particularly in the dangerously exposed area of the administration of justice). Yet it is at such times that from deep necessity men turn again with a courageous longing towards religion, seeking essential truth in it and hoping to derive from it the total renewal of life.

NOTES

HISTORICAL-PHILOSOPHICAL INTRODUCTION

[1] *Briefwechsel*, ed. Hans Schulz (Leipzig, H. Haessel, 1925), I, 306.
[2] *Ibid.*, p. 165.
[3] *Kantstudien*, VI (1901), 202.
[4] *Nachgelassene Werke*, II, 104.
[5] *Briefwechsel*, I, 130, 138.
[6] *Ibid.*, II, 417; compare also I, 377, and *Nachgelassene Werke*, II, 103–105.
[7] B, XVI.
[8] B, 263.
[9] B, 719.
[10] B, XIX.
[11] B, 857.
[12] B, 564.
[13] B, 868.
[14] Cf. *Sämtliche Werke*, I, 298.
[15] Compare, for instance, the anonymous but very informative essay "Confidential Nonpartisan Letters about Fichte's Stay in Jena" (*Vertraute unpartheiische Briefe über Fichtes Aufenthalt in Jena*, 1799).
[16] *Sämtliche Werke*, I–I, 305–306. Cf. also (from a later time) I–X, 177. [*Zur Geschichte der neueren Philosophie* (Munich lectures, 1827, or later): ". . . the Critique of Judgment, Kant's profoundest work, which would probably have given a different direction to his whole philosophy if he could have started instead of ending with it. . . ."—Trans.]
[17] First edition, pp. 121f.
[18] "The difference between Fichte's and Schelling's Systems of Philosophy, Preface" (*Differenz des Fichteschen und Schellingschen Systems der Philosophie, Vorerinnerung*).
[19] *Sämtliche Werke*, III, 17.
[20] *Critique of Pure Reason*, B, VIII.
[21] *Wissenschaft der Logik, Sämtliche Werke*, ed. G. Lasson, III, 33.

[22] *Ibid.*, IV, 25: "Under close inspection, the different propositions which have been set up as absolute laws of thought contradict each other and thus annul each other."
[23] *Encyclopädie* (3d ed.), §115; *Sämtliche Werke*, ed. G. Lasson, V. 129.
[24] *Sämtliche Werke*, IV, 28f.
[25] Cf. above, pp. 3f.
[26] *Sämtliche Werke*, VII, 361.
[27] *Ibid.*, p. 362.
[28] Cf. *Categories*, c 4 17a 1ff.; *De anima*, III 6, 430b 26ff.
[29] *Saint Thomas d'Aquin*, 2d ed. (Paris, Alcan, 1925).
[30] *Wahrheit*, I (Einsiedeln–Zürich, Benziger, 1947), 18.
[31] *Sämtliche Werke*, VI, 361.
[32] *Sämtliche Werke*, VII, 309.
[33] *Ibid.*, I, 434.
[34] *Ibid.*, I–I, 308.
[35] *Ibid.*, VII, 361f., 376.
[36] *Ibid.*, p. 298.
[37] *Ibid.*, I–IV, 203; I–VII, 357f.

TRANSLATOR'S NOTE

[a] See *First Introduction to the Critique of Judgment*, trans. James Haden (Indianapolis, Bobbs-Merrill, 1965), pp. 45f. This introduction, Kant says, ought to show how the work "fits in the totality of the doctrines" owing to "the idea of a system which will be completed only by the latter," i.e. by "the newly published," Critique. This Introduction was not accessible to Fichte in 1790.—Trans.

FIRST PART: FOUNDATION

1. SCIENCE AND OUR VIEW OF THE WORLD

[1] *Philosophischer Kritizismus*. Compare, e.g., the third edition, I, 88, 100, 180.
[2] *Logos*, I (1910–1911), 328.
[3] *Eth.*, II, 43 et schol.
[4] *Logos*, I, 332.
[5] *Ibid.*, pp. 330–331.
[6] *Von der Sendung der Philosophie* (Wiesbaden, Dieterich, 1946), p. 42.
[7] *Ibid.*, p. 19.
[8] *Logos*, I, 333.

Notes

[9] *Friedrich Nietzsches gesammelte Briefe*, 3d ed. (Leipzig, Insel-Verlag, 1902), I, 85 and 129.

[10] *Existentialisme chrétien* (Paris, Plon, 1947), p. 297. Cf. pp. 309, 318.

[11] "Rien, je crois, ne me prépara davantage à comprendre qu'il existe sur un certain plan des perspectives incompatibles, et qu'un esprit soucieux de justice et de vérité est tenu de les adopter tour à tour, sans qu'il lui soit possible d'espérer découvrir une formule unitaire qui les concilierait. J'étais conduit par là directement, et en deçà de toute réflexion technique, à reconnaître une certaine infirmité du jugement, et la nécessité, je n'ose dire de concevoir, mais d'affirmer un certain au delà du discours où une harmonie peut-être pressentie, et même en quelque façon restaurée, sans que la raison raisonnante se voie octroyer les satisfactions qu'elle réclame peut-être indûment." *Ibid.*, pp. 296-97.

[12] *Wissenschaft-Bildung-Weltanschauung* (Leipzig and Berlin, Teubner, 1928), p. 108: "daß die Wirklichkeit des Geistes für jede erdenkliche konkrete Lage den zugehörigen Weltaspekt als eine streng einmalige Sicht und Deutung fordert."

[13] *Kairos* (Darmstadt, O. Reichl, 1926), pp. 43f., 45.

[14] *Sämtliche Werke*, I, 284-285. Cf. V, 345.

[15] J. G. Fichte, *Briefwechsel*, ed. Hans Schulz, I, 377.

TRANSLATOR'S NOTES

[a] *Critique of Pure Reason*, 436.—Trans.

[b] Edward Irving (1792-1834), Scotch Presbyterian, preached the second coming of Christ. His followers founded the Catholic Apostolic Church. —Trans.

[c] Fichte used the word *Wissenschaftslehre* to designate philosophy as a strict discipline in contrast to the loose use of the word "philosophy" as a synonym for a vague declaration of intention or for an untutored doctrinaire platform.—Trans.

2. THE SUPERTEMPORALLY TRUE AND ITS FORMS

[1] *Die Ophthalmologie des Bhāvaprakāśa*, First Part (*Studien zur Geschichte der Medizin*, ed. K. Sudhoff and H. E. Sigerist, No. 10, Leipzig, J. A. Barth, 1930), pp. 14, 20.

[2] Cf. Paul Häberlin, *Naturphilosophische Betrachtungen*, I (Zürich, Guggenbühl and Huber, 1939), 164.

[3] Cf. Fichte, *Sämtliche Werke*, I, 367f.; Schelling, *Sämtliche Werke*, II–III, 132.

[4] Cf. Fichte, *Sämtliche Werke*, IV, 7.

[5] *Ibid.*, V, 185.

[6] H. Oldenberg, *Reden des Buddha* (Munich, Kurt Wolff, 1922), p. 291.

[7] *Sâdhanâ* (Munich, Kurt Wolff, 1921), p. 107. For further confirmation compare K. E. Neumann, *Die Reden Gotamo Buddho's* from the longer collection, *Dîghanikâyo* (Munich, R. Piper, 1907), I, 211.

TRANSLATOR'S NOTES

[a] *Faust*, I, line 1055.

[b] The word "object" derives from *obicere*—"to throw at." Jakob Böhme translated it, literally, as *Gegenwurf*, "thrown against us." The German word for object, *Gegenstand*, means literally what stands against us, or figuratively what objects to us. Medicus wrote: ". . . die Gegenstände so vorzustellen, wie sie uns entgegenstehen."—Trans.

[c] In 1806 Schelling wrote: "There is no kind of knowledge in which God could appear as object. As known object he would cease to be God. We are never outside God so that we could set him up before us as an object." (Aphorism 52. *Werke*, VII, 150) My translation.—Trans.

[d] *Faust*, I, lines 634f.

3. THE FAITH IN TRUTH UNDER THE CHANGES OF HISTORY

[1] *Sämtliche Werke*, IV-I, 210.

[2] Cf. Theodor Litt, *Von der Sendung der Philosophie*, pp. 49–51.

[3] *Sämtliche Werke*, IV, 386f.; *Nachgelassene Werke*, III, 32ff. Cf. above, p. 10.

[4] Cf. Benedetto Croce, *Logica come scienza del concetto puro*, 2d ed. (Bari, Laterza, 1909), pp. 219–221. English ed. (London: Macmillan, 1917) tr. by Douglas Ainslie, Part II, Chapter IV, subsection "On the critical and the polemical function of philosophy," pp. 320–324.

[5] Cf. Jonas Cohn, *Theorie der Dialektik* (Leipzig, Felix Meiner, 1923), p. 68.

TRANSLATOR'S NOTES

[a] Medicus is using the word *aufheben* in the double sense in which Hegel made use of it: at once to dispose of and to preserve.—Trans.

[b] Medicus quotes the saying in the original Italian:
> Quello ch'è non si può dire,
> puossi dir quel che non è.—Trans.

4. TRIALS IN THE AWARENESS OF TRUTH: TRIALS OF HUMANITY

[1] *Beyond Good and Evil*, No. 186.

[2] *Ibid.*, No. 229.

[3] *Ibid.*, No. 4; cf. No. 11.

[4] *Sämtliche Werke*, I, III, 330. [*System des transscendentalen Idealismus*. Preface. End of March, 1800.]

[5] Cf. above, p. 20.
[6] Von der Selbst-Überwindung ("Of the Overcoming of Self").
[7] Beyond Good and Evil, No. 259.
[8] Ibid., No. 241.
[9] Ibid., No. 260.
[10] Werke, Taschen-Ausgabe, IX, 400.
[11] Ibid., p. 402.
[12] Ibid., p. 404.
[13] Ibid., p. 456.
[14] No. 3.
[15] No. 2; cf. Werke, Taschen-Ausgabe, XI, 355–356.
[16] Werke, Taschen-Ausgabe, XI, 356–357.
[17] Beyond Good and Evil, No. 2.
[18] Ibid., No. 5.
[19] Ibid., No. 2.
[20] Ibid., No. 295.
[21] Ibid., No. 4.
[22] Ibid., No. 14.
[23] Ibid., No. 9.
[24] Ibid., No. 210.
[25] To Malwida von Meysenbug, October 18, 1888.
[26] Werke, Taschen-Ausgabe, XI, 355.
[27] Ibid., X, 259; cf. VII, 115, 400, 476.
[28] Ibid., VI, 235.
[29] Ibid., XI, 267.
[30] Ibid., p. 362.
[31] Cf. Taschen-Ausgabe, XI, 356.
[32] Ibid., VII, 241.
[33] Ibid., p. 243.
[34] Ibid., p. 324.
[35] Ibid., p. 293.
[36] Ibid., XI, 365.
[37] Ibid., p. 366. ["The right way" refers to Faust, I, l. 329.—Trans.]
[38] Taschen-Ausgabe, VII, 178–179.
[39] Aristotle, Eth. ad Eudem., VII, 14.
[40] Sämtliche Werke, ed. K. Sudhoff and W. Matthiessen, I–XI, 191; cf. I–VIII, 85.
[41] Sämtliche Werke, I–VII, 246.

⁴² Kant, *Prolegomena* § 14.
⁴³ *Sämtliche Werke*, I–VIII, 322.
⁴⁴ *Ibid.*, I–IX, 341. "Zu gleicher weis wie der engel kam zu Maria und sagt, du bist voller gnaden, . . . also werden uns die gnad heimlich mitgeteilt, und ein ietlicher behalt die gab, die ihm got zuschicket, dem das, dem ein anders, und lass ims sein ein englischen gruss, der so vil ist als dieselbig gab."
⁴⁵ *Ibid.*, I–VIII, 207. Und "der eins guten glaubens ist, der ist ein volbringer der werk gottes."
⁴⁶ *Ibid.*, I–VIII, 208; I–XI, 201; II–I, 80.
⁴⁷ *Taschen-Ausgabe*, VII, 243, Part Three, "Before Sunrise."
⁴⁸ *Taschen-Ausgabe*, II, 44.
⁴⁹ *Der Begriff des Politischen*, 3d ed. (Hamburg, Hanseatische Verlagsanstalt, 1933), p. 21.
⁵⁰ *Thus Spoke Zarathustra*, Part One, "Of Reading and Writing" [*Taschen-Ausgabe*, VII, 56].
⁵¹ *Ibid.*, Part Three, "Of the Great Longing."
⁵² *Taschen-Ausgabe*, XI, 354f.
⁵³ *Thus Spoke Zarathustra*, Part Three, "Before Sunrise."
⁵⁴ *Taschen-Ausgabe*, XI, 365.
⁵⁵ *Nachgelassene Werke*, I, 212f. Cf. II, 405.
⁵⁶ Cf. Benedetto Croce's *Logica come scienza del concetto puro*, 2d ed., the section "Critica della Logica formalistica," pp. 93–102. [Croce's critique of formalistic logic is the third chapter of the second part of his book.] English ed., Ainslie, Part I, Section II, Chapter III, "Critique of Formal Logic," pp. 133–147.

TRANSLATOR'S NOTE

ᵃ Medicus is probably thinking of *Faust*, I, l. 353.—Trans.

5. DIONYSOS AND APOLLO

¹ *Werke, Taschen-Ausgabe*, X, 346, 348.
² *Ibid.*, pp. 193, 76.
³ *Ibid.*, I, 160, 90.
⁴ *Ibid.*, p. 156.
⁵ No. 244.
⁶ No. 34.
⁷ No. 335.
⁸ No. 246.
⁹ *Werke, Taschen-Ausgabe*, X, 214f.
¹⁰ *Sämtliche Werke*, II–IV, 25f., *Philosophy of Revelation*. [Schelling con-

tinues: "God is by no means the opposite of finiteness. He is not, as some people imagine, the One who enjoys himself in the infinite. On the contrary, he manifests himself as the highest artistic nature by seeking what is finite (p. 26) and, as it were, by not resting till he has brought everything into a most apprehensible, comprehensible, finite form."]

[11] *Werke, Taschen-Ausgabe*, I, 63.

[12] Cf. Wilhelm Furtwängler, *Gespräche über Musik*, 8th ed. (Zürich, Atlantis Verlag, 1948, 1963), pp. 67ff.

[13] *Sämtliche Werke*, II–IV, 147.

[14] See K. Marti, Einleitung zum Deuteronomium I, 260 in Kautzsch-Bertholet, *Die Heilige Schrift des Alten Testaments*, 4 (Tübingen, Mohr, 1922–23). The scriptural passage quoted above and all the passages from Scripture which follow are from *The Holy Bible, Revised Standard Version* (New York Nelson, 1953). Copyright 1946 and 1952 by the Division of Christian Education of the National Council of the Churches of Christ in the U.S.A. and used by permission.

[15] *Encyclopedia of Philosophical Knowledge*, §2 and §5.

[16] In the poem *"Die Künstler"* ("The Artists"). [Written 1789, published 1803. Lines 64–65:
Was wir als Schönheit hier empfunden,
Wird einst als Wahrheit uns entgegengehn.—Trans.]

[17] *Discours de Métaphysique*, § 24.

[18] *Sämtliche Werke*, ed. G. Lasson, V, lxxvi. [Actually the last sentence of Hegel's opening address to his audience at the University of Berlin, October 22, 1818.—Trans.]

[19] *Vorlesungen über die Ästhetik* ("Lectures on Aesthetics"), ed. H. G. Hotho (*Werke*, X, i), 133, 134; 132.

[20] *Maximen und Reflexionen* ("Maxims and Reflections"), VI.

[21] *Werke, Taschen-Ausgabe*, X, 259; cf. IX, 435.

[22] *Ibid.*, X, 190.

[23] *Ibid.*, IX, 456.

[24] *Sämtliche Werke*, I, 505. [*Zweite Einleitung in die Wissenschaftslehre*. 1797. Cf. the translation by Peter Heath (Appleton-Century-Crofts, 1970) p. 74.]

[25] Compare also Thomas Mann, *Die Entstehung des Doktor Faustus* (Amsterdam, Bermann-Fischer, 1949), pp. 36–37.

TRANSLATOR'S NOTES

[a] See note 3, p. 44.

[b] Hegel's phrase (*Werke*, IX, 25), too often mistranslated as "progress *towards* the consciousness of freedom."—Trans.

c *Faust*, I, 11. 1814–1815:
   Ich bin nicht um ein Haar breit höher,
   Bin dem Unendlichen nicht näher.
The rhyme is the same as in *Faust*, I, 11. 461–462:
   Du, Geist der Erde, bist mir näher;
   Schon fühl ich meine Kräfte höher, . . .

6. TRUE KNOWLEDGE OF GOD

[1] *Sämtliche Werke*, I–VIII, 322.
[2] Cf. above, p. 57.
[3] Karl Sudhoff, *Paracelsus-Handschriften* (Berlin, Georg Reimer, 1899), p. 338.
[4] *Ibid.*, p. 411.
[5] *Ibid.*, pp. 373–374.
[6] *Ibid.*, p. 446.
[7] *Ibid.*, p. 259.
[8] *Les Deux Sources de la morale et de la religion*, 33rd. ed. (Paris, Presses Universitaires de France, 1941), pp. 112, 216, 222–223.
[9] *Ibid.*, p. 246.
[10] *Ibid.*, p. 247.
[11] *Ibid.*, p. 212.
[12] *Ibid.*, p. 226.
[13] *Ibid.*, p. 223.
[14] *Sämtliche Werke*, Erste Abteilung, Vol. VII, 157.
[15] *Werke*, IV–II, 152; compare II, 313.
[16] *Sämtliche Werke*, I–VII, 148–149.
[17] *Ibid.*, p. 149.
[18] *Ibid.*, p. 148.
[19] *Ibid.*, p. 149.
[20] Cf. Schelling, *Sämtliche Werke*, Zweite Abteilung, Vol. I, 263–264.
[21] Cf. above, p. 60.

TRANSLATOR'S NOTES

[a] *Sämtliche Werke*, VII, 150, aphorism 52. "In no kind of knowledge can God appear as something known (as an object). As known he ceases to be God. We are never outside of God so that we could posit him in front of us like an object."—Compare Schelling's Munich lectures on modern philosophy, the section on Descartes, *Werke*, X, 19–22.

[b] In German *vernünftiges Wesen*, which is not the same as *Verstandeswesen* or "intelligent being." The latter is merely a being capable of and practiced in cogent argumentation.—Trans.

7. ABOUT THE MYSTERY OF THE NON-FINITE

1 *Gesammelte Werke* (Munich, Kurt Wolff), VIII, 341.
2 *Confessions*, XI, 14.
3 *The Intelligent Individual and Society* (New York, Macmillan, 1938), pp. 66–67.
4 *Ibid.*, p. 6.
5 *Ibid.*, p. 30.
6 *Ibid.*, p. 32.
7 Cf. Bridgman, *op. cit.*, p. 68.
8 Last paragraph of chapter 46.
9 *Vertraute unpartheiische Briefe über Fichtes Aufenthalt in Jena* (published anonymously, 1799), pp. 56–58.
10 *Dawn of Day*, No. 168; *Werke, Taschen-Ausgabe*, V, 166.
11 *Être et Avoir* (Paris, Fernand Aubier, 1935), p. 145.

TRANSLATOR'S NOTES

a From the river Lethe, the dead drink oblivion, and "lethe" means forgetfulness. Lethargic means drowsy. But truth is not dependent upon psychological conditions. What is true is, as such, *un*forgettable even though we humans may forget it, owing to our finiteness. The truth as such is non-finite. It is *non*-oblivion—*a*letheia.—Trans.
b *Faust*, I, line 1346 and presumably 1783.—Trans.

8. THE PROBLEMATIC NATURE OF THE CERTAINTY OF SELF

1 *Être et Avoir*, pp. 9f., 119.
2 See already in Fichte, *Sämtliche Werke*, I, 504. See also Wilhelm Schuppe, *Der Zusammenhang von Leib und Seele, das Grundproblem der Psychologie* (Wiesbaden, J. F. Bergmann, 1902), pp. 26ff.
3 *Nouveaux Essais sur l'entendement humain*, IV, 7, § 7.
4 *Critique of Pure Reason*, B 422.
5 Marcel, *Être et Avoir*, p. 9. See above, p. 86.
6 *Encyclopädie* (3d ed.) § 94; *Sämtliche Werke*, ed. G. Lasson, V, 115.
7 Cf. Paul Tillich in *Logos*, XVI (1927), 70.
8 *Confessions*, V, 2; X, 27.
9 *Sämtliche Werke*, III, 39; VII, 421–422.
10 *Encyclopädie*, 3d ed., § 209. Cf. *Philosophie der Weltgeschichte*, ed. Georg Lasson, I, 83.
11 *La Conduite humaine et les Valeurs idéales* (Paris, F. Alcan, 1939), pp. 129–130.

[12] *Das Dämonische, ein Beitrag zur Sinndeutung der Geschichte* (Tübingen, J. C. B. Mohr, 1926), pp. 43–44.

TRANSLATOR'S NOTES

[a] See above, p. 80f.

[b] Diels, fragment 1, line 30. See Kirk and Raven, *The Pre-Socratic Philosophers* (Cambridge University Press, 1962), p. 267: Sextus, *adv. math.* vii, 111; Simplicius, *de caelo* 557, 25.

[c] Medicus is referring to lines 2556–2557 of the third part of the trilogy *Die Nibelungen*: "Kriemhild's Revenge."—Trans.

9. THE ROLE OF THE INTELLIGENCE IN THE LIFE OF THE SPIRIT

[1] Cf. above, p. 28f.

[2] Cf. *Critique of Pure Reason*, B, 310–312.

[3] *Sämtliche Werke*, I–V, 310. Cf. also Heinrich Luden's discussion with Goethe, August 19, 1806 (Goethe, Gedenkausgabe der Werke, *Briefe und Gespräche*, Zürich, Artemis-Verlag, 1949, XXII, 407f.). [Luden had just been appointed as professor of history at the University of Jena.—Trans.]

[4] *Sämtliche Werke*, ed. A. Buchenau, E. Spranger, and H. Stettbacher (Berlin and Leipzig, W. de Gruyter, 1927ff.), XIII, 32.

[5] *Ibid.*, pp. 14f.

[6] Cf. above, p. 69. Also, B. Croce, *Logica come scienza del concetto puro*, 2d ed. (Bari, Laterza, 1909), pp. 309–310, English ed., Ainslie, Part II, Chapter V, subsection on "Critique of the assertion of mystery in philosophy." Also Croce, *Filosofia della pratica* (Bari, 1909), p. 314; Ernst Troeltsch, *Gesammelte Schriften*, II, 2d ed. (Tübingen, Mohr, 1922), pp. 482–483; Karl Dunkmann, *Religionsphilosophie* (Gütersloh, Bertelsmann, 1917), pp. 168–169.

TRANSLATOR'S NOTE

[a] When the French army of occupation, which had overcome the resistance of the Bernese troops in March, ruthlessly crushed the peasant rising in Nidwalden. The new government of Switzerland, now no longer a loose confederacy of sovereign cantons but centralized as the Helvetian Republic, though not a mere puppet of the French, had to collaborate with them. —Trans.

10. PERSONAL WHOLENESS

[1] *Sämtliche Werke*, II–I, 301; cf. *ibid.*, p. 270.

[2] *Ibid.*, pp. 185f.

[3] *Die Überwindung des Hasses* (Zürich–New York, 1946, Europa Verlag),

Notes

p. 19; cf. also Theodor Litt, *Von der Sendung der Philosophie*, pp. 25 and 45f.

[4] *Emile*, Livre IV (Oeuvres complètes, avec des notes historiques par G. Petitain, Paris, Lefèvre, 1839, III, 302). ["... que ce qui doit marcher ensemble ne soit point séparé, et que l'homme, tout entier à tous les moments de sa vie, ne le soit pas à tel point par une de ses facultés, et à tel autre point par les autres."]

[5] *Sämtliche Werke*, ed. A. Buchenau, E. Spranger, and H. Stettbacher (Berlin and Leipzig, W. de Gruyter, 1927ff.), XVI, 18f.

[6] *Sämtliche Schriften*, XI (Stuttgart and Tübingen, J. G. Cotta, 1823), pp. 271-272.

[7] Cf. above, p. 95f.

[8] *Sämtliche Schriften*, VI (Stuttgart and Tübingen, J. G. Cotta, 1820), 327.

TRANSLATOR'S NOTES

[a] *Nathan the Wise*, Act III, Scene V.—Trans.

[b] *Aufbau* was one of the favorite terms of the Nazis.—Trans.

[c] *Jubiläums-Ausgabe* (Stuttgart and Berlin, J. G. Cotta), V, 55.—Trans.

[d] Schelling says of man: "He exists originally as the being which posits God, that is, he exists as a nature which is not for itself but is turned toward God or, as it were, enraptured in God."

[e] Goethe, *West-östlicher Divan*, Buch des Sängers, Talismane. Jubiläums-Ausgabe, V. 6.

[f] Franz Grillparzer, *Weh dem, der lügt*. Lines 1805-1806, near the end of the last act. The play had its (unsuccessful) first night in Vienna, March 6, 1838.—Trans.

[g] Medicus refers to the Second Part of Nietzsche's *Zarathustra*, the chapter "About Redemption" which, in this connection, should be read in its entirety. The immediate reference is to the following lines: "I see many a horror: to wit, men who lack everything, except that they have too much of one thing,—men who are nothing but a big eye or a big mouth or a big belly or anything else big,—I call them inverted cripples."

11. ABOUT THE SUPER-OBJECTIVE

[1] *Critique of Pure Reason*, A 105. (First edition, 1781)

[2] *Critique of Pure Reason*, B 304. (Second edition, 1787)

[3] *Ibid.*, 512.

[4] Cf. above, p. 81.

[5] Cf. Fritz Marti, "Göttermacht und Gottesfreiheit," in the collection of essays *Natur und Geist* (Erlenbach-Zürich, Rentsch, 1946), p. 147. English version: "The Power of the Gods and the Freedom of God," *Faith and Freedom*, Vol. 6, No. 18 (Summer 1953), Liverpool, England.

[6] *Kultur und Ethik* (Bern, P. Haupt, 1923), pp. 236, 251.
[7] περί κατασκευῆς ἀνθρώπου 24.
[8] *Lectures on the History of Philosophy*, ed. K. L. Michelet, III (*Werke*, XV), 205–206.
[9] *Sämtliche Werke*, I–VII, 148; X, 233; II–1, 282.
[10] *Ibid.*, I–X, 234; II–I, 278.
[11] *Critique of Pure Reason*, B XXX. [See below, p. 125, note 1.]
[12] *Sämtliche Werke*, II–I, 282.
[13] Cf. above, p. 76.
[14] Consult Schelling's *Philosophical Letters on Dogmatism and Criticism*, written 1795 (*Sämtliche Werke*, I–I, 281ff.). Among the "phenomena" to which the first words of Schelling's essay refer, one could list the fact that the anonymous author of the *Confidential Unbiased Letters* mentioned above (p. 84, note 9), when he first entered Fichte's classroom, counted himself as an "orthodox Kantian" (*loc. cit.*, p. 59).
[15] *De veritate*, art. 4, ad quintum; cf. *Summa contra gentiles*, I, 7.
[16] *De scientia Dei*, art. 11; *De veritate*, art. 12.
[17] *Critique of Pure Reason*, B, XXIX.

TRANSLATOR'S NOTES

[a] Hegel said in his *Propaedeutic* of 1808–1811 (*Werke*, XVIII, Berlin, 1840, page 153, § 30: "One can go beyond every given quantum and set a further limit. . . . Thus there arises the *progressus in infinitum* or the bad infinity." And in his *Logic* of 1812 (*Werke*, V, 97; 1834) he wrote: "That infinity remains encumbered with the beyond as unattainable, since it remains a mere *progressus in infinitum*. . . . This is a relapse into bad infinity." If, in contrast to his word "bad" we were to call the non-finite good, we should still remind ourselves that, like the infinite, the non-finite is not an object.

[b] For a vivid description of the spontaneous rising of thoughts see what Nietzsche has to say, in his *Ecce Homo*, about his experiences in writing the *Zarathustra*, § 3, *The Philosophy of Nietzsche* (N.Y., Random House, 1954), p. 896.—Trans.

[c] The translator had to break up Medicus' two cryptic sentences into six, and he took the liberty of inserting the phrase "the modern view." Kant certainly was not thinking of medieval intellectualism which would objectify the existence of God and the immortality of the soul. But, in the broader sense, that intellectualism also falls under Kant's critique.—Trans.

12. CONCERNING THE TRUTH OF FAITH

[1] *Critique of Pure Reason*, B, XXX.
[2] *Ibid.*, 855.
[3] *Ibid.*, 857.
[4] Cf. above, p. 111.

[5] *Critique of Pure Reason*, B, 401.
[6] *Ibid.*, XXX.
[7] "Une lettre de Dieu nous est parvenue. . . . Le péché pour lequel il n'y a point de pardon, c'est d'avoir mis en doute l'authenticité de cette lettre." —In the periodical *In extremis* published by Protestant students, Geneva, 1935, p. 72.
[8] "La foi en l'homme est implicitement foi en Dieu." Henri-L. Miéville, *Vers une Philosophie de l'Esprit ou de la Totalité* (Lausanne, Trois Collines; Paris, F. Alcan, 1937), p. 210.
[9] Cf. above, p. 89.
[10] *Gesammelte Werke* (Munich, Kurt Wolff), VII, 263; compare *Ibid.*, p. 234.
[11] *Abendstunde eines Einsiedlers; Sämtliche Werke*, ed. A. Buchenau, E. Spranger, and H. Stettbacher, I, 271 and 269.
[12] Cf. Plato, *Alcibiades*, I, 126C; *Epistle VII*, 332D.
[13] ". . . unification de la vie entière sous un principe divin."—*Wissenschaft und Glaube*, Beiträge von Emil Brunner et al. (Erlenbach-Zürich, Eugen Rentsch, 1944), pp. 47–48.

SECOND PART: THE REALM OF TRUTH

1. ON BEING AT ONE WITH ONESELF

[1] *Encyclopädie der philosophischen Wissenschaften im Grundrisse*, ed. Henning, *Werke*, VI, (Berlin, 1840), § 24, Zusatz 2, p. 52. ["Ordinarily we call truth the conformity of an object with our representation thereof. We presuppose an object, to which our representation should conform. However, in the philosophical sense truth, expressed in general and in abstract terms, means consistency of a content within itself. This is a meaning of truth quite different from the ordinary just mentioned. Incidentally, this deeper philosophical meaning is sometimes already found in ordinary language. Thus, for instance, one speaks of a true friend . . ."—Trans.]
[2] *Ibid.*; compare the *Science of Logic*, ed. Georg Lasson, *Sämtliche Werke* (Leipzig, 1923), III, 30f.
[3] Cf. above, pp. 9f. and 55f.
[4] Cf. above, p. 88.
[5] Cf. above, p. 10.
[6] *Sämtliche Werke*, VI, p. 297.
[7] *Ibid.*, p. 298.
[8] *Ibid.*, pp. 299–300.
[9] *Ibid.*, p. 294.
[10] Cf. also Aristotle, *Metaph.* IX, 10; 1051a 34–1052 a 11.

[11] Cf. above, p. 10.
[12] Hans Urs von Balthasar, *Wahrheit*, I (Einsiedeln–Zürich, Benziger, 1947), pp. 56, 54.
[13] *Ontologie ou Métaphysique générale*, 3d ed. (Louvain, Institut supérieur de Philosophie; Paris, Alcan, 1902), pp. 196 and 197.
[14] *Ibid.*, pp. 198 and 202.—"L'idéal, norme des jugements sur le vrai, est abstrait de l'expérience."
[15] For instance, *Quaestiones de veritate*, art. 2.
[16] *Wissenschaft der Logik*, ed. Georg Lasson (Leipzig, Felix Meiner, 1923), II, 408.
[17] *Grosse Denker*, ed. E. von Aster, 2d ed. (Leipzig, Quelle and Meyer, 1923), I, 325.
[18] *Ontologie*, p. 200: "connaissance de la vérité ontologique."
[19] According to Plato's report, *Theaetetus* 152a; compare Heinrich Barth, *Philosophie der Erscheinung*, I (Basel, B. Schwabe, 1947), 54.
[20] *Ibid.*, p. 261.
[21] *Tractatus de multum nobili et prima universali scientia, quod nihil scitur*. Lugdunum, 1581, p. 112.
[22] *An Enquiry Concerning Human Understanding*, IV, 2.
[23] *Sämtliche Werke*, 1, 482.
[24] *Ibid.*, VIII, 372. (1806)
[25] *Nachgelassene Werke*, II, 98.
[26] *Sämtliche Werke*, ed. Hartenstein (1867–1868), VIII, 26.
[27] *Sämtliche Werke*, ed. Buchenau, Spranger, and Stettbacher (1927ff.), XII, 157.
[28] *Ibid.*, XII, 9; compare 45.
[29] *Sämtliche Werke*, I, 286.
[30] B, 303.
[31] *Sämtliche Werke*, IV, 386f.; cf. above, pp. 10 and 44.
[32] *Sämtliche Werke*, IV, 387.
[33] *Sämtliche Werke*, ed. Buchenau, Spranger, and Stettbacher (1927ff.), XIII, 25.
[34] *Sämtliche Werke*, VII, 330.
[35] *Sämtliche Werke*, ed. Buchenau, Spranger, and Stettbacher, XII, 95.
[36] *Sämtliche Schriften*, IX (Stuttgart and Tübingen, J. G. Cotta, 1822), 164, 174.
[37] *Sämtliche Werke*, ed. Buchenau, Spranger, and Stettbacher, IX, 53, 115.
[38] *Ibid.*, XII, 84.
[39] *Ibid.*
[40] *Ibid.*, pp. 153–154.

[41] *Sämtliche Werke*, VII, 384.
[42] *Ibid.*, pp. 384–385; compare also IV, 583.
[43] *Neue Schweizer Rundschau*, September 1946; also compare the book edition (Basel, Benno Schwabe, 1947), pp. 49f.
[44] *Weltgeschichtliche Betrachtungen* ("World-historical Contemplations"), ed. Jakob Oeri, 3d ed. (Stuttgart, W. Spemann, 1918), p. 94; *id.*, Leipzig, Alfred Kröner Verlag, 1955, pp. 95–96.
[45] Book VII, 520, 521.
[46] Book V, 473.
[47] *Sophokles, Tragödien*, German translation by Emil Staiger (Zürich, Atlantis Verlag, 1944), pp. 236, 238.—*Antigone*: lines 203–230, 454–455, 508–509.

TRANSLATOR'S NOTES

[a] Hegel writes *Bestimmung* or *Begriff*. Students of Hegel know his distinction between *Begriff* and *Idee*. Our reader is less likely to misunderstand Medicus and Balthasar if the word "idea" rather than "concept" is used. Balthasar speaks of the "transcendent idea" of things and says man "must learn and try to see things as they are before God, for God, in God." (*Wahrheit*, p. 54)—Trans.

[b] "Non per aliud cognosci debet, quod perfecte cognosci debet: sed per seipsum, ab ipsomet cognoscente immediate."—Trans.

2. THE FOUNDATION IN THE REALM OF TRUTH

[1] *Nachgelassene Werke*, II, 103f.; compare Fichte's letter of March 31, 1804, to F. H. Jacobi (*Fichtes Leben und literarischer Briefwechsel*, Sulzbach, Seidelsche Buchhandlung, 1831; Leipzig, Brockhaus, 1862).
[2] Cf. above, p. 78.
[3] *Nachgelassene Werke*, II, 613.
[4] *Sämtliche Schriften*, VI (Stuttgart and Tübingen, J. G. Cotta, 1820), 139.
[5] *Sämtliche Werke* (Hartenstein, 1867–1868), VII, 150.
[6] *Sämtliche Werke* (Buchenau–Stettbacher, 1927ff.), VIII, 164.
[7] Fifth unaltered edition (Freiburg im Breisgau, J. C. B. Mohr, 1878).
[8] *Archiv für Gewerbepathologie und Gewerbehygiene* (Berlin, Julius Springer), VIII, 238.
[9] *Sämtliche Werke*, VII, 480; cf. also the last verse of Goethe's poem "The Awakening of Epimenides."
[10] Hans Barth, *Wahrheit und Ideologie* (Zürich, Manesse Verlag, 1945), p. 183. [For many years, Barth had been literary editor of the *Neue Zürcher Zeitung*, the leading paper in Switzerland, before he became professor of philosophy at the University of Zürich, across the street from the Institute of Technology, whence Medicus retired in 1946.—Trans.]

[11] *Über das Recht*, Briefwechsel mit einem Juristen, übersetzt von A. Skarvan (Heidelberg and Leipzig, Waibel und Co., 1910).

[12] *Das Kapital* (Moscow, Marx-Engels-Lenin-Institut, 1932–1943), III, 106.

[13] E.g., *Archiv für Gewerbepathologie und Gewerbehygiene*, I (Berlin, Julius Springer, 1930), 9, 17; *Schweizerische Medizinische Wochenschrift*, 63. Jahrgang (Basel, Benno Schwabe, 1933), No. 37; *ibid.*, 66. Jahrgang (1936), Nos. 44, 48, 49; *Aufgaben der kausalen Forschung in Medizin, Technik und Recht* (Basel, Benno Schwabe, 1936), 114, 130f., 143f., 174 and passim.

[14] With regard to this compare Theodor Litt, *Wege und Irrwege geschichtlichen Denkens* (Munich, Piper, 1948), p. 143.

[15] *Wirtschaft und Recht*, 2d ed. (Leipzig, Veit und Co., 1906), pp. 219f.

[16] *Die Tat* (Zürich), March 23, 1948.

[17] July–September, p. 413.

[18] Second Part, "The Most Silent Hour."

[19] Compare Max Brod, *Unambo*, a novel about the Judeo-Arabic war (Zürich, Steinberg-Verlag, 1949), pp. 227f.

[20] Cf. above, p. 165.

[21] *Sämtliche Werke*, V, 184.

[22] The phrase was coined by Pestalozzi, in his birthday talk of January 12, 1818.

TRANSLATOR'S NOTES

[a] Medicus wrote this in 1951, having lived in Switzerland since 1911, having married a Swiss and having been naturalized. He wrote it after the terrifying experience of what happened in his native Germany under Hitler, and he was well aware of the Swiss system of taxation by direct vote of the people who also decide by ballot how the taxes are to be spent. In the United States we are often not so happy to contribute, through the withholding tax, to the expensive tastes of Congress or the White House.—Trans.

[b] Friedrich Julius Stahl, born in 1802 as a Jew, converted to Lutheranism in 1819, published his *Philosophy of Right* in two volumes (1830–37), trying to demonstrate the divine origin of law and of the state. In 1832 he became professor at Würzburg, in 1834 at Erlangen, and in 1840 at Berlin. He was one of the main leaders of Prussian conservatism and sat in the supreme church council (Oberkirchenrat) as well as in the Reichstag. He died in 1861.

[c] Writing in Switzerland, Medicus could afford to quote the original, in the third legal language of the Swiss, before giving his German translation. I here copy the Italian text, from which I have translated. "Per il fascista, tutto è nello stato. In tal senso il fascismo è totalitario, e lo stato fascista, sintesi e unità di ogni valore, interpreta, sviluppa e potenzia tutta la vita del popolo. . . . Il fascismo vuol rifare non le forme della vita umana, ma il contenuto,

l'uomo, il carattere, la fede. E a questo fine vuole disciplina, e autorità che scenda addentro negli spiriti, e vi domini incontrastata."—Trans.

[d] It is obvious that Fichte speaks of ideas not in the sense of Berkeley, for whom the word idea designates anything that happens to be in a mind, but in the sense of Plato and Kant, for whom ideas are unconditional challenges. —Trans.

[e] The American reader will remember Upton Sinclair's *Jungle*.—Trans.

3. CONCERNING INJUSTICE AND THE RESISTANCE TO IT

[1] *De veritate*, art. 2.

[2] Cf. above, p. 108f.

[3] Kurt Wolzendorff, *Polizei und Prostitution* (Tübingen, Laupp, 1911), pp. 11f.

[4] Hermann Oldenberg, *Reden des Buddha* (Munich, Kurt Wolff, 1922), p. 309.

[5] Cf. above, p. 148f.

[6] *Sämtliche Werke*, IV, 412.

[7] Cf. Julius Ebbinghaus, *Zu Deutschlands Schicksalswende*, 2d ed. (Frankfurt am Main, 1947), pp. 43, 53. And compare with that Kant's "Erörterung des Begriffs einer Tugendlehre," in *Die Metaphysik der Sitten* (1797), Zweiter Teil: Metaphysische Anfangsgründe der Tugendlehre; Einleitung I (Cassirer edition VII, 188; Berlin, 1916).

[8] Cf. Fichte, *Nachgelassene Werke*, II, 538–540.

[9] *Weltgeschichtliche Betrachtungen*, ed. J. Oeri (Stuttgart, Speemann, 1918), p. 36; id., Leipzig, Alfred Kröner Verlag, 1955, p. 39.

[10] *Sämtliche Werke*, II–I, 553.

[11] *Sämtliche Werke*, II–II, 282.

[12] Mark 8: 36; Phil. 3: 20.

[13] *Sämtliche Werke* (Buchenau, Spranger, and Stettbacher), XII, 145.

[14] *Ibid.*, p. 98.

[15] *Ibid.*, pp. 119–120.

[16] Cf. above, p. 157.

[17] § 270.

[18] *Sämtliche Werke* (Hartenstein, 1867–1868), VII, 125. Cf. Werner Haensel, *Kants Lehre vom Widerstandsrecht* (Berlin, Ergänzungsheft der Kant-Studien, Pan-Verlag, 1926), p. 67.

[19] *Morale et Politique ou les Vacances de la Probité* (Neuchâtel, La Baconniere, 1940), pp. 19–20. "La religion de la Force est assurément une religion fort séduisante."

[20] *Im Schatten von morgen*, German translation by W. Kaegi (Bern and Leipzig, Gotthelf-Verlag, 1936), p. 124.

[21] *Ibid.*, p. 127.

[22] *Frammenti di Etica* (Bari, Laterza, 1922), p. 157: "L'uomo nel suo pratico operare." [See Livingston's not always trustworthy translation, *The Conduct of Life,* p. 275 (New York, Harcourt Brace, 1924)] Similarly, Pestalozzi, *Sämtliche Werke* (Berlin, de Gruyter, 1938), XII, 52: "States flourish and perish like man himself. They are nothing but man himself as he flourishes publicly and perishes publicly."

[23] *Grundlinien der Philosophie des Rechts,* § 100.

[24] *Ibid.*, § 257.

[25] *Lo Stato Organismo etico* (Rome, Athenaeum, 1914), pp. 4, 71, 83; *Diritto e Stato nella Morale idealistica* (Padova, Cedam, 1950), pp. 126, 191–192, 204.

[26] *Sämtliche Werke* (Hartenstein, 1867–1868), IV, 252.

[27] *Sämtliche Werke,* II–I, 553. [See above, p. 177, note 10.]

[28] *Grundlage des Naturrechts nach Prinzipien der Wissenschaftslehre, Sämtliche Werke,* III, 206: "Die Menschheit sondert sich ab vom Bürgertume, um mit absoluter Freiheit sich zur Moralität zu erheben; dies aber nur, inwiefern der Mensch durch den Staat hindurchgeht."

[29] *Das System der Rechtslehre, Nachgelassene Werke,* II, 538: "Jeder Mensch geht durch den Staat hindurch, aber er geht nicht in ihm auf."

[30] *Sämtliche Werke,* VI, 369.

[31] *Grundlinien der Philosophie des Rechts,* § 258.

[32] *Sämtliche Werke,* VII, 392.

[33] *Nachgelassene Werke,* II, 539–540. [See above, p. 176, note 8.]

[34] *Ibid.*, pp. 540f. Compare also *Sämtliche Werke,* IV, 436ff.

[35] *Sämtliche Werke,* IV, 583. [See above, p. 151, note 42.]

[36] *Essais,* III, 1.

TRANSLATOR'S NOTES

[a] Demonic reality is not restricted to what is obviously devilish. The devil need not show his hoof. There is an old saying that wherever God has a church, there beside it the devil builds a chapel. And often that chapel is bigger and more sumptuous than the church. Yet the two doors should make even a simpleton hesitate as to which establishment to enter. The cleverer device of the devil is to make use of but one door and to lay his snares inside the church. On one of Michael Pacher's Sankt Wolfgang panels of 1477 one can see the saint preaching from a high pulpit on the right, but in the top left corner the devil perches between two architectural ribs and whispers to those willing to listen. Cleverer yet would be to present vice as virtue. Thus Hitler taught the demonic doctrine that the virtue of obedience suffices because it embraces all others. The cleverest of all is not to use the mouths of madmen or scoundrels but to let honorable men preach devilish doctrine.

Notes

Then the demonic is at its best and most efficacious, especially when these honorable men are honestly convinced that what they preach is righteous. Did not our "reasons" for the Vietnam war sound "right"? See also Medicus' quotation from Tillich, page 96, note 12.—Trans.

b *Der Turm* (1924). First Act, Second Scene.—Gedichte und Dramen. Ausgewählte Werke in zwei Bänden. (Frankfurt, S. Fischer Verlag, 1957), I, 237.—Trans.

4. CONCERNING HUMANITY AND INHUMAN "DUTIES"

1 *König Maximilian II. von Bayern und Schelling: Briefwechsel*, ed. L. Trost and F. Leist (Stuttgart, Cotta, 1890), pp. 196, 199–201. Cf. also Schelling, *Sämtliche Werke*, I–X, 261, and II–I, 569–570.

2 Cf. above, p. 180.

3 Cf. above, p. 154ff.

4 Of April 23, 1852. *Briefwechsel*, 278. Cf. above, p. 177.

5 *Wertwissenschaft* (Stuttgart, Frommann, 1932), p. 605.

6 Cf. above, pp. 182f.

7 *Die Erzählungen der Chassidim* (Zürich, Manesse-Verlag, 1949), p. 838.

8 An expression of Kant's, *Anthropologie in pragmatischer Hinsicht* (1798), *Sämtliche Werke* (Hartenstein, 1867–1868), VII, 431: "Physiological anthropology inquires into that which *nature* makes of man, pragmatical into that which *he*, as a freely acting being, makes of himself, or can and ought to make."

9 *Sämtliche Schriften*, VI (Stuttgart and Tübingen, J. G. Cotta, 1820), 139. [Compare the continuation of Pestalozzi's passage, note 4, p. 157.]

10 Cf. above, pp. 149f.

11 Cf. above, pp. 95f.

12 Cf. above, pp. 172f.

13 *Sämtliche Werke* (Hartenstein, 1867–1868), IV, 281, 282, 269, 284. Compare V, 32; VII, 22, 192, 199.

14 *Gebrochenheit*, an expression from Hebbel's preface to his play *Maria Magdalene*.

15 Cf. above, p. 86.

16 A formulation of Schiller's. Compare Kant, *Critique of Practical Reason*, §6, note: "Thus he judges that he can do something because he is aware that he ought to do it."

17 Letter to F. H. Jacobi of the 30th of March, 1818.

18 *Sämtliche Werke* (Hartenstein, 1867–1868), VII, 162ff. [Medicus means §55 of the *Metaphysische Anfangsgründe der Rechtslehre* which is the first part of his long work of 1797, *Die Metaphysik der Sitten*, or *Metaphysics of Morals*. Kant says this "right" can furnish only "an approximation" of what could be called just.—Trans.]

[19] *Ibid.*, p. 137. Cf. also above, pp. 175 (note 7) and 180f.
[20] *Nachgelassene Werke*, III, 427. [1807]
[21] *Sämtliche Werke*, II–I, 486.
[22] Letter to Elise Lensing, December 5, 1843.
[23] *Sämtliche Werke*, V, 185, 211. [For 185 see note 21 to our page 170 and 5 to our page 37. On his page 211 Fichte reprints what he said on pp. 184–185.—Trans.]
[24] *Sämtliche Werke* (Hartenstein, 1867–1868), IV, 285.

TRANSLATOR'S NOTES

[a] Medicus uses the phrase from Schelling's aphorism 46 (*Werke*, VII, 149). See p. 92, note 9.—Trans.
[b] Hitler's phrase: "tausendjähriges Reich."—Trans.
[c] *Faust*, II, lines 11954–11965.—Trans.
[d] *Werke, Säkular-Ausgabe* (Stuttgart and Berlin, J. G. Cotta, 1904), I, 45.

5. INHUMAN TRUTHS AND HUMAN UNTRUTHS

[1] *Sämtliche Werke* (Hartenstein, 1867–1868), VII, 235.
[2] *Ibid*, pp. 308f.
[3] *Sämtliche Werke*, IV, 289–290.
[4] *Nachgelassene Werke*, III, 99.
[5] Cf. above, p. 109.
[6] *Diesseits und Jenseits* (Winterthur, Mondial-Verlag, 1947), II, 78: "Der Liebende ist einverstanden mit Gott."
[7] *Prolegomena to Ethics*, ed. A. C. Bradley (Oxford, Clarendon Press, 1890), p. 344.
[8] Cf. above, p. 202.
[9] *Sämtliche Werke* (Hartenstein, 1867–1868), VII, 22.
[10] *Nachgelassene Werke*, III, 73.
[11] *Ibid.*, pp. 193f.
[12] C. Amiet, *Über Kunst und Künstler* (Jahresgabe der Bernischen Kunstgesellschaft für 1948), 12.
[13] Oxford, Clarendon Press, 1885, II, 237.
[14] *Ethik des reinen Willens* (Berlin, B. Cassirer, 1907), p. 528.
[15] *Frammenti di Etica* (Bari, Laterza, 1922), pp. 33–37. [See Chapter VIII, "On Telling the Truth" (pp. 52–61), in the translation (which I found often untrustworthy) of Arthur Livingston, *The Conduct of Life* (New York, Harcourt, Brace and Co., 1924).] Compare *Filosofia della Pratica* (Bari, 1909), pp. 95–96. [In Douglas Ainslee's translation, *Philosophy of the Practical* (London, Macmillan, 1913), pp. 135–139.]

Notes

16 *Sämtliche Werke* (Hartenstein, 1867–1868), VII, 236.
17 *Ibid.*, pp. 309, 310, 311. [*Über ein vermeintliches Recht aus Menschenliebe zu lügen.* 1797.]
18 Cf. above, p. 173.
19 *Gesammelte Werke*, VIII, 163.
20 *Sämtliche Werke*, IV, 167.
21 *Sämtliche Werke* (Hartenstein, 1867–1868), VII, 235.

TRANSLATOR'S NOTES

a "Metaphysische Anfangsgründe der Tugendlehre." "Über ein vermeintes Recht, aus Menschenliebe zu lügen."—Trans.

b Alles geben die Götter, die unendlichen,
Ihren Lieblingen ganz,
Alle Freuden, die unendlichen,
Alle Schmerzen, die unendlichen, ganz.
Goethe, "Vermischte Gedichte"

c See page 209 above, note 15. Croce's philosophy of the Spirit has four parts: Aesthetics, Logic, Philosophy of the Practical, Theory and History of Historiography.

d In the first act of *The Devil's Disciple* by George Bernard Shaw, Mrs. Dudgeon says to the parson who appealed to her heart: "My heart! My heart! And since when, pray, have *you* begun to hold up our hearts as trustworthy guides for us? . . . We are told that the heart of man is deceitful above all things, and desperately wicked."

6. THE CLAIM WHICH THE DEPTHS OF TRUTH MAKE ON MAN

1 *Handzeichnungen europäischer Meister aus der Albertina*; Einführung von Walter Ueberwasser (Bern, Iris-Verlag, 1948), p. 7.
2 Max Brod, *Diesseits und Jenseits* (Winterthur, Mondial-Verlag, 1947), II, 165.
3 *Das Buch Hiob und das Schicksal des jüdischen Volkes* (Zürich, Steinberg, 1946), pp. 206–207.
4 *Ibid.*, pp. 174–175.
5 *Ibid.*, pp. 176.
6 *Ibid.*, p. 210.
7 *Ibid.*, pp. 221–222.
8 Compare also Fritz Marti in the collection of essays, *Natur und Geist* (Erlenbach-Zürich, Rentsch, 1946), pp. 146f.
9 *Sämtliche Werke*, I–VII, 149. [See note 16, p. 76.]
10 *Jenseits von Gut und Böse*, No. 2.
11 *Ibid.*, No. 43.

¹² Cf. above, pp. 48f.
¹³ *Die fröhliche Wissenschaft*, No. 271. Compare *Also Sprach Zarathustra*, "Der Notschrei." [Fourth Part, "The Cry for Help."]
¹⁴ *Das Tibetanische Totenbuch*. From the English edition of the *Lama Kazi Dawa Samdup*, edited by W. Y. Evans-Wentz, translated by L. Göpfert-March, with a psychological commentary by Carl Gustav Jung (Zürich, Rascher, 1935), pp. 51f.
¹⁵ *Ibid.*, pp. 16f.
¹⁶ *Ethics*, IV, 64 and *Corollary*. Compare Schelling, *Sämtliche Werke*, I–VII, 409.

TRANSLATOR'S NOTE

ᵃ "für lauter Kreuz und Christ/Ihn eben und sein Kreuz vergisst." *Der ewige Jude*. Werke IV, 238 (Artemis, 1962).

7. ABOUT THE GOAL OF MANKIND

¹ Compare Kant's *Prolegomena to Any Future Metaphysics Which Will Be Able to Come Forth as Science*.
² No. 33, *Werke, Taschenausgabe*, III, 51.
³ "Of Old and New Tablets," No. 11.
⁴ *Ibid.*; compare "Of the Faithless."
⁵ *Philosophie der Weltgeschichte*, ed. Georg Lasson (1917), I, 132. Cf. above, p. 135.
⁶ *Ibid.*, p. 136.
⁷ *Ibid.*, p. 137. "Der Geist ist mit seinem Begriffe versöhnt."

TRANSLATOR'S NOTE

ᵃ A term borrowed from Kant and Fichte.—Trans.

8. ABOUT HUMANITY: ITS ONTOLOGICAL GROUND, THE DANGERS TO IT, AND ITS HEIGHT

¹ Cf. above, pp. 89f.
² *Soliloqu.* I, 1, 3. Cf. I, 15, 29. *De immort.* 12, 19.
³ Cf. above, p. 82.
⁴ Cf. above, p. 98.
⁵ Cf. above, p. 83.
⁶ Cf. above, p. 80.
⁷ Cf. above, pp. 27f and 58.
⁸ Cf. above, pp. 81ff.
⁹ Cf. above, p. 86.

Notes

[10] Gabriel Marcel, *Être et Avoir*, p. 118. "On ne comprend que sur la base de ce qu'on est."
[11] *Sämtliche Werke*, I–VII, 359.
[12] *Ibid.*, p. 363.
[13] *Ibid.*, p. 364.
[14] Cf. above, p. 203.
[15] *Sämtliche Werke*, I, 36. Cf. Aristotle's *Nicomachean Ethics*, VII, 7, 1150a.
[16] *Pensées* (Text de Léon Brunschveig), No. 418.
[17] Cf. above, pp. 135 and 230f.
[18] Cf. above, p. 136.
[19] Cf. the quoted letter of Fichte to Goethe, quoted above, p. 23.
[20] "Les grandeurs de sens contraire ne s'annulent pas."—Louis Meylan, *Les Humanités et la Personne* (Neuchâtel and Paris, Delachaux et Niestlé, 1939), p. 58.
[21] ". . . la lumière qui jaillit du mystère." *Rencontre, Revue littéraire* (Lausanne, September–October, 1950), 55.
[22] *Sämtliche Werke*, IV, 166.
[23] *Sämtliche Werke*, V, 403.
[24] Elisabeth·Förster-Nietzsche, *Der junge Nietzsche* (Leipzig, Kröner, 1912), p. 169.
[25] Wilhelm Lütgert, *Die Liebe im Neuen Testament* (Leipzig, Deichert, 1905), p. 124.
[26] Cf. above, pp. 192ff.
[27] Cf. Martin Werner in the collection of essays *Das Ewige in der Religion* (Schwarzenburg, Verlag Gerber-Buchdruck, 1948), p. 153.
[28] Cf. Gabriel Marcel, *Être et Avoir*, pp. 99ff.: "March 11, 1931. Charity as presence, as absolute availability. . . ." *Homo Viator* (Paris, Aubier, 1944), p. 28: ". . . that which I consider the essential characteristic of a person, that is, his availability"; p. 31: "The available being stands in contrast to one who is occupied or hampered by himself."
[29] Victor Hugo, *La Légende des Siècles, A l'homme*:
. . . mon coeur, qui cherche son chemin,
N'accepte le divin qu'autant qu'il est humain.
[30] *The Sacrifice*, Scene XI.

TRANSLATOR'S NOTES

[a] Compare Augustine: *de vera religione*, 39:72: "Try to reach that whence the very light of intelligence is lit."
[b] Compare Augustine, *de vera religione*, 39, 72: "If you find your nature

mutable, rise above yourself. But when you do transcend yourself, remember that you are transcending the ratiocinating soul" (the intellect).

c Medicus says "heilsam" and "Heil vermittelnd." To translate Heil as salvation would sound too otherworldly.—Trans.

d Members of German student fraternities would wear a ribbon in the fraternity colors. The ribbon extended from the right shoulder to the left hip. Its origin was the sword bandoleer. The ribbon was worn over the vest and under the jacket. While the student also wore a cap of the same colors, it was the ribbon which corresponded to our fraternity pin.—Trans.

9. CONFIRMATIONS

[1] Cf. above, p. 29.

[2] Cf. above, p. 170.

[3] Cf. above, pp. 157f.

[4] Much the same is said, though on the ground of different presuppositions, by Max Brod, *Diesseits und Jenseits* (Winterthur, Mondial-Verlag, 1947), II, 105.

[5] *Sâdhanâ: The Realization of Life* (New York, Macmillan, 1916), p. 107.

[6] Cf. Schelling, *Sämtliche Werke*, I, VIII, 210.

[7] *Sâdhanâ*, pp. 75–76.

[8] Cf. above, pp. 192f.

[9] John 17:4.

[10] Cf. above, p. 243.

[11] Cf. above, pp. 226f.

[12] Cf. above, pp. 125f.

[13] *Les Humanités et la Personne* (Neuchâtel, Delachaux et Niestlé S. A., 1944), p. 257.

[14] Cf. above, pp. 136 and 104f.

[15] Compare Schelling, *Sämtliche Werke*, II–I, 248; II–III, 187–188. [Schelling says *zurechtgestellt* which means "set up in the right order." Medicus uses the noun *Zurechtstellung*, "rectification."—Trans.]

TRANSLATOR'S NOTES

a See Schiller's poem "Deutsche Treue," *Säkular-Ausgabe* (Stuttgart and Berlin, J. G. Cotta, 1904), I, 262.

b Source unidentified, presumably Conrad Ferdinand Meyer.

c Der Regen fällt nicht ihm, die Sonne scheint nicht ihr,
  Du auch bist anderen geschaffen und nicht dir.

d *The Gay Science* (1881–82) §270 and §335. *Zarathustra* (1884–85) Part IV, "The Honey Sacrifice."—See already in 1874, *Schopenhauer as Educator*, second page and the whole first chapter.

10. RELIGION AND CULTURE

1 *Sämtliche Werke* (Hartenstein, 1867–1868), VI, 267.
2 Cf. above, p. 29.
3 Cf. above, p. 128.
4 Cf. above, pp. 131 and 247f.
5 Critical edition of F. M. Schiele (Leipzig, Dürr, 1902; 2d ed., Felix Meiner, 1914), 17. *Sämtliche Werke*, III–I, 357.
6 Cf. above, p. 121.
7 Compare Kautzsch-Bertholet, *Die Heilige Schrift des Alten Testaments*, 4th ed., I, 44.
8 B, 723.
9 Gabriel Marcel, *Existentialisme chrétien* (Paris, Plon, 1947), p. 304: "Penser, formuler, juger, au fond, c'est toujours trahir."
10 Kuno Fiedler, *Schrift und Schriftgelehrte* (Bern-Leipzig, P. Haupt, 1942), p. 37. [In his chapter on the "Idolatry of Scripture," Fiedler continues the words quoted by Medicus from *Scripture and Scribes*, p. 37: "All the consequences appear which, as experience shows, idolatry inevitably brings with it: estrangement from God, religious deafness, superstition, enmity to truth, fanaticism, spiritual torpor, moral sloth, self-righteousness and every kindred trait.

"To be sure, the transition from one kind of interpretation to the other occurs quite differently in individual men and, at all events, quite (p. 38) imperceptibly, which is precisely the precariousness of the occurrence. From the simple statement 'Moses says' which we still meet in Jesus (e.g., Matthew 19:8) one slips into the well-known 'Scripture says,' and from there it is no longer far to 'God says,' a phrase in which the evil is already fully ripe."—Trans.]
11 Cf. Kant, *Sämtliche Werke* (Hartenstein, 1867–1868), VI, 286; VII, 380.
12 *Sämtliche Werke* (Buchenau, Spranger, and Stettbacher, 1927ff.), XIII, 15. [See note a, page 102.]
13 No. 129.
14 *Werke, Taschenausgabe*, IX, 107.
15 "Of a Thousand and One Goals." Jean-Paul Sartre says much the same in *L'Existentialisme est un Humanisme* (Paris, Nagel, 1947), especially p. 89.
16 Especially in the ninth [the last] chapter [on "What is noble?"].
17 No. 123. (In Thomas Mann's *Doctor Faustus*, towards the end of Chapter 27, Adrian Leverkühn, informed "from the very best source," seems to have come upon the tracks of such guesses.)
18 No. 125.
19 *Werke, Taschenausgabe*, VI, 375. [As an appendix to *The Gay Science*, Nietzsche published his *Lieder des Prinzen Vogelfrei*. Literally, *vogelfrei* means free as a bird, but figuratively it can also mean an outlaw who, "free

as a bird," is anybody's prey. By 1882 Nietzsche was rapidly acquiring that status, among his contemporaries. The very first of his songs is addressed "to Goethe" and, respectful in poetic form, makes sport of the last eight lines of the second part of Goethe's Faust:

Goethe: Prose rendering:

Chorus mysticus   Mystic choir

Alles Vergängliche   Everything transitory
Ist nur ein Gleichnis;   is but a parable.
Das Unzulängliche,   What is inadequate
Hier wird's Ereignis;   here turns event.
Das Unbeschreibliche,   The undescribable
Hier ist's getan;   here it is done.
Das Ewig-Weibliche   The ever-feminine
Zieht uns hinan.   lifts us aloft.

Nietzsche:

An Goethe   To Goethe

Das Unvergängliche   The everlasting
Ist nur dein Gleichnis!   is but your parable.
Gott, der Verfängliche,   God, the delusive one,
Ist Dichter-Erschleichnis. . . .   is poets' fraud.

Welt-Rad, das rollende,   World-wheel, the rolling one,
Streift Ziel auf Ziel: grazes goal after goal:
Not—nennt's der Grollende,   Necessity—says the rancorous,
Der Narr nennt's—Spiel. . . .   the fool calls it—play.

Welt-Spiel, das herrische,   World-play, the imperious,
Mischt Sein und Schein:—   mixes being and seeming:—
Das Ewig-Närrische   the ever-foolish thing
Mischt uns—hinein!   mixes us in!

—Trans.]

[20] *The Gay Science*, Nos. 285 and 341.
[21] *Werke, Taschenausgabe*, VIII, 10.
[22] Cf. above, p. 52.
[23] Compare Friedrich Büchsel, *Die Johannesbriefe* (Leipzig, A. Deichert, 1933), p. 58f. [Büchsel, Professor of Theology at the University of Rostock, dedicated his book "to Fritz Medicus in Zürich." The gist of the exegetic pages to which Medicus refers can be found in Büchsel's free rendering of the sense of two verses, 19 and 20, of the third chapter of John's First Letter: "19. Active, sincere love gives us the certainty that we are sincere human

beings, that is, men inwardly tied to God. If nevertheless our conscience condemns us as sinners, that certainty, by means of being centered in God, can convince our conscience, 20. that the grace of God is much greater than we dare to believe in our humiliation and that, our sin notwithstanding, God does not forget our love and does not reject us although we are sinners."
—Trans.]

[24] Martin Buber, *Die Erzählungen der Chassidim* (Zürich, Manesse Verlag, 1949), pp. 288f. Am. ed. *Tales of the Hassidim* (New York, Schocken Books).

[25] *Die Erzählungen der Chassidim*, p. 158.

[26] Many examples in *Vishnu-Narayana: Texte zur indischen Gottesmystik*, trans. R. Otto (Jena, Diederichs, 1923). For example, pp. 123, 147ff.

[27] K. Haas, *Amida Buddha* (Leipzig, Dieterich, 1910), p. 56.

[28] *Ibid.*, pp. 63–66. Cf. also Martin Buber, *Die Erzählungen der Chassidim*, pp. 18, 397.

[29] *Sämtliche Werke*, I–VII, 261.

[30] Cf. above, pp. 226f.

[31] H. Oldenberg, *Reden des Buddha* (Munich, Kurt Wolff, 1922), p. 136. John 1:47; compare 7:17.

[32] *Critique of Judgment* §86.

[33] *Sämtliche Werke* (Hartenstein, 1868), VI, 284.

[34] Paul Tillich, "Zwei Wege der Religionsphilosophie," in the collection of essays, *Natur und Geist*, pp. 222f, 225. Cf. also Martin Buber, *Die Erzählungen der Chassidim*, p. 421.

[35] Romain Rolland, *Das Leben des Ramakrishna*, trans. P. Amann (Erlenbach-Zürich, Rotapfelverlag, 1929), p. 265. Compare 36–37.

[36] Fritz Marti, "Göttermacht und Gottesfreiheit," in the collection of essays, *Natur und Geist*, p. 158. English version published (1953) in *Faith and Freedom: A Journal of Progressive Religion* (Liverpool, England) under the title "The Power of the Gods and the Freedom of God."

[37] Cf. above, pp. 92–93.

[38] Cf. above, pp. 78 and 99.

[39] Rolland, *Das Leben des Ramakrishna*, p. 284.

[40] *Apology*, 28 and 29.

[41] Wilhelm Lütgert, *Die Liebe im Neuen Testament* (Leipzig, Deichert, 1905), p. 243.

[42] *Geschichtlicher Sinn und Kirchlichkeit* (*Beiträge zur Förderung christlicher Theologie*, III, 4 Gütersloh, Bertelsmann, 1899), 98.

[43] Cf. also Gabriel Marcel, *Homo Viator* (Paris, Aubier, 1944), pp. 223–224.

[44] Cf. above, p. 135. [Concept, not in the ordinary sense, but in that of

Hegel, as "consistency of a content within itself." See Note 1, p. 135. —Trans.]

⁴⁵ Cf. above, p. 119.

⁴⁶ *Zwei Wege der Religionsphilosophie*, p. 227.

TRANSLATOR'S NOTES

ᵃ Medicus says *unendlich*. The phrase "infinite task" could sound depressing. To be sure, our task is endless, but it is not hopeless. There are no finite solutions. But if we acknowledge our fallibility, then it is precisely by means of our merely finite endeavors and decisions that we can fulfill our non-finite task, again and again. This is in line with what Medicus says in the remainder of the paragraph.—Compare also pages 261f.—Trans.

ᵇ Goethe, *Torquato Tasso*, Act V, Scene 1, lines 2848–49.

ᶜ See p. 102, note a.

ᵈ German distinguishes between *Geisteswissenschaft* and *Naturwissenschaft*, i.e. between the systematic knowledge of matters of the spirit, on the one hand, and matters of nature on the other. We have no adequate English formula for *Geisteswissenschaft*. The closest may be the humanities.

ᵉ Quantus tremor est futurus,
   Quando judex est venturus,
   Cuncta stricte discussurus!
. . . .
   Quid sum miser tunc dicturus?
—From the *Dies irae*, The Roman Missal, Sequence of the Mass for the Dead.

ᶠ Medicus may have had in mind St. Francis' *perfetta letizia* (Little Flowers, VIII).—Trans.

ᵍ See above, p. 105; Lessing, *Nathan the Wise*.

ʰ Schelling called God *das allerfreieste Wesen*, "the very freest being," *Die Weltalter, Sämtliche Werke*, I–VIII, 308. Also compare Exodus 33:23.

ⁱ Cf. Karl Rahner, S.J., *Worte ins Schweigen* (Innsbruck, Rauch, 1965), p. 7: "How could you be the God of my life if you were not more than the God of *my* life?"—The very title of this beautiful book is significant: Words into Silence.

ʲ ". . . le silence éternel de la Divinité." Cf. above, p. 221, Alfred de Vigny.

INDEX OF NAMES

Amida Buddha, 274
Amiet, Cuno, 207
Anaximander, 44
Angelus Silesius, 251
Anselm of Canterbury, 46
Aristotle, 8f., 233, 291,[39] 299,[10] 309[15]
Augustine, 56, 82, 90, 232, 257, 276

Baader, Franz von, 214, 236, 241
Bacon, Francis, 36
Balthasar, Hans Urs von, 10, 137
Barth, Hans, 163
Barth, Heinrich, 139
Baumgartner, Mathias, 138
Bergson, Henri, 74f., 78
Bridgman, Percy Williams, 82f.
Brod, Max, 206, 218, 221, 302,[19] 310[4]
Buber, Martin, 190, 273f., 313,[24] 313[34]
Büchsel, Friedrich, 312[23]
Buddha, 38, 173, 226, 274
Burckhardt, Jacob, 152, 177

Claparède, Edouard, 181
Cohen, Hermann, 208
Cohn, Jonas, 187, 290[5]
Croce, Benedetto, 182, 208f., 229, 292,[56] 296[6]

Dante, 104, 156
Dehmel, Richard, 92
Democritus, 46
Descartes, René, 86ff., 106, 122, 233, 251
Deutero-Isaiah, 219f.
Dionysius of Syracuse, 152
Dunkmann, Karl, 296[6]

Ebbinghaus, Hermann, 303[7]
Einstein, Albert, 78
Escarra, Jean, 167
Esser, Albert, 27
Eucken, Rudolf, 142

Fichte, Johann Gottlieb, 1f., 4–7, 9ff., 22f., 44, 46, 51, 61, 71, 84, 92, 103, 120, 135–138, 140f., 143f., 146, 148, 151, 154, 157, 163, 170, 174, 183f., 194, 198f., 200, 203, 207, 210f., 214, 238, 163, 170, 174, 183f., 194, 198f., 298,[14] 303[8]
Fiedler, Kuno, 267
France, Anatole, 79
Francis of Assisi, 173, 271
Freud, Sigmund, 278
Frisch, Max, 151ff.

Goethe, Johann Wolfgang, 23, 28, 65, 69f., 85, 104, 106, 138, 194, 205, 224, 251, 260, 296[3]
Göring, Hermann, 119
Green, Thomas Hill, 206
Gregory of Nyssa, 120
Grillparzer, Franz, 109, 204

Haas, Hans, 313[27]
Häberlin, Paul, 289[2]
Haensel, Werner, 303[18]
Hebbel, Friedrich, 96, 200, 305[14]
Hegel, G. W. F., 5f., 8, 10, 69, 88, 95, 103, 121, 135–138, 179, 229f.
Heraclitus, 39, 101
Hitler, Adolf, 20, 59, 155, 201
Hobbes, Thomas, 86
Hofmannsthal, Hugo von, 171, 176

Hugo, Victor, 245
Huizinga, Johan, 181f.
Hume, David, 139
Husserl, Edmund, 17ff., 24, 26, 42

Ibsen, Henrik, 204, 281
Isaiah, 219f.

Jacobi, Friedrich Heinrich, 43, 76
Jeremiah, 68, 218
Jesus, 120, 128, 145, 173, 252, 275, 280f.
John the Evangelist, 275
Jung, Carl Gustav, 226

Kant, Immanuel, 1–5, 8, 16, 22, 54, 69, 71, 76, 87f., 116, 120, 122–125, 127, 137, 139ff., 154, 181f., 183, 194, 196f., 201ff., 206, 209ff., 214ff., 229, 234, 236, 258, 276, 291,[42] 303,[7] 305,[8] 311[11]
Kōa Shōnin, 274

Leibniz, Gottfried Wilhelm, 11, 55f., 69, 87f.
Lessing, Gotthold Ephraim, 105
Litt, Theodor, 18, 21, 290,[1] 296,[3] 302[14]
Lotze, Hermann, 228
Louis IX, 172
Luden, Heinrich, 296[3]
Lundberg, Birger, 166
Lütgert, Wilhelm, 243, 281f., 309,[25] 313[41]
Luther, Martin, 73

Machiavelli, Niccolò, 177, 198
Mann, Thomas, 48, 71, 83, 293,[25] 311[17]
Marcel, Gabriel, 20f., 85f., 234, 241, 267, 309,[10] 309,[28] 313[43]
Marti, Fritz, 278, 297[5]
Marti, Karl, 293[14]
Martineau, James, 208
Marx, Karl, 164ff.
Mauriac, François, 244
Maximilian II of Bavaria, 186
Mercier, Désiré, 137f.
Meyer, Conrad Ferdinand, 251[a]
Meylan, Louis, 238, 255, 309[20]

Miéville, Henri-Louis, 129, 299[8]
Molière, 6, 171
Montaigne, Michel de, 185
Munnynck, Marc de, 132
Mussolini, Benito, 119, 162, 180

Niethammer, Friedrich Immanuel, 1
Nietzsche, Friedrich, 20, 47–55, 57–66, 68, 70f., 74, 85, 168, 181, 185, 229f., 242, 252, 268–271, 277

Otto, Rudolf, 313[26]

Paracelsus, 56ff., 73f., 279
Parmenides, 87, 101
Parodi, Dominque, 95
Pascal, Blaise, 237
Paul, Saint, 260
Pestalozzi, Johann Heinrich, 33, 102f., 110ff., 132, 141, 147–151, 157, 160, 167, 178f., 181, 192, 250, 268, 271, 302,[22] 304[22]
Pindar, 252
Plato, 31, 54, 71, 86, 152, 163, 234, 280, 299,[12] 300[19]
Protagoras, 139
Pythagoreans, 6

Raphael, 34
Ramakrishna, 245, 271, 276, 278, 280
Ravà, Adolfo, 183
Rembrandt, 144f.
Riehl, Alois, 16
Rolland, Romain, 256
Rousseau, Jean-Jacques, 110

Sanchez, Franciscus, 139
Sartre, Jean-Paul, 192, 311[15]
Savioz, Raymond, 241
Schelling, Friedrich, 5f., 10f., 48, 56, 65–68, 73–76, 78, 100, 103, 106f., 122f., 177, 179, 183, 186f., 199, 224, 229, 234, 275, 289,[3] 308,[16] 310,[6] 310[15]
Schiller, Friedrich, 15, 66, 69, 196, 199, 246, 305[16]
Schleiermacher, Friedrich, 5ff., 196, 261
Schmitt, Carl, 59

Index of Names

Schön, Theodor von, 236
Schopenhauer, Arthur, 63ff., 70f., 230
Schubert, Franz, 34
Schuppe, Wilhelm, 295[2]
Schweitzer, Albert, 118
Sertillanges, Antonin Gilbert, 10
Shakespeare, William, 104
Siegmund-Schultze, Friedrich, 109
Socrates, 71, 280
Sophocles, 152
Spinoza, Baruch, 17, 46, 226
Spitteler, Karl, 150
Stahl, Friedrich Julius, 160
Stahl, Georg Ernst, 20
Stammler, Rudolf, 165
Susman, Margarete, 221, 224

Tagore, Rabindranath, 38, 82, 131, 214, 245, 250ff., 281

Thales, 6, 44f.
Thomas Aquinas, 10, 123f., 137f., 171
Tillich, Paul, 22, 96, 277, 283, 295[7]
Tolstoy, Leo, 164
Troeltsch, Ernst, 296[6]

Ueberwasser, Walter, 307[1]

Vigny, Alfred de, 221
Vivekananda, 280
Vives, Ludovicus, xi

Wagner, Richard, 63
Werner, Martin, 244, 309[27]
Wolff, Christian, 143
Wolzendorff, Kurt, 303[3]

Zangger, Heinrich, 162, 165
Zwingli, Huldrych, 73

INDEX OF TOPICS

Page references to the main passages are in italics

Absolute, the, 140, 143, 202, 227, 266, 275
Abstraction, 17, 24f., 80, 86, 99, 102, 120f., 125f., 205, 208f., 240
Action, moral, 28f., 192f., 211
Accident; see Contingency
Administration of justice, 32, 98, 157, 159–64, 167–70, 189, 213, 247, 283
Aesthetics, 100, 217
Aim; see Purpose
Alienation (self-estrangement), 90f., 96, 109f., 237, 260
Anxiety, 79, 128, 258, 276
Appearance (phenomenon), 9f., 30, 37, 119, 124f., 127, 137, 144
    false, 32, 50, 62f., 203
Apollinic, 63, *65–68*
Appropriateness, 3, 203
Art, 57, 63, 69, 98, 131, 189, 199, *248*, 259
    work of, 3f., 25, 30ff., 65, 100, 144f., 207, 217, 264, 266
Atheism, 277f.
Authority, external, 128, 163, 191, 267
Autonomy, 106, 108, 115, *117f.*, 122, 171, 183, 248, *257ff.*

Basis
    of action, 96
    economico-legal, 156, 165ff., 187, 235, 247
    of humanity, 114, 155ff., 188, 191, 195, 240, 245
    in nature, 118, 155, 234f., 237, 241, 245
    of society, 155, 160, 164, 167

Beautiful, the, 32, 69, 250
Being at one with oneself; see Oneness
Bible, 5, 262, 266ff.
Biological understanding, 40
Biologism, 49ff., 54, 63, 65, 71, 225, 252, 269, 271
Body, 86, 176, 234, 249
    one's own, 86, 234, 241

Capitalism, 164ff.
Care, social, 279
Causal connection, 81, 83, 116, 234f.
Certainty, 17, 28, 43, 54, 70, 82, 87f., 135, 265
    immediate, 33, 125ff., 129f., 214, 254f., 265
    religious, 100, 129
Challenge (the call, appeal), 23, 35, 93, 127, 143, 147, *158*, 166–170, 175, 181, 214, 244, 255
Christianity, 38, 57, 64, 73, 79, 118, 177, 181f., 221, 230
Church, 73f., 116
Classical, 68
Coercion (force), *35ff.*, 60, 92, 142, 157–60, 167f., 178, 193, 247
Collective
    existence, 92f., 157, 179, 192
    guilt, 112, 175
Commandments, 68, 177, 181, 212f., 218
Communication of the truth, 209
Community, 35, 44, 77, 79, 90f., 96, 127f., *141f.*, 146, *173ff.*, 194, 207, *241ff.*, 271, 279, 282
    of nations, 93, 177, 224, 236

316

Index of Topics

Conceptual form, 42f., 63, 69f., 80, 87, 99, 116, 211
Conditionality
  historical, 19, 43, 45, 78, 129, *172–76*, 190, 193, 196f., *200f.*, 234, 239, 253, 258, 261f., 264f., 267, 283
  of man, 6, 69f., 77, 210, 261
Confidence (trust), 180ff., 221, 274
Conscience, 29, *108*f., 128, 149f., 166, *171ff.*, 178, 182, 184f., *189f.*, *192*, 238, 242f., 259, 273, 281
  social, 166, 242
Consciousness, 6, 29, 33f., 39f., *42*, 56, 60, 66, 69, 75f., 107, 115, 140, 155, 166, 232, 239, 264f.
Constitution of state, 181–84
Content, 88, 108, 119, 126–29, 221, 233, 257, 265
  and form, 16f., *65–70*, 73, 108, 117, 162, 200, 265
Contingency, 6f., 20, 30, 42, 50, 67, 88, *105ff.*, 257
Continuity of history, 24, 39f.
Contrastlessness, 75, 225f., 233
Contrasts (oppositions), 43, 76, 212, 225f., 253, 255, 262, 271, 282
Conviction, 101, 150, 170, 228
Copy theory of knowledge, 139
Creativeness, 26, 62f., 65f., 119, 229
Creed as commitment of faith, 15, 213, 266
Critical thinking, 43, 45, 84, 104, 124, 129, 282f.
Critique of Judgment (Kant), *1–4*, 9, 123, 137, 154, 276
Critique of Practical Reason (Kant), 1–4, 123
Critique of Pure Reason (Kant), *1–4*, 16, 82, 123f., 139, 143, 265, 296[2]
Cubism, 131
Cultural
  catastrophes, 95, 112
  heritage, 112, 197, 243
  life, 24, 31, 43, *65f.*, *111ff.*, 147, 238, 259, 262, 264, 267, 271f., 283
Culture, 24, 26, 30, 65f., 71f., 93, 99f., 107, *116f.*, 121, 145, 163, 176, 231, 236, 261f., 272, 275, 280, 282f.
  faith in, 48, 264, 266

Death, 9, 79, 157, 204f., 252
  believers in, 11
Decision, 34f., 41, 54f., 63, 76, 94f., 107f., 146, 162, 189, 212f., *223*, 227, 235, 237, 265, 283
Dedication (devotion), 34, 75
Demonic powers, 95f., 112, 119f., 175f., 193f., 196, 230, 249
Denominations and religions, 100, 116f., 228, 249, 256, 276
Depth
  of being, 37, 42, 55, *68f.*, 71, 109, 130, 138, *143*, 170, 244, 260, 278
  of human existence, *34ff.*, 42, 57, 68, 89, 106, 131, 140, 143, *159f.*, 175, 186, 204f., 237, 247, 249, *255ff.*, 259, 266, 271, 274, 278, 280, 282
  of the life of the spirit, 44, 68f., 131, 282
  of truth, xi, 31, 56, 73, 97f., 103, 126, 146, *222ff.*
Devil, 48, 71, 120, 225
Dharma, 251
Dictatorships, 162, 258f.
Dignity, 113, 166, 172, 182ff., *187f.*, 191, 197f., 203, 277
Dionysiac, 47f., 50f., 55, 59, 62f., 66ff., 71, 74, 225
Dogmas, religious, 5, 79, 100, *116*, 121, 127, 258, 276, 278
Doubt, 126–29, 249, 256, 264ff.
Dualism, 75, 262
Duty, 32, 37, 111f., 173ff., 177–80, *192–202*, 206f., 243f., 279, 281

Economy, 32, 113, 156, 163ff., 167, 187, 191
Education, 30, 32, 35, 77, *91ff.*, 95, 103, *110ff.*, 128f., *147f.*, 157, 159, 166, 183, 191, 213, 236, 281
Ego; *see* I
End; *see* Purpose

End in itself, 113, 141, 148, 179, 184
Enlightenment, 129, 196f., 267
Entelechy, 40, 251f.
Error, 29, 49, 66, 115f., 161, 164, 232, 249, 271
Evil, 193, 211f., 222f., 226, 247 254, 268f.
Existence, 11, 30, 66, 87f., 94, 125f., 135, 190, 226f., 269
  animal, 235
  external, 86–90, 94, 244
  human, 11, 74, 77, *86–89*, 94, 107, 112, 125f., 144f., 157f., 173, *191f.*, 235f., 244, 247, 255, 262, 269, 275, 280f.
  responsible, 212, 241
  of God, 277f.
Expediency, 3, 203
Experience, 116, *137f.*, 144, 212, 234
  an (*Erlebnis*), 3f., 6f., 32, 35f., 112
  living (*Erleben*), 5f., 16, 28ff., 33, 61, 99f., 103f., 107, 129, 137f., 143, 217, 228, 257, 260, 282
  religious, 275f.
Experiment, 127

Faith, 11, 15f., 24f., 41, *43–46*, 49f., 57, *69f.*, 118, 122, *125–32*, 150, 198, 218, 221, 228, 254f., 258, *260*, 264, 266f., 270, 274
  imagery of, 45, 76, 127–30, 218f., *221ff.*, 226, 228
  in truth, 45f., 49f., 62, 70, 89
Faithfulness, 182, 241ff., 246
Family, 281f.
Fanaticism, 131
  of truth, 204
Fascism, 162, 180
Fate, 79, *96*, 106, 108, 172, 174, 195, 205, 220ff., 252
Fatherland, 150f., 173f.
Finiteness, 70, 81, 85, 116, 121, 135, 239f.
Form, 16f., 32, *65–71*, 73, 75, 88, 108, 184, 201, 213, 283
Formation of self, 90f., 110, 125f., 160, 236f.
Formulation, 79, 83, 99f., 212, 239, 267

Freedom, 33, 37, 39, 43, 45, 67f., 76*ff.*, *125–29*, 149, 151, 166, 171*f.*, 179, 230, 247
  abuse of, 253
  basis of, 156
  of conscience, 108
  in history, 261
  illusive, 237
  intellectual, 34–37, 77, 115
  liberating, 193
  national, 174
  responsible, 75, 223
  restrictions of, 100
  superhistorical idea of, 184
Fundamental concepts, 16f., 80, 82–84

Generalization, 212f.
Geometry, 18f., 48, 80f., 86f.
Goal; *see* Purpose
Goals come to man, 119
God, 5, 61, 66, 68, 96, *107*, 135, 145, 218, 221ff., *224f.*, 275–82
  as artist, 66
  certainty of, 74, 128f., 219f., 275
  children of, 259
  as dictator, 258f.
  loves his enemies, 255
  existence of, 277f.
  honor of, 219f., 255
  image of, in man, 123, 207, 267, 279
  as *intellectus archetypus*, 265
  as Judge, 273
  makes no judgments, 53, 55f.
  knowledge of, 5, 75f., 79, 120, 180, 224f.
  life of, 10
  in man, 75, 107
  nature in, 11, 234f.
  is no object, 75f., 120, 125
  peace of, 260, 262, 267
  the personal, 118ff.
  presence of, 57f., 73, 79, 257, 268, 271, 279, 281
  representation (image) of, 127f., 220, 238f., 276
  wants no human sacrifice, 262
  service of, 73, 183, 220, 250
  makes use of sin, 244

Index of Topics

is not somebody, 118
the suffering, 250, 252, 279
is truth, 9f., 49, 89, 232
Will of, 257f.
Golgotha, 252
Good, the, 29, 158, 193f., 202, 250
Grace, 119, 123, 145, 249
Group egotism, 223, 263
Guilt, 90, *112*, 164, 169, 193, 195f., 212, 214f., 220, 240, 243f., 252, *274f.*
of the time, 193, 196, 243f.

Hatred, 109f., 196, 253f.
Hazard; see Contingency
Height
of personal life, 35, 89, 94f., *108f.*, 205f., 227, *237f.*, 262
of the time, 6, 23, *25*, 39, 45f., 95f., 117, 163, 173, 175, 188, 237f., 259, 269
Heritage, historical, 41, 46, 195f., 229
Heroes, 200
History, 17–20, 24f., *40–43*, 48, 67, 70, 93f., 107, 113, 145f., 172ff., 180, 183, 187, *194–97*, 218, 230, 245, 256ff., 261, *263ff.*, 272, 280
of philosophy, 6, 58f., 229
Holy, the, 69
Home, *105–108*, 201
Honor of God, 219f., 256
Human existence; see Existence
Humanity (*Menschlichkeit*), humanness, on being human, xi, 18, 28, 33ff., 54, *61*, 102, 162f., *176f.*, 180
and alienation, 97
basis of, 156f., 167, 190f., 195, 235, 240, 242, 244f.
and community, 142f.
and community of nations, 92f.
and feeling, 23
through freedom, 157f., 237, 261
and justice, 157f., 165–72
and knowledge, 89, 140f.
needs no laws, 213
as love, 206, 241, 250
as root of morals, 214
and mythology, 47f., 239
not objective, 239, 244
from ontological necessity, 223
and power, 149f., 167f.
and state, 150f., 187ff., 191f., 196ff.
through supertemporal ideas, 147, 238
tragic, 199
transcendental dignity of, 276f.
through truth, 57f., 282f.
as unity (oneness), 126f., *132*, 136, 147ff., 255ff., 262
and good will, 206f.
and "the world," 172f.

I, 4f., *122*, 126, 136, 182, 216, 234, 252f.
the thinking, *87f.*, 106f., 122, 126
the true, *42*, 237
Idea
moral, 183
of the true, 16, *27f.*, 48, 66, 75, 78, 81, 85, 97f., 135f., 210f., 243, 271, 282
Ideas
historical, 17f., *43f.*, 67
superhistorical, 18, *43f.*, 67
Ideal demands, 29, 204f.
Idealism, 10, 68, 70, 86, 190
Ideals, *109*, 202f., 205, 262
Identity with oneself, 8f., 90f., 136
Ideology, 61, 108, 163f., 166, 181f.
Imagery (*Vorstellung*), 76, 115f., 127, 139f., 143, 218
Imagination, 26, 39, 131, 233, 241
Immediacy, 5, 8, 16, 26, 28, 32, 127, 139, 174, 209, 227, 252f., 267f.
Imperatives, 106, 194, 205, 213, 241, 279
Imperialism, intellectual, 95
Impersonality
of nature, 109, 236
of ratiocination, 26, 35f., 79, 97, 107, 110, 112, 118, 247, 249
Independence, 90, 108f., 117, 160, 174, 178, 207, 212, 254
Individual, the, 40, 75–78, 122, 159f., 179, 183f., 194f., 241, 256

Infinite (Non-finite), the, 70, 80–83, 85, 111, 116, 122, 177, 222
Infinity, the bad, 88f.
Infliction of punishment, 159, 168f., 246f.
Inhumanity, 18, 34, 89, 92f., 174, 176f., 183, *189ff.*, 192f., 199, 205f., 213f., *243ff.*, 254, 258, 262, 277f.
Injustice, 157, 161–67, 170f., 175, 178, 199, 253
Inner affairs of a state, 177
Intellectual struggles, 78, 94f.
Intellectualism, xi, 9, 55, *121–24*
Intelligence (*Verstand*), 10, *16–20*, 24, 29, *34–38*, 51, 58, 63, 69f., 75–79, 81f., 89, *97–104*, 105ff., *109–12*, 115–24, 131, 141f., *144–47*, 210f., 232ff., 246f., 255, 257, 263f., 266
truth of; see also Ratiocination
International community, 92f., 177, 224, 236
Invitation, 33ff.
Inwardness, 74, 89, *129f.*, 132, 163, *211*, 219, *241f.*, 253
Irrationality, 15
Israel, 68, 218f., 278

John, Gospel and letters of, 145, 180, 252, 274ff., 281
Joy, perfect, 274
Judgment, 55f., 58, 88, 135, 138f., 233f.
Just, the, 32, 98, *155–70*, 189, 247
Justice, 32f., 157–70, 182, 247
Justice; see Administration of

Knowledge, 75f., 88, 122–26, 255
methodical, *15–23*, 51, *63f.*, 77f., 115ff., 141, 229, 246, 259
objective, 5, 15, 33, 35, 64, 75, 110, 115f., 234
perfect, 58, 69, 124, 164
principles of, 81–85, 122ff., 234
Laws of thought, 8
Legal order, 160, 163f., 167, 172
Legal security; see Security of law
Libertinism, 258, 283
Liberty; see Freedom

Lie, 57, 62, 203f., *208–11*, 215, 219, 222
Life, *4f.*, 9, 30, *47–55*, *59–62*, 66, 86, 98f., 140, 221, *225*, 271, 281f.
meaning of, 30f., 62, 79, 143, 145, 167, 170, 174, *206*, 227, *235f.*, 244, 248f., 256, 259ff., 262ff., 274f.
personal, 35, 98, 110, 118f., 126, 141
travail of, 113f., 166f.
worth living, 17, 60f., 108f., *156ff.*, 167, 176, 205f., 213, 222, 278f.
Living reality, 1, 72, 208
Logic, 8, 50, 52, 61, 84, 100, 116, 136
Love, 34, 38, 74, 76–79, *148f.*, 173, *175*, 214f., 216, *241–44*, 250, 252–56, *266*, *271*, 281
of enemy, 173ff.
of God, 119, 219–22, 227, 274f., 280
Loving activity, 74, 250, 271

Man, 75–79, 92f., 111, *209*, 224
his art, 248
as citizen, 182ff., 188ff., 243
his conscience, 238
his creations, 268f.
his education, 95
and evil, 226
faith in, 129f.
as free, 157f.
God present in, 23
and love, 241f.
modern, 217f.
and mystery, 241
and myth, 57, 128
his nature, *107*, 242
"noble," 49
overtaxed, 205
paltry, 158, 254
as social being, 163
and the supertemporal, 238
and truth, 88f., 140f., 146f., 222f.
unreliable, 237
and values, 232
whole, xii, *17*, 20–23, 31f., 58,

Index of Topics

121, 125, 130, 132, 136f., 139, 219
Marriage, 266, 281f.
Martyrdom, 106, 172, 175, 193
Mathematics, 15, 35, 64, 82f.
Maxim, 194, 202, 206, 208, 212
Maya, 37, 63
Member of society, 76, 92f., 108, 112, 171, 174, 201, 207, 241f., 243, 279
Messianism, 221
Metaphysics, 50f., 58, 65, 71, 79, *122ff.*, 136, 143, 181, 228f., 231
Military service, 192f.
Misery, 200f., 250
Mission, personal, 172, 249, 252, 280f
Misunderstanding, 101f.
Monachism, 173f., 200
Moral
 action, 29, 192f., 211
 commandments, 59, 198f., 203, 206
 law, 178, 194, 198f.
Moralism, 205, 214, 275
Morality, *28ff.*, 98, 157, 166, 170, 179, *182ff.*, 188, 192, *194*, 198f., *246*, 275, 279
 noble, 49, 59, 65, 229, 269
Mystery, 58, 80, 85ff., 116, 121, 241
Mythology, 56f., 63, 116, 119, *125*, 127, *239*, 244, 262, 267, 277

National Socialism, 18, 20, 59, 181, 224
Natural science, 15, 64f., 116
Nature, 4, 11, 36, 40, *56f.*, 105, 156, 195, 224, 234f., 242, 244, 276
 deities, 244f.
 in God, 224, 234f., 241
 teleology, 276
Necessity, 7f., 66f., 193
 of the purely human, 41, 47, 60, 94, 106f., 146, 165, 183, 213f., 216, 249, 260, 269
Neighbor, 215
Neoscholasticism, 9f., 122, 137f.
New Testament, 68, 145, 180, 213, 254f., 260, 271, 280f.
Non-finite; *see* Infinite

Norms, 8, 45, 49, 63, 89, 165, 167, 182, 199, 211, 214, 270, 283
Obedience, 44, 162, 175f., 182, 258f., 262, 267
Object, 3f., 16, 28ff., *33–36*, 39f., 58, 61, *86*, 109, 115–18, *120f.*, 123–129, 138, 174, 195, 201, 217, *234f.*, 254, 265, 277
Objective spirit, 41, 156, 184
Objectivity, 15, 20, 35, 39f., 138, 240, 282
Old Testament, 68, 218–21, 254, 267
Omnipotence of state, 150, 163, 185
Oneness (being at one with oneself), 57, 132, 135f., 141–44, *147–150*, 171, *173*, 175, 180, 216, 219, 221, *230*, *238*, 240f., *247f.*, 259
Ontological truth; *see* Truth
Order of imagery, 117, 127
Organism, 40, 275

Passion, bound by, 90, 109f., 237
Past, 39, 95f., 212, 238, 268
Patriotism, 149, 178f., 243, 253
Peace of God, 260, 262, 267
Pedagogy, 77, 141, 147f., 160
Penal law, 149, 168
Penalty, 34, 159, 182
Perfection, 31f., 261f.
Personal being; *see also* Unity of substance of, 77, 90, 97, 105, 248, 283
Personality, 21, 34f., *76f.*, 79, 97, 105, 107, 111, *117–20*, 128, 167, *172*, 203, 214, *237*, 247, 249, 252, *271*, 281
Phenomenon; *see* Appearance
Philosophy, 15, 22f., 43–48, 95, *101–104*, 140, 265f.
Philosophizing, 44–47, 102f.
Politics, 59, 109, 172, 188, 192
Possibilities, individual, 22, *33ff.*, 42, 89, 95f., *107ff.*, 111f., 173, *205*, 210, 249, 254, 262, 272, 282
 as obligation, 187
Power, 32f., 47, 59, 92, *95ff.*, 149–152, 156, *158ff.*, 164, 167f., *175–79*, 183, 187, 218, 237, 263
 divine, 256, 276

of spirit, 25f., 38f., 42, 111f., 130f., 165, 189f., 264
Primitive thinking, 233
Principles, first; see Fundamental concepts
Problematic nature of science, 16–20, 27–30, 56, 146f., 234
Progress, 70f., 75, 264
Proof, 73, 122f., 125
Prophets, 31, 68, 219f., 228, 254, 278
Prose, 30, 56, 97, 100, 260, 267
Punishment inflicted, 159, 169, 246f.
Purpose (goal), 71, 103f., 171, 176, 203, 208f., 216, 246f., 276
Purposiveness, 232

Question, 23, 44f., 64, 74, 80, 88, 265f., 268

Rationalism, 19, 65, 143
Rationality, 15
Ratiocination (*Verstand*); see also Intelligence
 truth of, 16, 31, 34, 58, 80f., 84f., 96ff., 141, 146f., 189, 210, 217, 234, 257, 266
Reality, 1, 19, 30, 32, 89, 109f., 125f., 165f., 190
Realm
 of ends, 194, 196–99, 202
 of truth, 95, 151ff., 175
Reason (*Vernunft*), 54, 60, 71, 75–79, 83f., 87, 94, *122f.*, 142–47, *154f.*, *171*, 200, 212, 223f., 233, 253, 260, 263f., *269–72*, 282f.
Reasonable, the (*das Vernünftige*), 138, 179
Rebellion, 178
Receptive, 119
Relations between men, 271, 278f.
Relationship, 143, 258, 272, 275, 281f.
Relativism, 258, 266, 275
Religion, 69, 74, 100, *103f.*, *116f.*, 180, 228, 256–64, 266f., 272–283
Religions, great, 244f., 249, 278
Religious personality, 281

Representation (*Vorstellung*); see Imagery
Research, scientific, 42f., 46, 189, 210
Resistance, right of, 180ff., 197
Responsible existence, 241
Responsibility, *21*, 41f., 44, 77, *92ff.*, 105, 109, 112, 118, 126, *140f.*, 171, *208f.*, 223f., 235, 237, 272, *275*
 social, 33, 92, 112, 158, 171ff.
Restlessness, 94, 196, 262f., 280
Revelation, 30, 37, 68, 98, 207, *218ff.*, 228, 248, 252, 255, *257f.*, 268
Right, 24f., 59, 160, 163f., 176, 178f., 198

Sacrifice, 36, 79, 172, 251f., 256
Safeguarding of existence, 212
Salvation, 280
Scholasticism, 10, 123f., 137
School, 93, 110f., 160
Science, *15–23*, *25ff.*, 42f., 51, *63ff.*, 77, 99, 115, 131, 228, 246, 259
Science; see Problematic nature of science
Sciences other than natural, 15, 27, 99ff., 258, 272
Security, 212f.
 of law, 160–63
Seemingness; see Appearance
Self
 -affirmation, 87, 251f.
 -alienation; see Alienation
 -certainty, 85, 87ff., 91f., 94, *107*, 110, 112f., 125f., 207, 265
 -formation; see Formation
Service, 89, 98f., 105f., 141, 250
Servility, 177
Set, 83
Sin, 244, 268, *273ff.*
Skepticism, 122, 263, 266
Social
 order, 33, 155–58, 160–63, 170f., 194, 249, 279
 practice, 158, 160, 165–70, 239
Socialmindedness, 76, 158, 166
Sophistics, 71, 139
Space, 18, 83, 85ff.

Index of Topics

Spirit, 7, 69, 71, 73f., *86*, 97, 111, 124, *148*, 152, 176, 191, *230f.*, 265
Spontaneity; *see* Independence
State, 91, *149–53*, 156–59, 161ff., 169, *174–93*, 195, 197, 201, 243
  constitution, 181–84
  mechanism, 186
  morality, 181–85
  omnipotence, 150, 163, 185
Subject, 30, 90, 125, 201, 252, 277
Subjectivism, 6f., 77, 122, 247f., 269f.
Subjectivity, *20*, 29, 37, 77, *125f.*, 155f., 169, *176*, *207*, 229, 234, 247f.
Substance, personal; *see* Personal substance
Suffering, 32, 34, 159, 199, 219f.
Superhistorical, 26, 41f., 44, 67, 147, 199, 265
Superobjective, 117, 126–29, 147, 278
Superstition, 74, 256, 258, 266, 278
Supertemporal, 24, 27f., *39–46*, 79, 119, 157, *192*, 194, 238, 279
Symbol, 31, 56, 66, 79, 103, *116f.*, 224, 228, 239, 258, 282f.
Synthesis, 83, 117, 228, 231

Task
  human, *88ff.*, 106f., *109–12*, 130, 149, 173, 182, 188, 230, 236, 255, 260, 279
  infinite, 56, 107, 136, 230, 260
  of the time, 18, 43, 67, 128f., 174
Taste, aesthetic, 247f.
Technology, 121, 239
Temptation, 92f., 111, 172, 175, 235, 260, 262
Thing in itself, 9, 138, 140, 143
Thomism, 138
Time, 15, 25, 39, 79, 82f., 143, 150, 191, 195, 213, 239f.
Timelessness, 8, 15, 18, 24ff., 197, 239
Totalitarian state, 162f., 174, 184, 189
Tragic events, (tragedy), 63, 178, 199, 243, 283

Transcendence, 107, 127, 138, 255, 276ff., 282
True, the, 16, 28f., 34, 66f., 75, 78, 192, 223, 233, *266*, 282
True being, xi, 10, 31, 44, 51f., 55, 58, 70, 135
Truth, xif., 9f., 18–23, *27f.*, 45, 48–63, 65ff., 69–73, 94ff., 109–12, 139, 151, 176, 203f., 206, 210, 216, 250
  liberating, 190, 222, 276
  metaphysical, 137
  ontological, 10, *55*, 73, 75, 97f., 126, *135–39*, *143–46*, 171, 179, 190f., 196, 200, 221, 225f., 232f., *239*, 246ff., 254, 259, 265, 278, 282f.
  relative (conditional), 16, 29, 37f., 48, 80–85, 247, 257, 275
  unconditional, 16, 20, 22, 28f., *31*, 36ff., 50, 58ff., 75f., 80–85, 87, *98*, 109, *146f.*, *239*, 254, *256f.*
Truthfulness, 64, 203, 209
Trust, 91, 180ff., 221, 274
Twilight of the Idols (Nietzsche), 54, 62, 70

Unconditional certainty, 88
Unconditionality, 54, 69f., *89*, 108f., 111, 146f., 163f., 183, *187*, 190, 200, 209f., 227, 232f., *256f.*, 265, *277f.*, 280f., 283
Unity
  nature of, 110, 125, 130, 249, 256, 259f., 262, 264
  of personal being, 76, *111*, 115f., 121, 125f., 132, 210, 259, 263
  synthetic, 115f.
Untruth, 47f., 97, 191, 208f., 211, 215f., 225
Urges, life of, 90, 97f., 109, 119, 235ff., 283

Validity, 50, 58f., 117, 160, 227, 232f., 270
  universal, 35, 101, 272
Value contrasts, 31f., 41f., 44, 50–55, 59ff., *78f.*, 94, 145f., 189f., 212, 223–27, 232f., 253, 261, 265f., *269ff.*

Values, 18, 49, 59, 112, 118ff., 136, 141, 145f., *154f.*, 162, 167, 170, 183, 189f., 192, 194, 223, 229f., 247, 261, *269*, *272f.*, 279, 282
Vocation (calling), 73, 131f., 148

War, 34, 91f., 173–76, 184, *192f.*, 196–99, 243, 252
Weakness, human, 164, 173, 211f., 214f.
Wholeness, 76, 110f., 121, 249, 256, 259f.
Will, 29f., 75, 118f., 127, 175f., 179, 201, 213
for truth, 225, 257, 271
for power, 47, 55, 59, 71, 95, 229f., 245
good, 29, 98, 202f., 279
Wisdom, 18, 141
World, 36, 56, 70f., 88f., 96, 129, 147, 173f., 200, 204, 223, 257, 262, 275
around us (environment), 93f., 108, 112, 237
overcoming the, 34, 256, 260
World reason, 270
World-view, *15–23*, 42f., 61, 77f., 101, 116